POSTCARD HISTORY SERIES

Yavapai County

ON THE FRONT COVER: PRESCOTT, GURLEY STREET, C. 1910 (HAND COLORED POSTCARD). This street was named after John A. Gurley, who would have been the first territorial governor of Arizona if he had not died before taking office in August 1863. Gurley was a Republican US congressman from Ohio from 1856 to 1863. President Lincoln named Gurley territorial governor of Arizona but after his death replaced him with John N. Goodwin. (Published by M. Reider Publ., author's collection.)

ON THE BACK COVER: JEROME, UNITED VERDE WORKS, C. 1910 (HAND COLORED POSTCARD). After a new smelter was constructed in Clarkdale, the smelter seen here was removed to make way for an open pit mine. At the United Verde Pit, some ore was as much as 40 percent copper, and silver was more than 200 ounces per ton. (Published by E.W. Carroll, courtesy John Taylor.)

Postcard History Series

Yavapai County

Rick Sprain
Introduction by Nancy Burgess

ARCADIA
PUBLISHING

ISBN 978-1-4671-2450-8

Published by Arcadia Publishing
Charleston, South Carolina

Printed in the United States of America

Library of Congress Control Number: 2016942231

For all general information contact Arcadia Publishing at:
Telephone 843-853-2070
Fax 843-853-0044
E-mail sales@arcadiapublishing.com
For customer service and orders:
Toll-Free 1-888-313-2665

Visit us on the Internet at www.arcadiapublishing.com

*To my wife Nicole, who has stood by me unquestionably
as I took on this seemingly endless adventure*

Contents

ACKNOWLEDGMENTS

I never would have completed this book without the help of local historians, historical societies, friends, and most of all, other postcard collectors who have a passion to collect and share their cards. I would first like to thank Kelly Graham and the Skull Valley Historical Association. Kelly was one of the first people I spoke with, and his enthusiasm was infectious. He allowed me access to the collections at the Skull Valley Archives, and he was instrumental in introducing me to others in Yavapai County who were more than willing to assist me. John Taylor, who has one of the best mining postcard collections out there, took his own time and scanned dozens of old cards out of his collection for this book. Both Andrew Christenson, curator, and Cynthia Gresser, executive director of the Smoki Museum, allowed me to scan the postcards in the museum's collection. Also, Andrew, who has a wonderful collection of local cards, allowed me to use his personal collection for the book. Bagdad's Bob Delgado single-handedly saved the town's and mine's histories and started the town's museum and archives. Tony Meager opened up his spectacular personal collect of Arizona postcards for me. We spent hours going through his cards and scanning a good chunk of his Yavapai collection. I would also like to thank John Bradshaw. John was kind enough to give me access to his father Bob Bradshaw's massive postcard file. Lastly, I'd really like to thank Nancy Burgess. She allowed me to go through her personal collection of cards in so many volumes that I lost count. With her vast knowledge of Yavapai County history and her own passion for postcards, Nancy was the only person who I wanted to write the introduction for this book.

All images in this book are from my personal collection unless otherwise noted.

Introduction

If you are about to start reading *Yavapai County*, you are most likely interested in one or all of the following: Yavapai County history; images of Yavapai County; images of a particular place; or postcards in general. Almost anyone who picks up a copy of *Yavapai County* has probably at some point in time purchased, sent, or received a postcard.

It was not until May 1893 at the Columbian Exposition in Chicago that the first souvenir postcards were seen. These chromolithographed images were printed on the backs of US postal "penny" cards and could be mailed at the 2¢ letter rate. The government made a penny on the sale of each one. They were packaged in sets and were enormously popular, partly due to the fact that they were in color. Many were taken home and saved and were never mailed. The people who purchased these were the first postcard collectors.

Collecting postcards was a popular way for those who traveled to create albums of their visits around the world or across the country or even to the big city in their own home state. Special postcard albums were marketed, encouraging the purchasing, sending, and receiving of postcards. Today, deltiology (the collection of postcards) is the third most popular collecting hobby in the world, surpassed only by the collection of coins and stamps.

Each postcard tells a part or all of a small story. Not only is the image interesting to collectors and historians, but the message, the stamp box, the information printed by the publisher, and the printing technique used for the postcard are also of interest. If the card was used and mailed, the stamp and postmark and the names of the addressee and the writer, if present, are also of interest. Taken together, all of these small pieces of information tell a story about a time and a place.

As the concept of the souvenir postcard caught on, photographers from all over the world sent their images to large companies which specialized in printing postcards. Prior to World War I, millions of color lithograph postcards were printed in Germany, which mastered the art of postcard printing, sometimes using up to 40 colors in the printing process. These cards were manufactured during what is called the "golden age" of postcards. After World War I, companies such as Albertype and Curteich-Chicago C.T. Art-Colortone produced thousands of domestic postcards for the ever-growing souvenir and advertising postcard markets.

Locally, itinerant photographers would travel through communities and neighborhoods or set up outdoor studios, taking portraits of the family on the front porch, the children in a wagon or on a pony or the cowboy on his horse. Many of these images were printed as Real Photo Postcards (RPPCs) and delivered to the subjects of the photograph on the same or the next day.

For many, the "Wild West" of the late 19th and the first half of the 20th century was a mystery. The introduction of Arizona postcards gave newcomers and visitors the opportunity to tell the folks back home what Arizona was really like, and the cities and towns of Yavapai County were soon represented by the picture postcard. At the same time, regional and local communities were realizing that postcards were a cheap and easy way to advertise their businesses, economic development opportunities, recreation, transportation routes, and historic and scenic attractions.

Since the beginning of the 20th century, postcard collectors have sought out the beautiful scenes of Arizona, but only recently have collectors sought out postcards as a historic record offering a treasure trove of images and comments. The first scenic views of Arizona were published starting about 1900 by commercial publishers in the eastern United States. The cards were often lovely, hand-colored views of the Grand Canyon and other now well-known scenes. Also, about 1900, local photographers began producing more specialized postcards that focused on the important buildings, events, and places of their communities. These are a treasure for today's collectors.

Postcards have provided a way for cities and towns to recapture their history through photographs. The photographic and physical history of a place can often be reconstructed almost exclusively through postcards. Many of the best photographs produced by professional or semi-professional photographers were printed as postcards, either through a major publishing company or locally. In *Yavapai County*, the author has chosen postcards that represent as many of the diverse places in Yavapai County as possible, representing cities, towns and communities, mining, recreation, lakes and rivers, roads and highways, the railroads, and other scenic, interesting, and sometimes obscure attractions of Yavapai County, Arizona.

In 1864, Yavapai County was one of the original four counties in Arizona Territory; it is believed to be the largest county ever created at that time in the United States, containing approximately 65,000 square miles. Because all or portions of five other counties—Apache, Coconino, Gila, Maricopa, and Navajo—were carved out of the original land area of Yavapai County, it is known as "Mother of Counties." Today, Yavapai County consists of 8,125 square miles. Prescott has been the county seat of Yavapai County since 1864. In May 1864, the territorial capital was established at Prescott. The territorial capital remained in Prescott until 1867, when it was moved to Tucson for 10 years before returning to Prescott from 1877 to 1889. The territorial capital was then moved permanently to Phoenix. Arizona became a state on February 14, 1912.

In the first decade of the 20th century, many Yavapai County merchants jumped on the postcard bandwagon. Some merchants sold postcards printed with local or regional advertising or subjects, along with the name of their business. A spinner-style postcard rack on the counter in the J.S. Acker and Co. store in Prescott in a 1916 photograph shows local views, including Washington School.

The same image would often be chosen from the same printer by more than one merchant in a community, and so the same postcard might show up with different publishers' business names on the front or the reverse of the card. The image also might be produced over a long period of time. Yavapai County merchants that published their own postcards included Brisley's Drug Store, Heil Drug Store, the Owl Drug and Candy Company, Timmerhoff's, Corbin and Bork, Robinson's Newsstand, and Acker's Book Store, all in Prescott. Others include B.B. Shimonowsky & Bros. at the Fort Whipple Post Exchange; Boyd Drug Co. and druggist Lynn Boyd; E. W. Carroll; Yavapai Drug Company; R.A. Smith and the Jerome Drug Company in Jerome; George H. Francis in Humboldt; and the Clarkdale Pharmacy in Clarkdale.

Fred Harvey Company, L.L. Cook, Frasher's Foto, Petley Studios, and Bob Bradshaw produced numerous Yavapai County postcards for businesses, communities, and tourist attractions.

The images and detailed captions presented in *Yavapai County* provide an incredible insight into the places and spaces and the life and times of Yavapai County since the first scenic views of Arizona were published more than 100 years ago. Enjoy!

—Nancy Burgess

One

Towns and Communities of Yavapai County

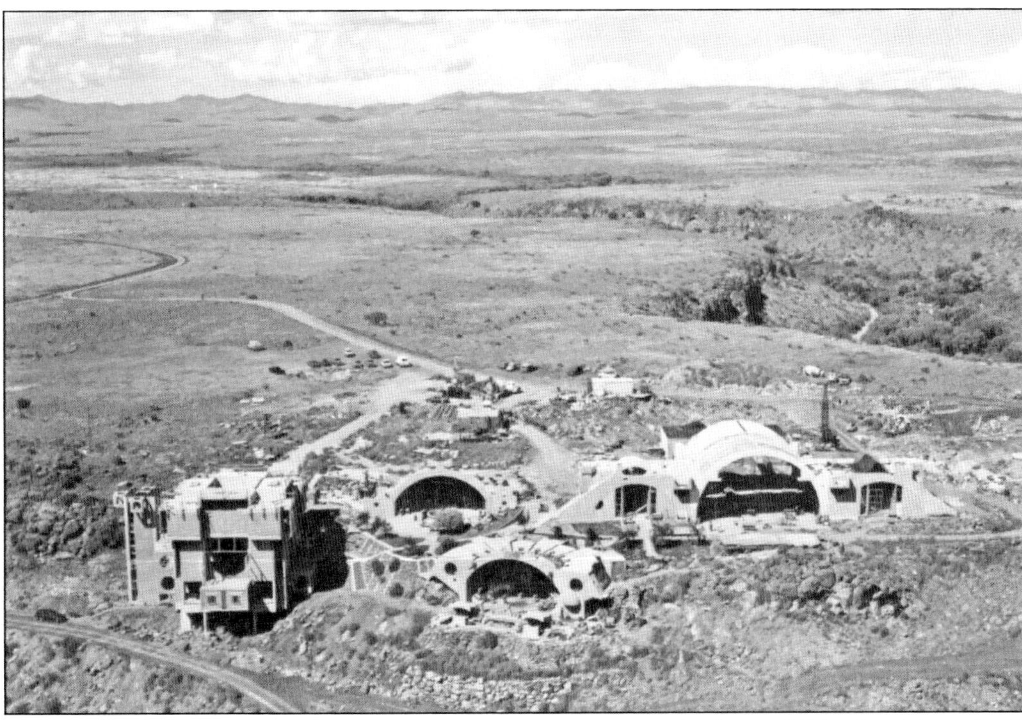

Arcosanti, 1970s–1980s (Real Photo Postcard). The brainchild of architect Paolo Soleri, Arcosanti was designed as a self-sustaining urban environment. Ground-breaking was in 1970 on 25 acres near Cordes Junction, and the community was originally to have a population of about 5,000 people. Now the population varies from 50 to 150 people, depending on the number of volunteers and students on site. Participants come from around the word for the five-week workshop on art, architecture, and urban planning. Tourists can even make reservations for overnight stays in one of the complex's many suites. (Published by the Cosanti Foundation, photograph by Landis Aerial Surveys, Inc.)

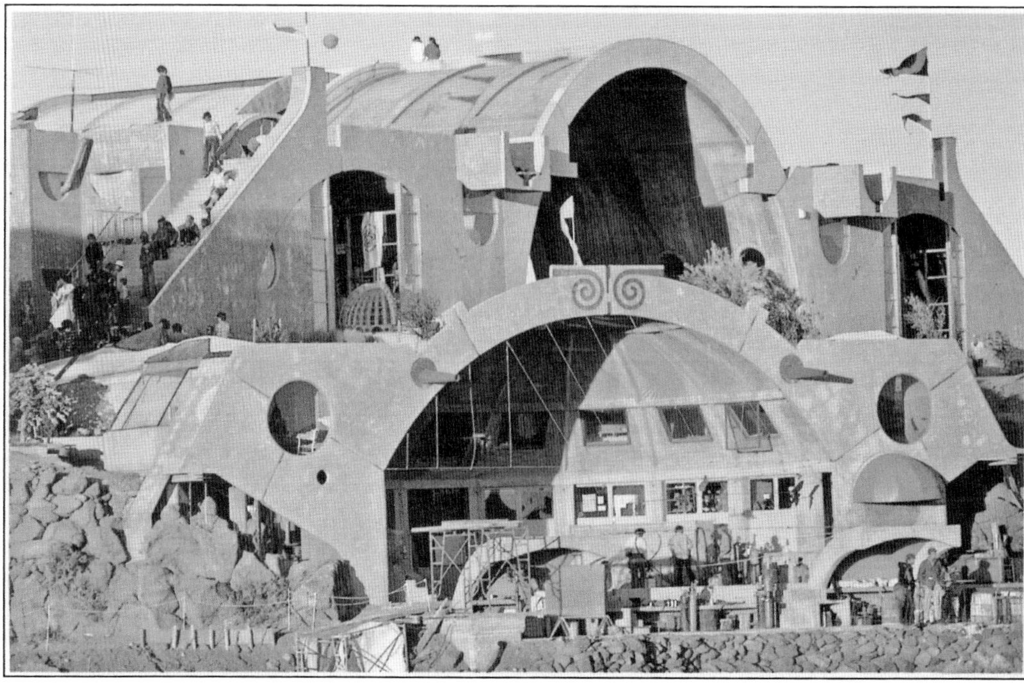

ARCOSANTI, POSTMARKED DECEMBER 9, 1996 (REAL PHOTO POSTCARD). The bronze casting foundry apse is in the foreground, while the housing and vault are in the background. Still a work in progress, Arcosanti has never been fully completed. It would eventually become famous for its bronze castings. (Published by the Cosanti Foundation.)

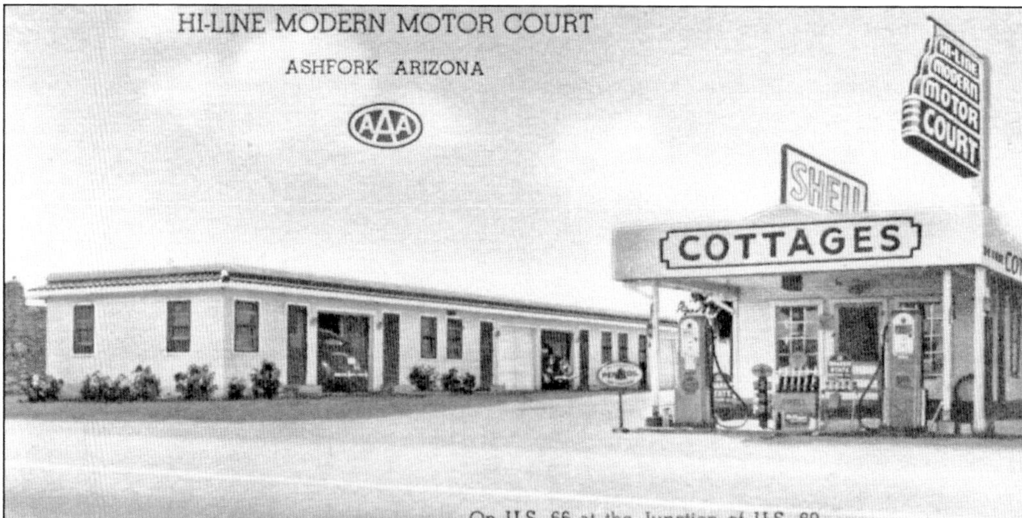

ASH FORK, HI-LINE MODERN MOTOR COURT, C. 1950S (ADVERTISING POSTCARD). Opening in 1936 along Highway 66, the motor court has seen many changes over the years. The gas pumps were eventually removed and the station turned into the motel's office. Renamed Hi-Line Motel, it has since closed, and the buildings have become run down. It was advertised as "Your Home Away from Home. Where U.S. 66 meets U.S. 89 to Prescott and Phoenix, New, strictly modern cottages with and without equipped kitchenettes. Tiled showers and closed attached garages."

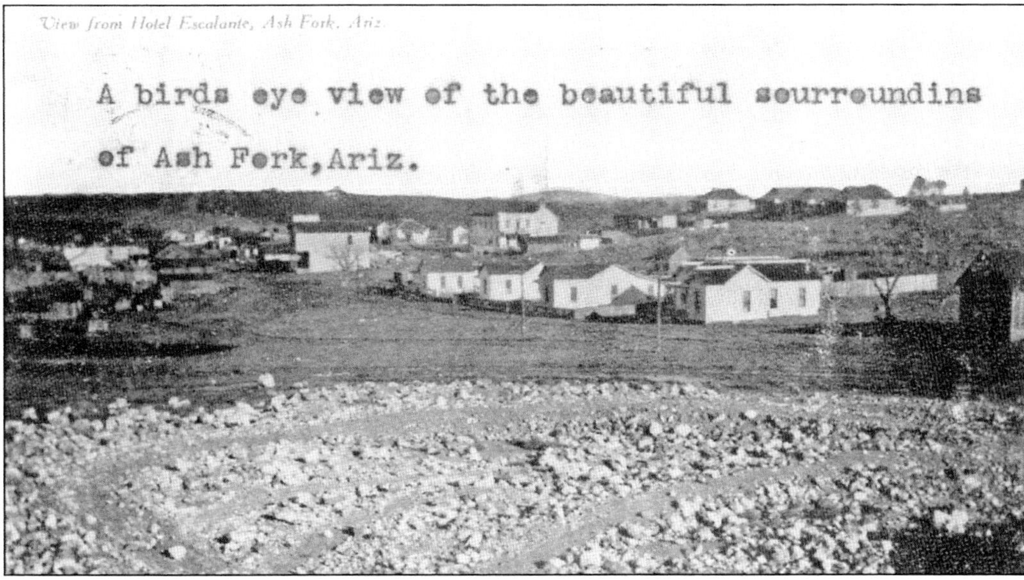

ABOVE: ASH FORK, VIEW FROM HOTEL ESCALANTE, POSTMARKED APRIL 15, 1907 (DIVIDED BACK POSTCARD); BELOW: ASH FORK, BIRD'S-EYE VIEW, C. 1915 (HAND COLORED POSTCARD). Located at the intersection of Highways 40 and 89, Ash Fork's existence began as a railroad siding for the Atlantic & Pacific Railroad in the early 1880s. It was once a popular stop along the Santa Fe Railroad and a resting place for weary travelers along Route 66. The town started a downward spiral when the railroad moved its main line in 1960, and later the highway was widened and skirted the town. Ash Fork has seen a small resurgence in the last few years with the many stone quarries opening around the town. Ash Fork has even proclaimed itself "the Flagstone Capital of the world." (Above, published by Fred Harvey; below, published by Fred Harvey, courtesy Nancy Burgess.)

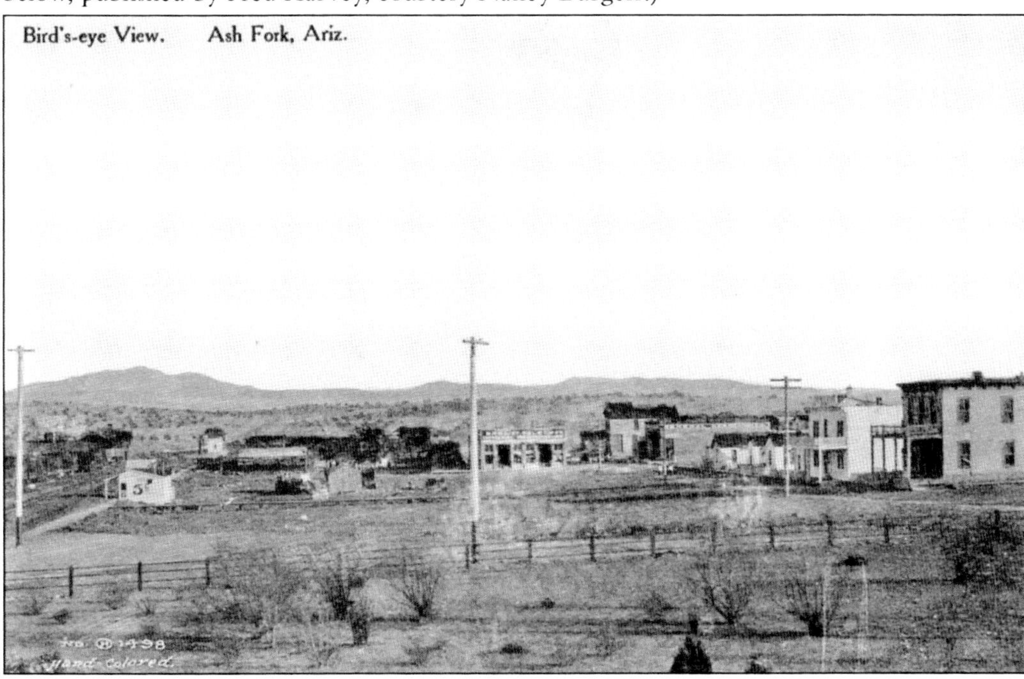

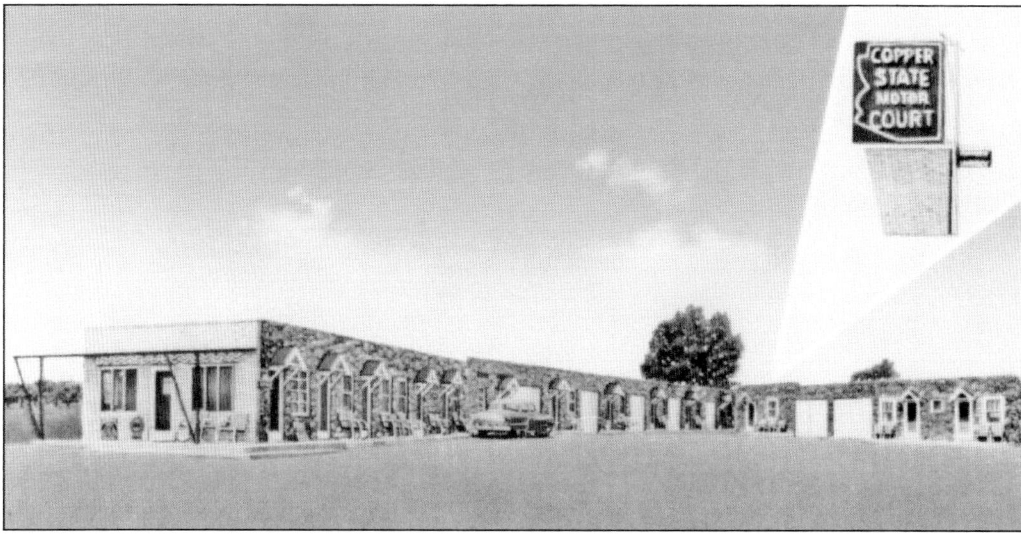

Ash Fork, Copper State Motor Court, Postmarked 1962 (Advertising Postcard). Built in the early 1930s to fill a growing need for the motorcar travelers along Route 66, the old hotel is still open today and looks amazingly as it did back in the 1930s. Even with the evolving traffic patterns throughout the years, the Copper State has never closed its doors. The back of the card reads, "12 Clean Comfortable Units and Lobby—Cross Ventilated—Tubs and Showers—Englander Beds—Safe Panel Ray Heat—Recommended by AMA & ATA." (Published by MWM Company.)

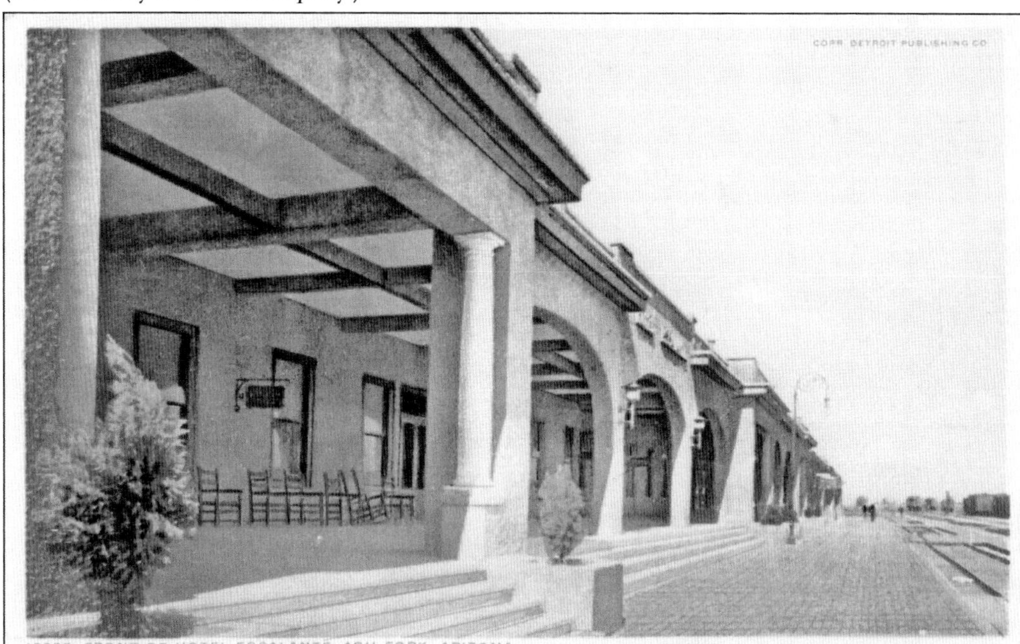

Ash Fork, Front of Hotel Escalante, c. 1908 (Advertising Postcard). The hotel and station was an L-shaped building covering a space of 420 feet by 200 feet with a beautiful courtyard, gardens, and the only grass lawn in town. All that is left today of the Escalante are some old concrete slabs where the hotel once stood. There is a scale model of the Escalante at the Ash Fork Museum. (Published by Fred Harvey.)

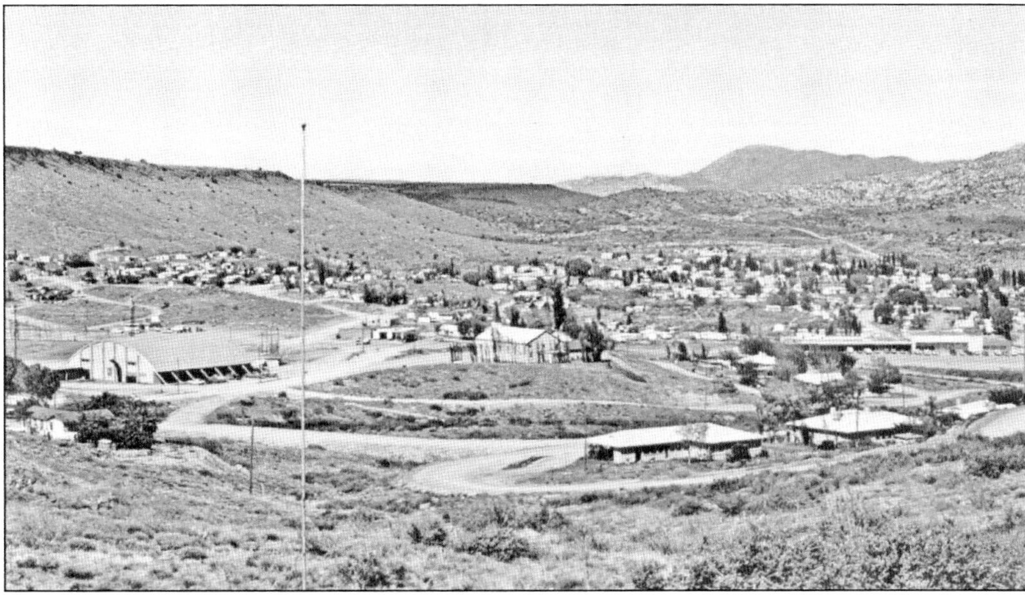

Bagdad, Town Site of Bagdad, c. 1960 (Real Photo Postcard). The town now has a population of about 2,500 people, which includes mine employees and their families as well as school district employees and local business operators. The original town site was located a few miles away and was moved to its present location when the mining operation expanded. (Published by Kingman Photo Services, photograph by David C. Lincoln.)

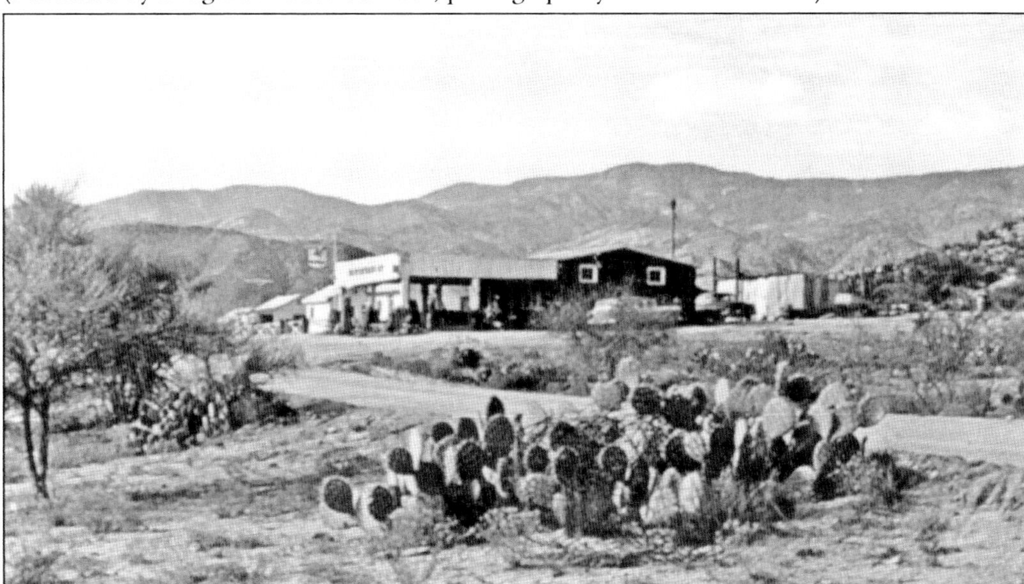

Bumble Bee, General Store and Gas Station, c. 1950s (Real Photo Postcard). The old gas station, having served its last customer many years ago, is now just another empty and dilapidated building left in Bumble Bee. The card's reverse reads, "General Store & Stage Coach Station, Established in 1860. Oldest post office in state. The mail exchange station between Prescott and Phoenix since territorial days. The store is a museum of pioneer relics. The entire town is now owned by Charles and Helen Penn." (Published by Penn Publications, photograph by Hal Carstens.)

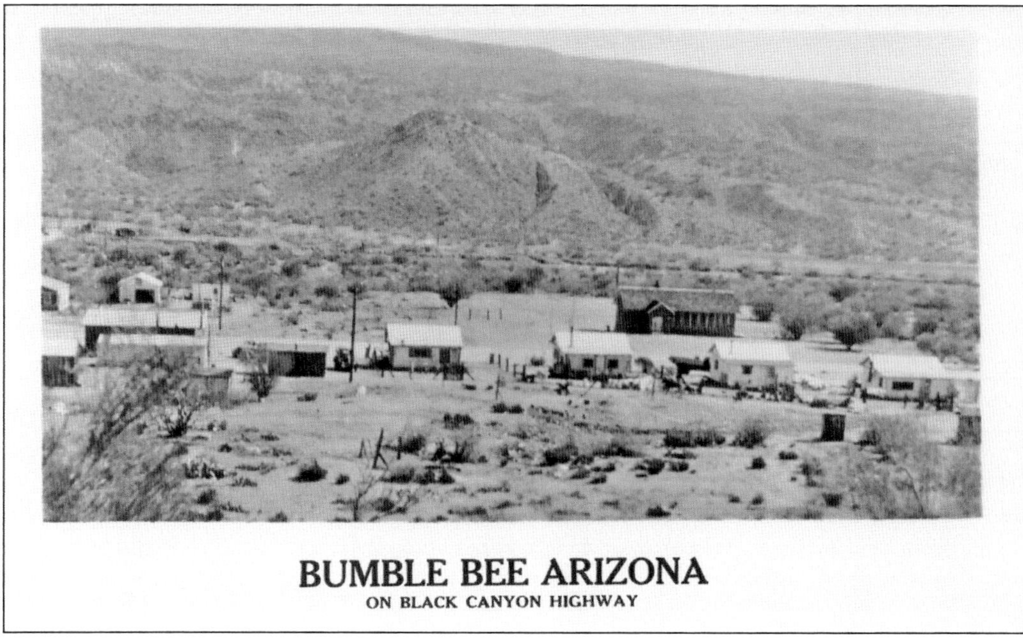

Bumble Bee, Postmarked September 29, 1951 (Real Photo Postcard). Originally known as Snider's Station, Bumble Bee served as a stage stop between Prescott and Phoenix. The town changed the name to Bumble Bee in 1879 when the post office opened. Now a ghost town, Bumble Bee is a few miles off of Highway 17 along the old Black Canyon Highway.

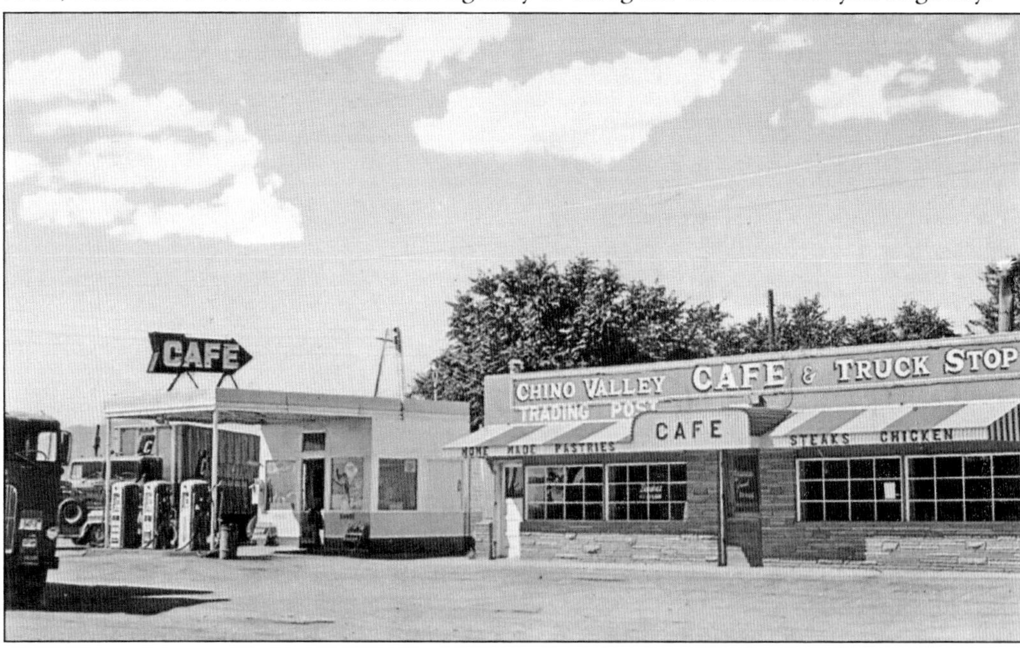

Chino Valley, Chino Valley Trading Post, Postmarked September 10, 1965 (Advertising Postcard). The back reads, "Chino Valley Trading Post, U.S. Highway 89, Chino Valley Arizona, 16 miles north of Prescott, Richfield Truck Stop and Cafe, Excellent home cooked meals and pastries. Tires and repair service." (Published by Dean Riggins, courtesy Tony Meager.)

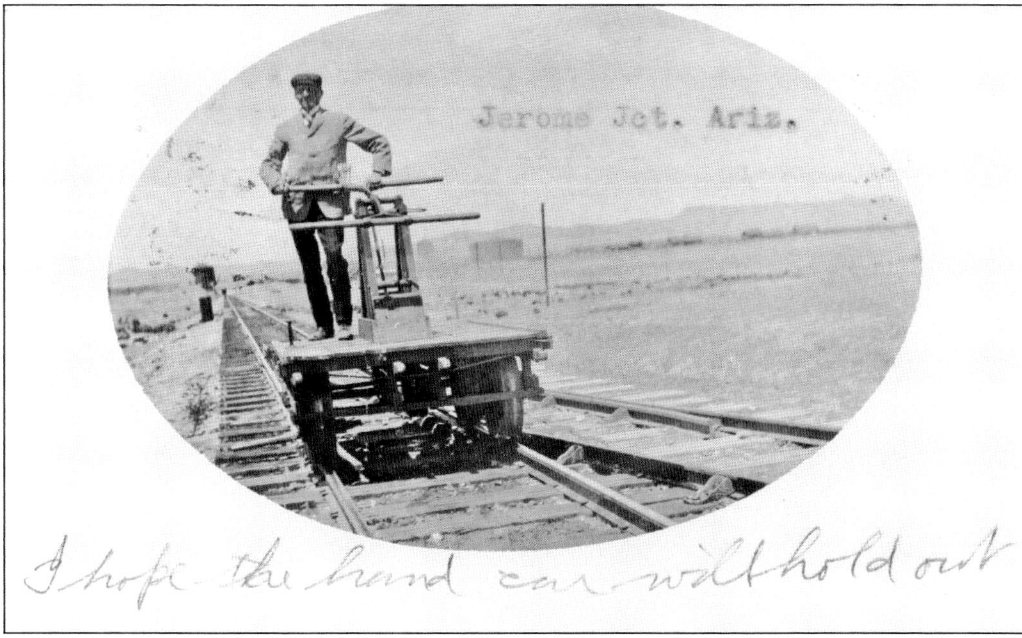

Chino Valley–Jerome Junction, Hand Car, Postmarked August 1908 (Divided Back Postcard). Established in 1894 as a railroad stop between Prescott and Jerome, Jerome Junction was originally known as Junction. The name was not officially changed to Jerome Junction until 1914. In 1920, the name was changed to Copper, and in 1923, it was absorbed into the town of Chino Valley. Written on the front the card is "I hope the hand cart will hold out." (Courtesy Nancy Burgess.)

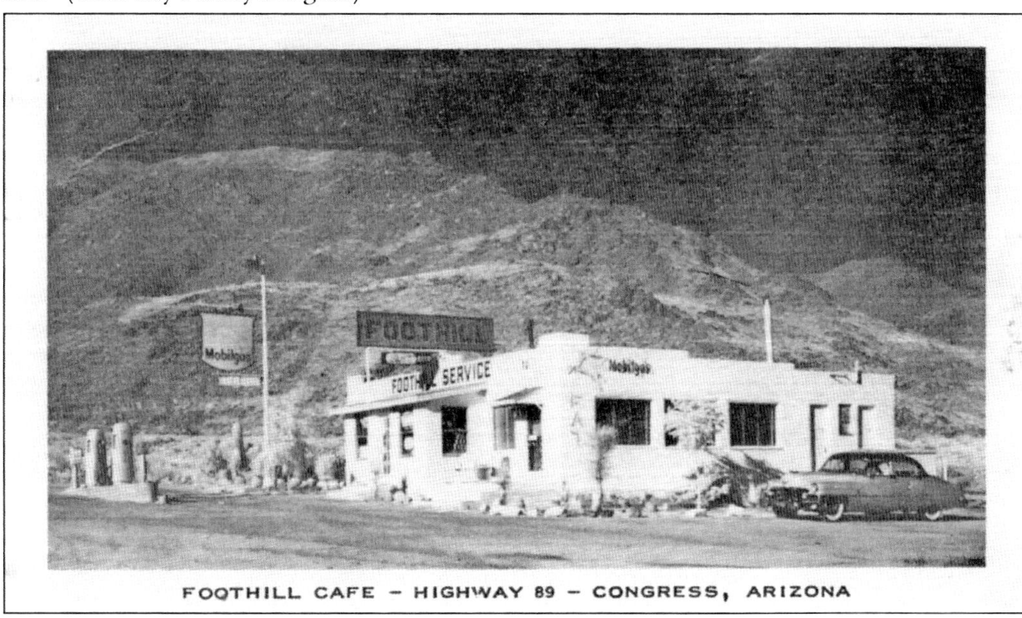

Congress, Foothill Café, Postmarked September 1, 1954 (Real Photo Postcard). The location of the old Foothill Café and Mobil service station no longer looks anything like it did back in the 1940s, 1950s, or 1960s. Now it is the Arrowhead Bar and Grill, a popular stop for locals and tourists alike. (Courtesy Nancy Burgess.)

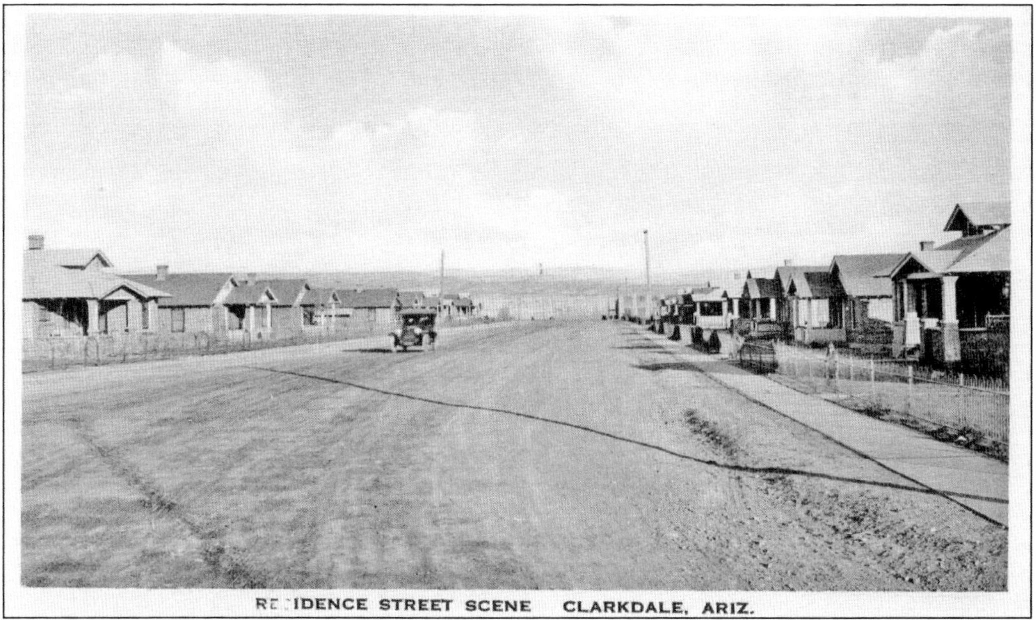

CLARKDALE, RESIDENCE STREET SCENE, C. 1920S (ALBERTYPE POSTCARD). Constructed between 1914 and 1930, the "Upper Town" homes were rented to United Verde Copper Company employees based on their positions within the company. Rents ranged from $5.15 a month for a laborer to $6.50 for mechanics. Utilities were $1 for electricity and $2 for telephones. (Published by the Clarkdale Pharmacy.)

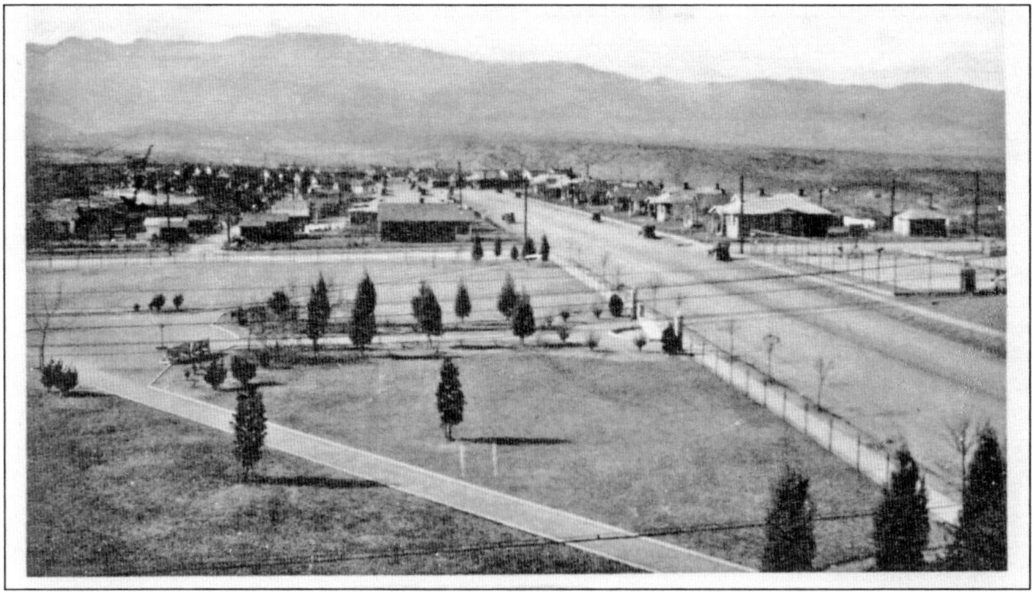

CLARKDALE, UPPER TOWN, C. 1920S (ALBERTYPE POSTCARD). Clarkdale was started by United Verde Copper Company in 1912. A company town, Clarkdale was the first master-planned community in Arizona. The town was built on a ridge above the Verde River overlooking the smelter where copper ore was brought down from Jerome. Clarkdale was named after William A. Clark, owner of the United Verde Copper Company. The company was purchased by Phelps Dodge Mining Company. (Published by the Clarkdale Pharmacy.)

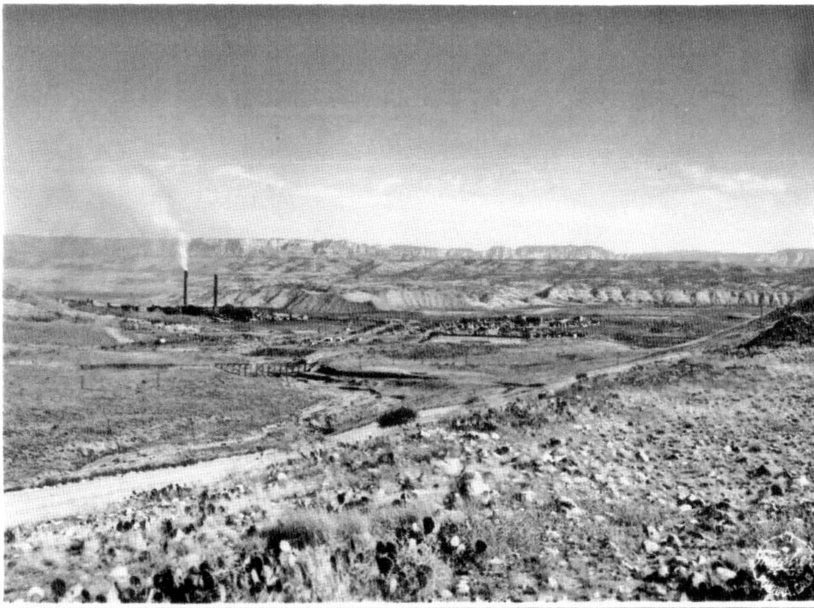

CLARKDALE, BIRD'S-EYE VIEW, C. 1930S (REAL PHOTO POSTCARD). The twin smokestacks in the background are from the United Verde Copper Company Smelter. Building of the smelter began in 1912, and it opened in May 1915. The pollution caused by the smelters killed the valley's once-thriving agricultural business, forcing many farms out of business. Some lucky ones were able to relocate to the Sedona area and start their lives over. (Published by Frashers, Inc.)

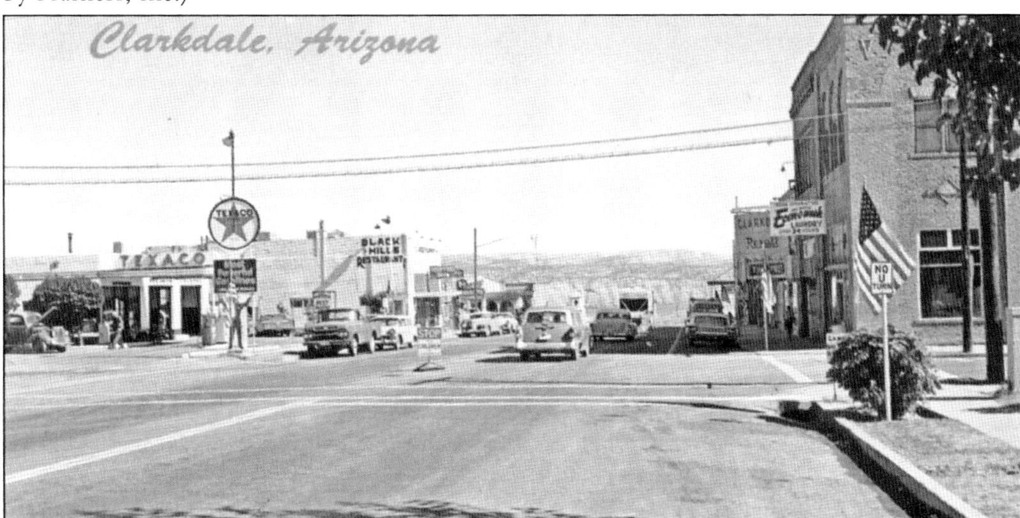

CLARKDALE, DOWNTOWN CLARKDALE, DATED ON BACK APRIL 3, 1964 (REAL PHOTO POSTCARD). Clarkdale was bought and sold a number of times beginning in 1953. Over the next few years, the citizens of Clarkdale became fed up with management of the town and banded together to incorporate their town. With the blessing of the Yavapai County Board of Supervisors, Clarkdale broke free as a company town and incorporated on July 1, 1957. (Published by the Bradshaw Studios, photograph by Bob Bradshaw.)

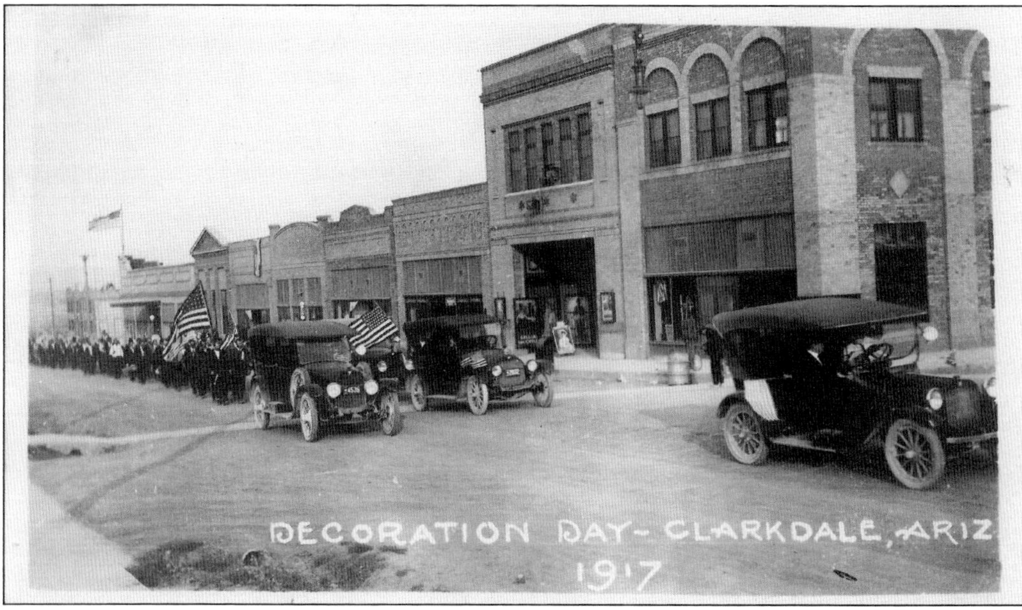

CLARKDALE, DECORATION DAY, C. 1917 (REAL PHOTO POSTCARD). This is one of the last two images taken on Decoration Day (Memorial Day) 1917 in downtown Clarkdale showing the Clarkdale Business Block. Downtown has not changed much over the years and still has the charm of 80 years ago. One can still stroll through the town streets and enjoy its restaurants, bars, and art galleries, and on a nice summer evening sit on the grass of the city's park and listen to a concert on the bandstand. (Courtesy Nancy Burgess.)

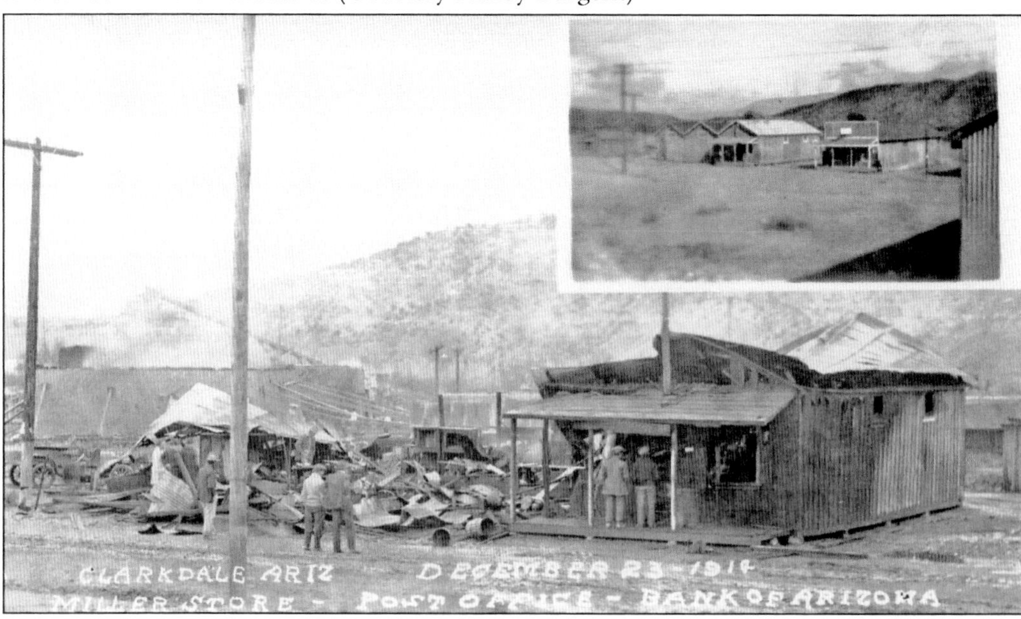

CLARKDALE, DOWNTOWN FIRE, DECEMBER 23, 1914 (REAL PHOTO POSTCARD). According to the *Weekly Journal-Miner* of December 30, 1914, the early-morning fire caused by an unattended stove in a store caused the destruction of the Bank of Arizona, post office, and T.F. Miller Company buildings. Ironically, the Miller store had just completed a brick building and was soon to start moving its stock to the new location. (Courtesy Nancy Burgess.)

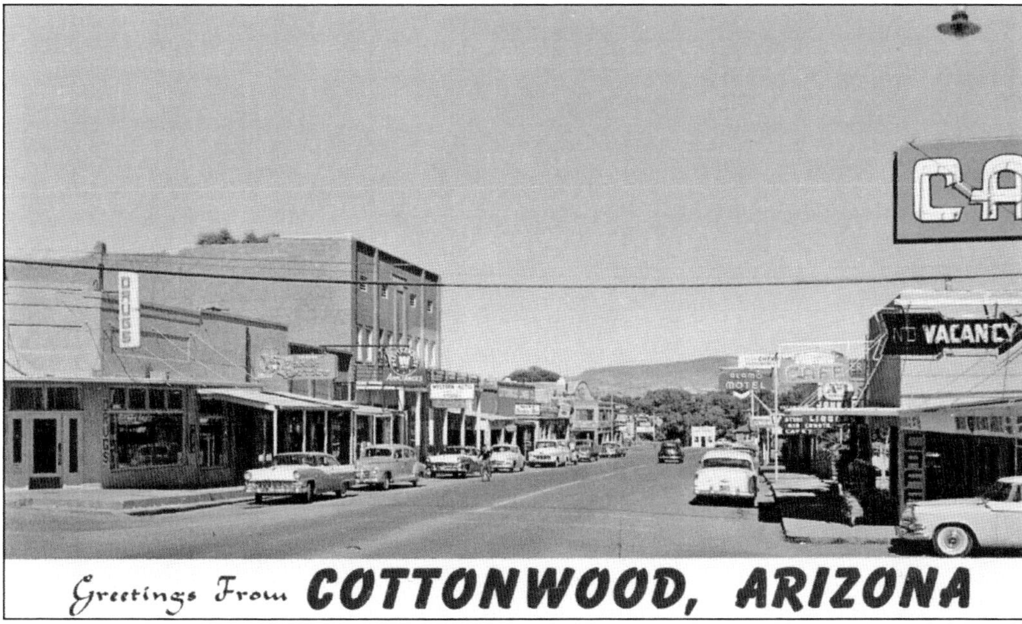

COTTONWOOD, DOWNTOWN, 1950s–1960s (REAL PHOTO POSTCARD). Downtown Cottonwood is now home to some wonderful restaurants, quaint shops, and local wineries. Located in the Verde Valley, Cottonwood was settled as a farming community and provider of goods for the soldiers at Fort Verde. (Published by Dexter Press, photograph by Bob Bradshaw.)

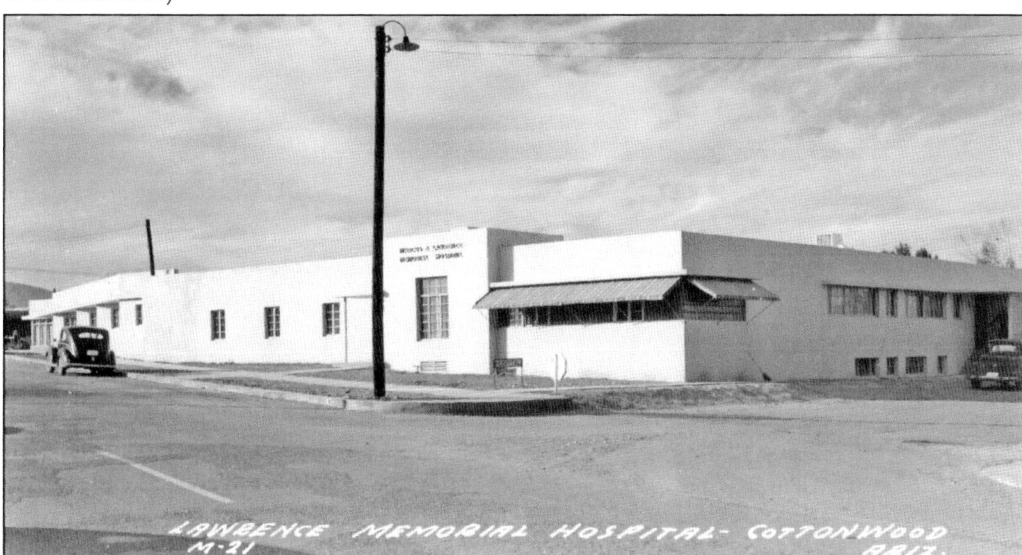

COTTONWOOD, LAWRENCE MEMORIAL HOSPITAL, C. 1945. (REAL PHOTO POSTCARD). In 1939, Carrie Lawrence donated a large sum of money to the heath care community of Cottonwood to have a hospital named after her son, Marcus J. Lawrence. Many years later, the hospital was renamed Verde Valley Medical Center after it became known that Lawrence was murdered by a jealous boyfriend who found out Lawrence was sleeping with his girlfriend. Lawrence was known to be a local gambler and playboy when he was beaten to death in Prescott in 1938. (Published by L.L. Cook Co.)

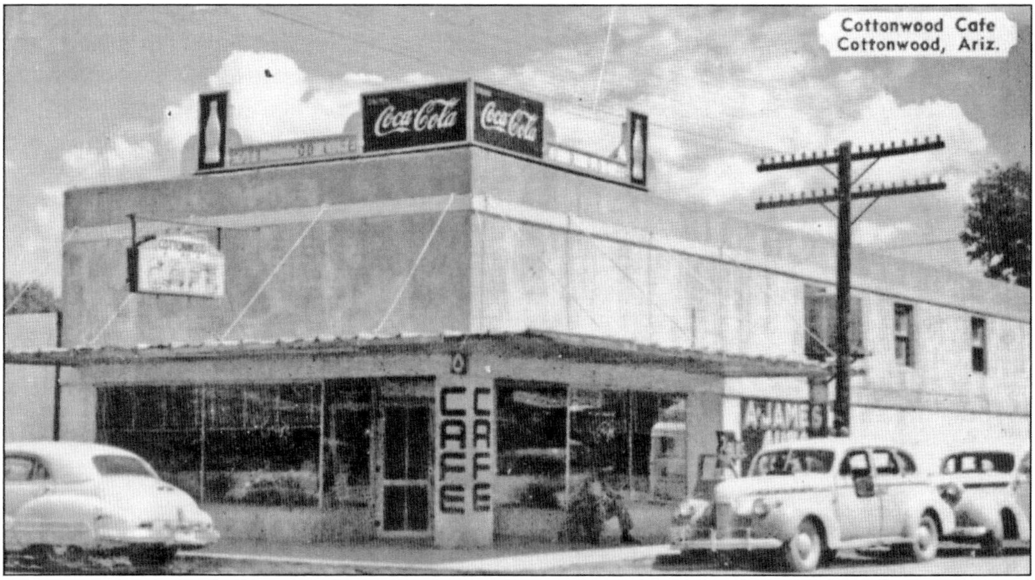

COTTONWOOD, COTTONWOOD CAFÉ, C. 1950 (REAL PHOTO POSTCARD). Built in 1933 after a fire decimated four businesses and a home on the corner of North Main and East Pinal Streets, the Cottonwood Café was a fixture in Cottonwood until it closed in the 1960s. In more recent years, the building has been a wine bistro, Greek restaurant, women's clothing store, frame shop, and pet store. On the back of the card is written, "Where Bill & I ate our dinner 1950." (Published by Clear-Vue, David Lionell Press.)

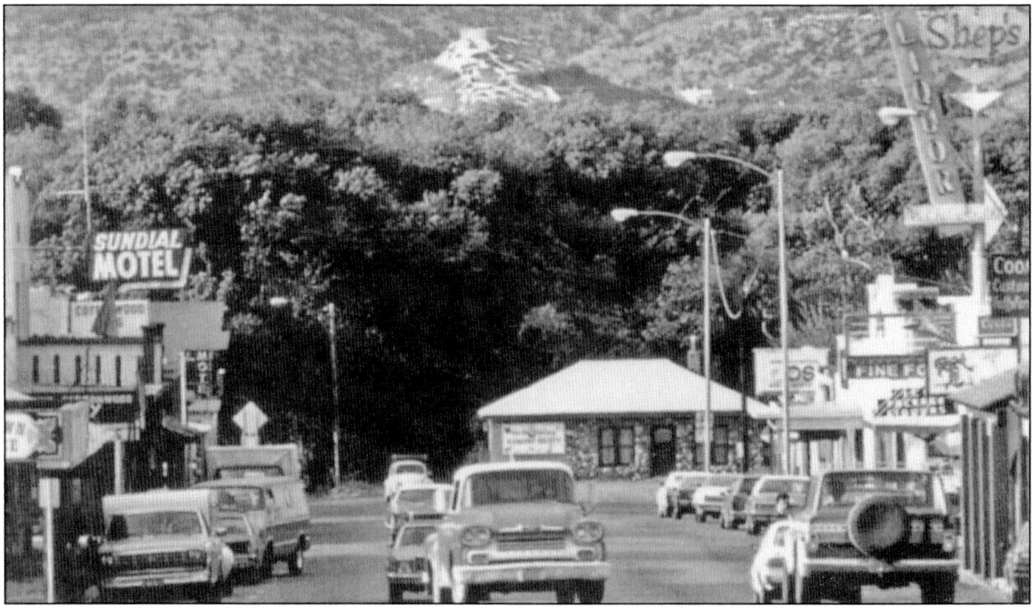

COTTONWOOD, DOWNTOWN COTTONWOOD, C. 1970S (REAL PHOTO POSTCARD). Downtown Cottonwood is pictured with Tuzigoot National Monument in the background. Due to the decline in mining operations through the 1940s and 1950s, Cottonwood saw its population plummet from about 4,000 to just a few hundred. The city incorporated in 1960, and as of 2013, the population has rebounded to well over 11,000 people. (Published by the Bradshaw Studios, courtesy of John Bradshaw and Bradshaw Color Studios.)

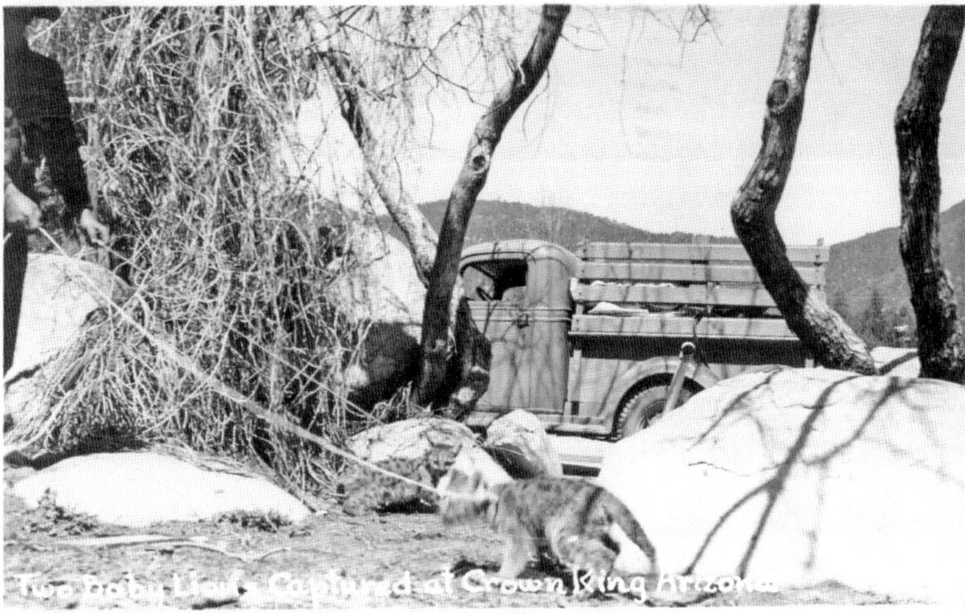

CROWN KING, MOUNTAIN LION CUBS, POSTMARKED OCTOBER 12, 1939 (REAL PHOTO POSTCARD). Two mountain lion cubs are captured at Crown King. Located high in the Bradshaw Mountains along the Senator Highway, Crown King still boasts a population of just over 100 year-round residents, well below its heyday of a few thousand in the late 1800s. The community was named after the Crowned King Mine and shortened its name to Crown King in 1888. At the height of the mining boom, Crown King had over 500 structures, including boardinghouses, saloons, several company stores, and even two Chinese restaurants. To handle the growing mine operations, a railroad was built in 1904. But due to financial failure, the railroad was abandoned in 1926. The old railroad bed is still in use today, not as a railroad but as the main access road to Crown King.

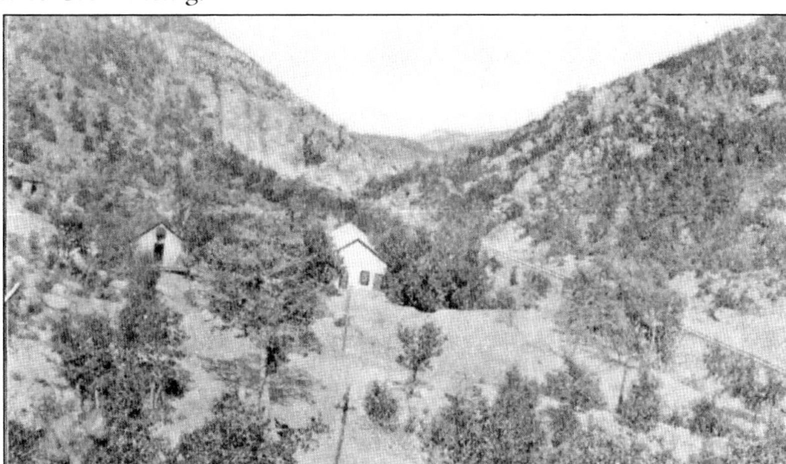

View, Crown King, Arizona

CROWN KING, C. 1915 (DIVIDED BACKPOSTCARD). An old house and barn stand alone on a hillside near Crown King. Although the town is not visible in this postcard, one can get an idea of how remote the town site is. Even today, the road to Crown King is dirt and is about an hour's drive from the nearest paved road.

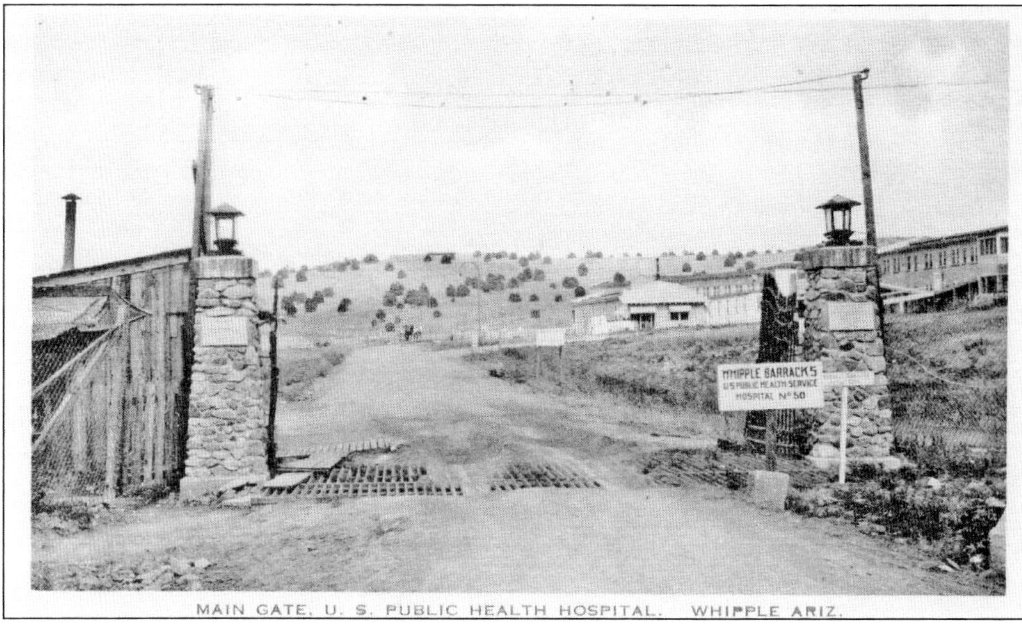

FORT WHIPPLE, MAIN GATE, C. 1920S. (ALBERTYPE POSTCARD). From his office in Santa Fe in October 1863, Gen. James Henry Carleton ordered a new military post be opened in Arizona to protect miners and settlers from a perceived Indian threat. The fort was to be named Fort Whipple after Amiel W. Whipple, who in the 1850s conducted a survey from Arkansas to Southern California to locate the best route for a railroad. The original Main Gate is still standing today on the grounds of Yavapai College. (Published by B.B. Shimonowsky & Bro., Post Exchange.)

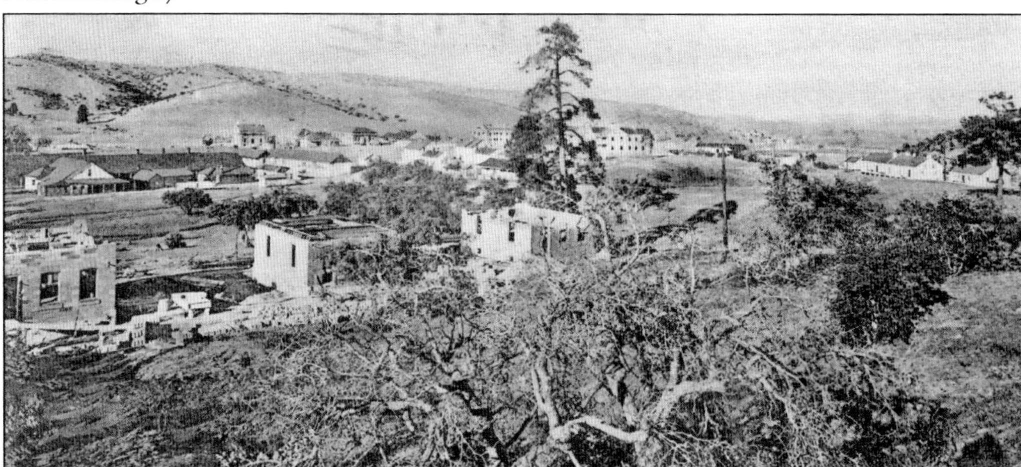

FORT WHIPPLE, WHIPPLE BARRACKS, POSTMARKED FEBRUARY 27, 1909 (HAND-COLORED POSTCARD). In May 1864, the army camp had moved from Chino Valley, where the first fort had been established, to its present site along Granite Creek. By the early 1870s most of the dilapidated old fort was demolished to make way for new barracks for the troops, along with officers' quarters, storehouses, and offices. The mid-1880s saw a shift of hostilities towards southern Arizona, with a large portion of troops following from Fort Whipple. For two years, 1885 and 1886, Fort Whipple became home to the 10th US Cavalry, known as the "Buffalo Soldiers." (Produced by Brisley Drug Co.)

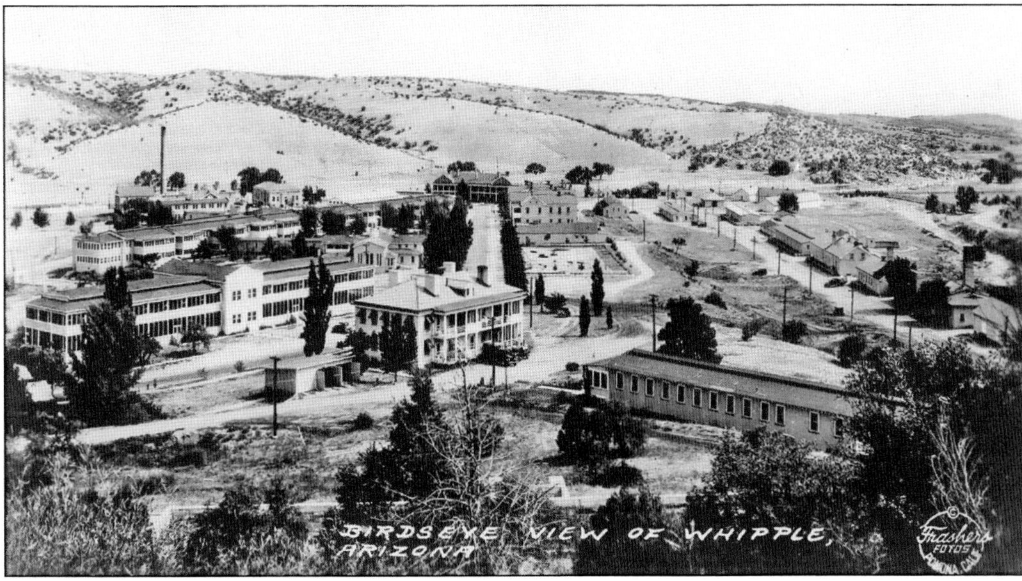

FORT WHIPPLE, C. 1930S (DIVIDED BACK POSTCARD). Fort Whipple had a second life in 1918 when it was activated as a US Army hospital. With the end of World War I, the Army needed facilities to treat its men returning from Europe who had contracted tuberculosis and who suffered from gassings during battle. In 1920, the US Public Health Service took over operations of the facilities to use as hospital for veterans. Today, Whipple is still serving America's veterans as a hospital run by the Veterans Administration. (Published by Frashers, Inc.)

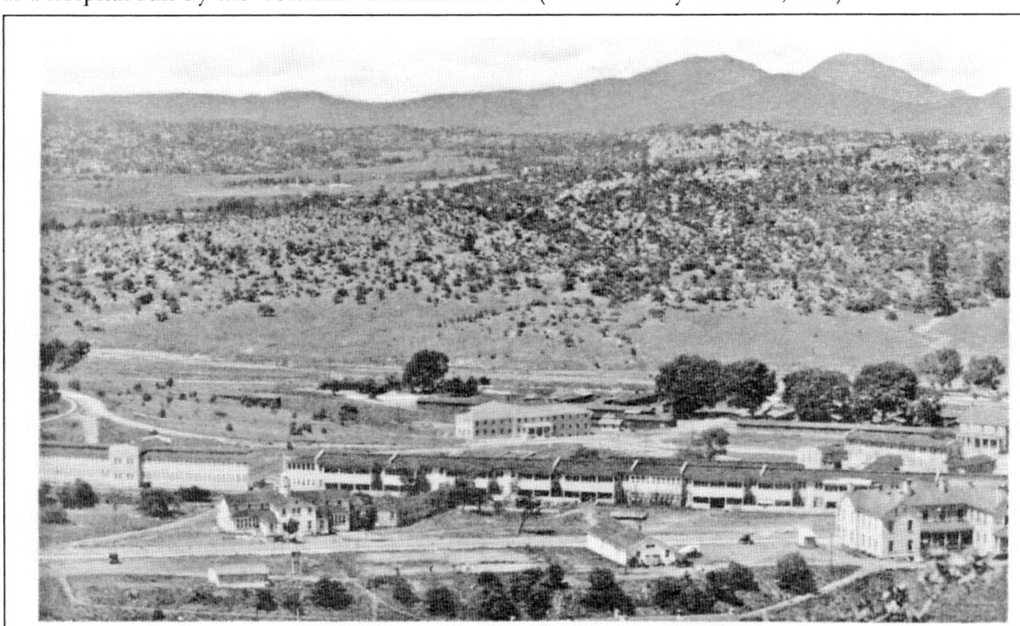

FORT WHIPPLE, HOSPITAL, C. 1920S (ALBERTYPE POSTCARD). On December 6, 2003, Pres. George W. Bush signed legislation that changed the name to Bob Stump Department of Veterans Affairs Medical Center. Stump served four terms in the Arizona House of Representatives from 1959 to 1967 and five terms in the Arizona State Senate from 1967 to 1976. (Produced by Brisley Drug Co.)

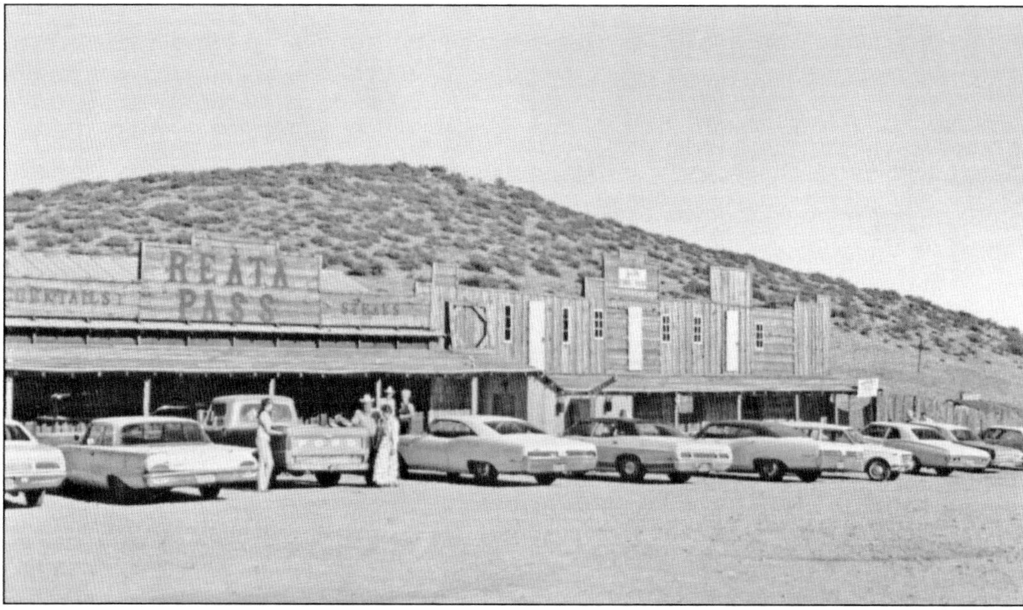

HUMBOLDT, REATA PASS STEAKHOUSE, C. 1963 (ADVERTISING POSTCARD). A local favorite for many years closed its doors over 20 years ago and reopened as the Reata Pass Auction House. The steakhouse also had a stage where local performers did skits and melodramas. The original Reata Pass was located northeast of Phoenix and was an old stage stop from Phoenix to Fort McDowell on the Verde River.

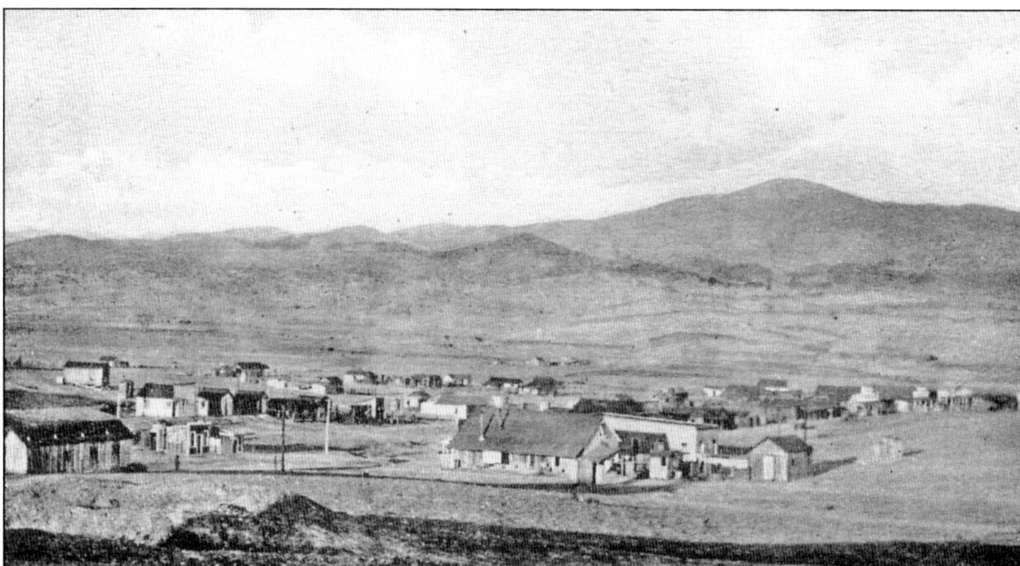

HUMBOLDT, TOWN VIEW, C. 1910 (ALBERTYPE POSTCARD). The original post office opened as Val Verde in 1899 but was renamed Humboldt in 1905 after the German explorer Baron Alexander von Humboldt. By 1907, Humboldt's population had grown to over 1,000 people. With the growth, the town boomed. It now had upwards of 15 bars, a number of bordellos, five restaurants, stores, hotels, banks, bakeries, along with every unsavory character a boom town could draw. (Courtesy Nancy Burgess.)

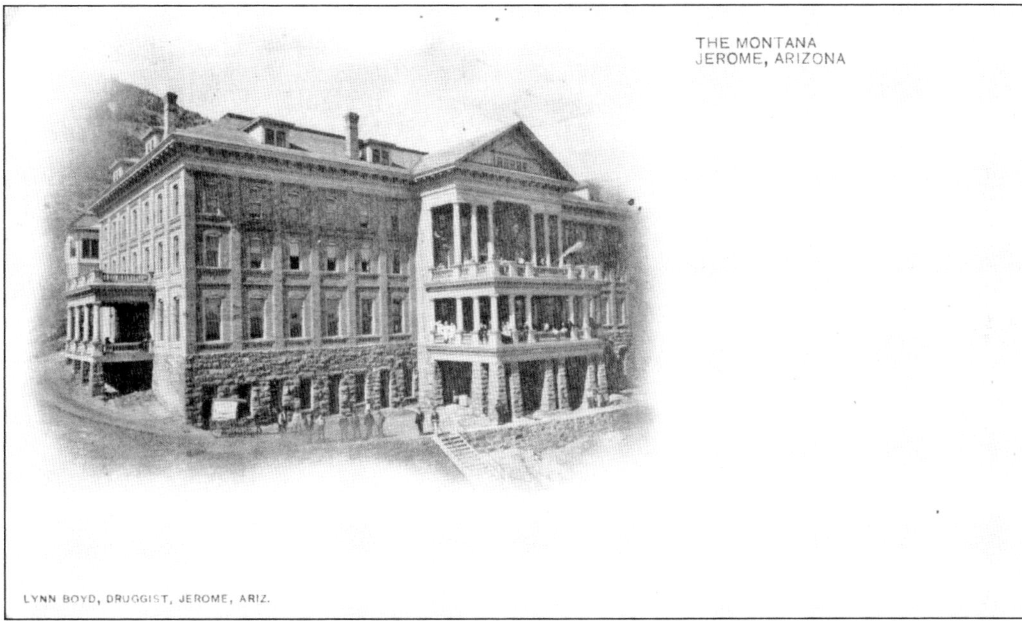

JEROME, THE MONTANA, C. 1904 (UNDIVIDED BACK POSTCARD). Built for his employees, Sen. William A. Clark opened the Montana Hotel in 1900. According to the *Coconino Sun* newspaper from March 5, 1915, the Montana Hotel was "one of the largest and most complete hostelries in the state." It burned to the ground on Sunday, February 29, 1915. (Produced by Lynn Boyd Drug.)

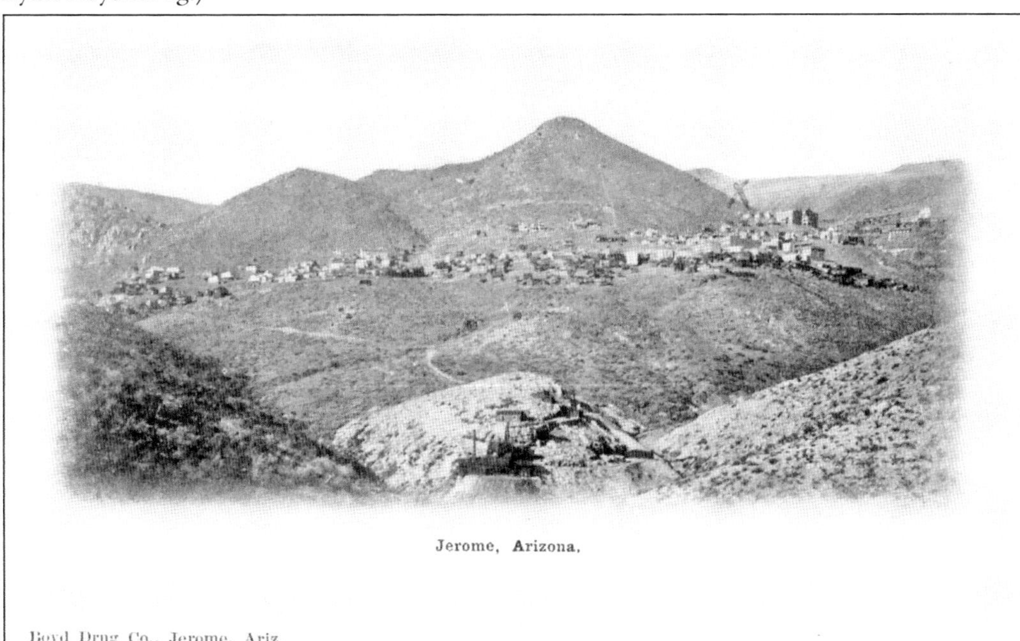

JEROME, TOWN VIEW, C. 1904 (UNDIVIDED BACK POSTCARD). Someone many years ago handwrote on the back of the card, "The mine is just around the corner and is marked by 'X' The large building just to the right of 'x' is the Montana Hotel." (Produced by Lynn Boyd Drug.)

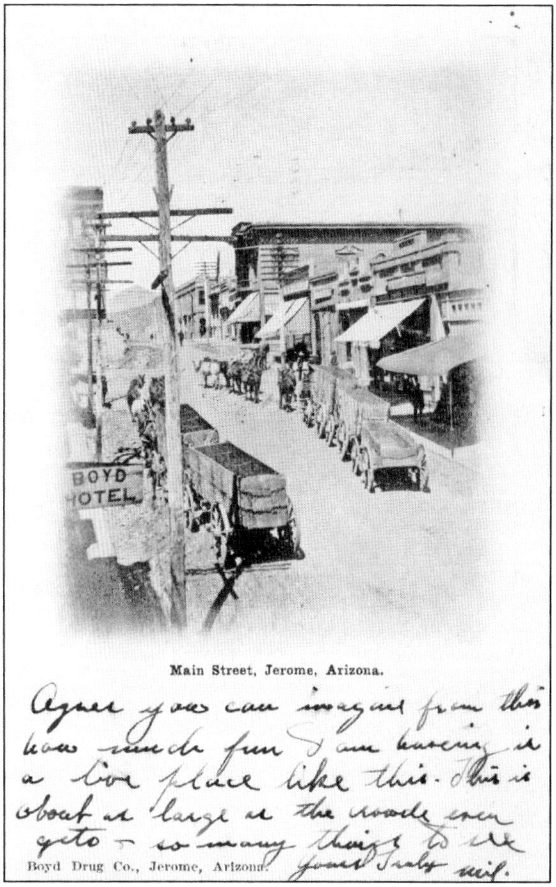

LEFT: JEROME, ORE WAGONS, POSTMARKED SEPTEMBER 20, 1907 (DIVIDED BACK POSTCARD); BELOW: JEROME, MULE TRAINS, C. 1910 (DIVIDED BACK POSTCARD). Long before a car traveled on Main Street in Jerome, ore wagons were a common site. Handwritten on the face of the card at left is, in part, "Agnes you can imagine from this how much fun I am having in a live place like this. Yours Truly Neil." (Left, produced by Lynn Boyd Drug; below, published by R.A. Smith–Jerome, courtesy Nancy Burgess.)

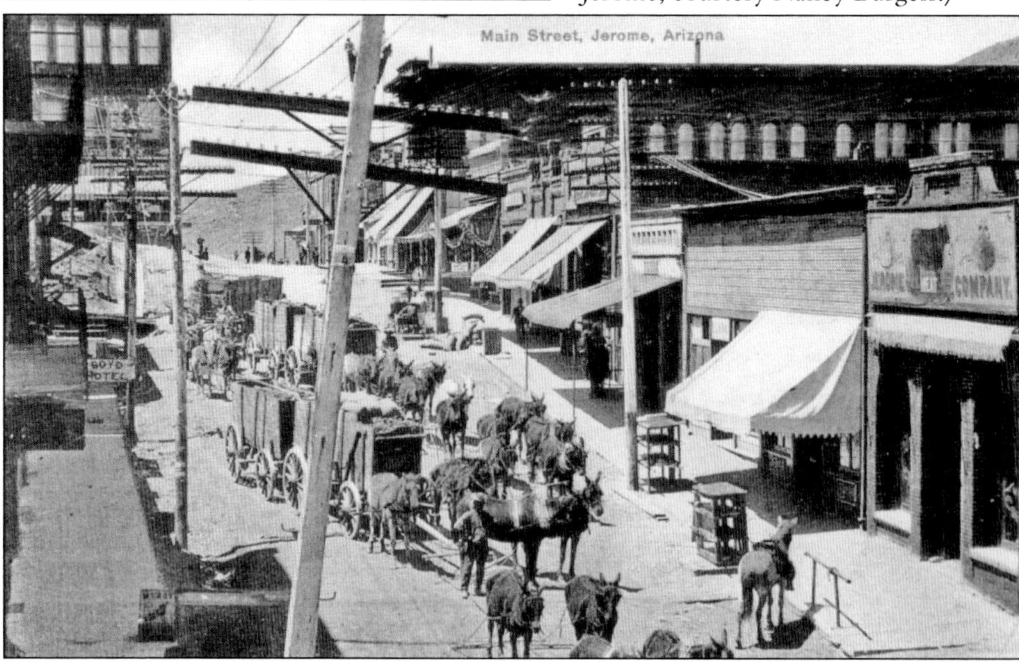

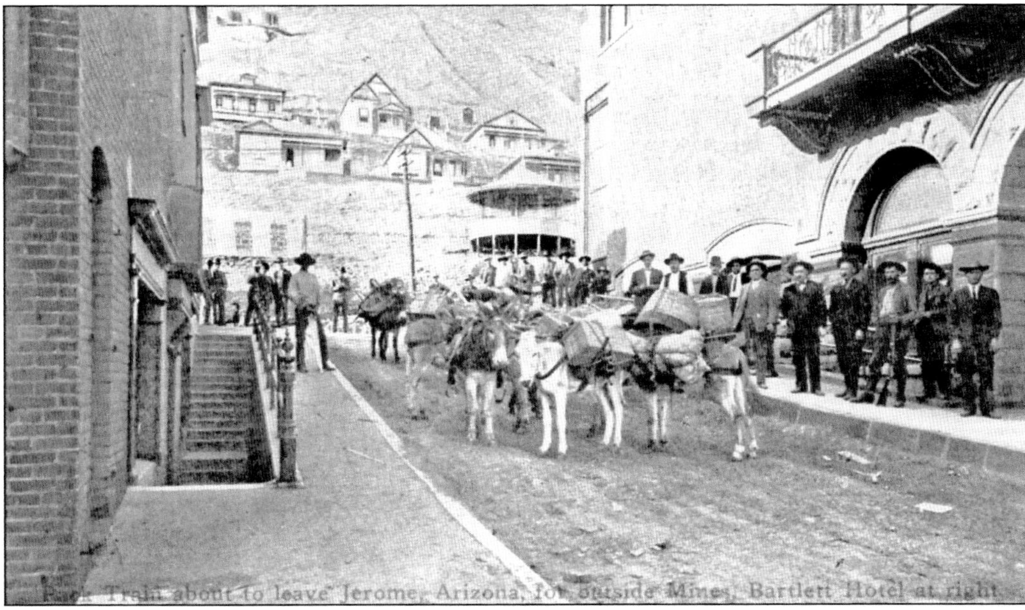

JEROME, PACK TRAIN, POSTMARKED JANUARY 18, 1912 (HAND-PAINTED POSTCARD). The caption at the bottom of the card reads, "Pack train about to leave Jerome, Arizona, for outside Mines, Bartlett Hotel at right." Although a few automobiles were in Jerome at the time, most mines were still only reachable by wagons or mules. (Published by E.W. Carroll, Jerome.)

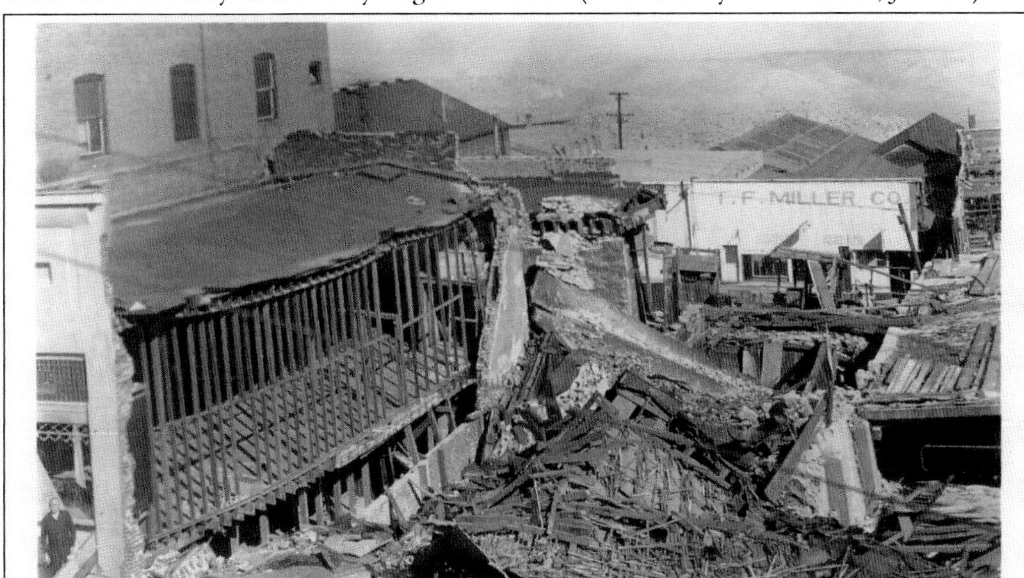

JEROME, COLLAPSING CITY, C. 1937. (REAL PHOTO POSTCARD.) Handwritten on the back of this card is the following: "Looking over the wreckage to the next st. Next to the T.F. Miller garage is the Post Office and that is as bad as the main for 2 blks or worse. The Post Office is going to be at the other end of town, no stores on 1 side of Main St. for 2 blks, and the other side is almost 5 ft higher and the sidewalks are starting to sink so we not only have a different town but we have a Board walk which reminds me of Atlantic City or somewhere else. Freda." (Courtesy Nancy Burgess.)

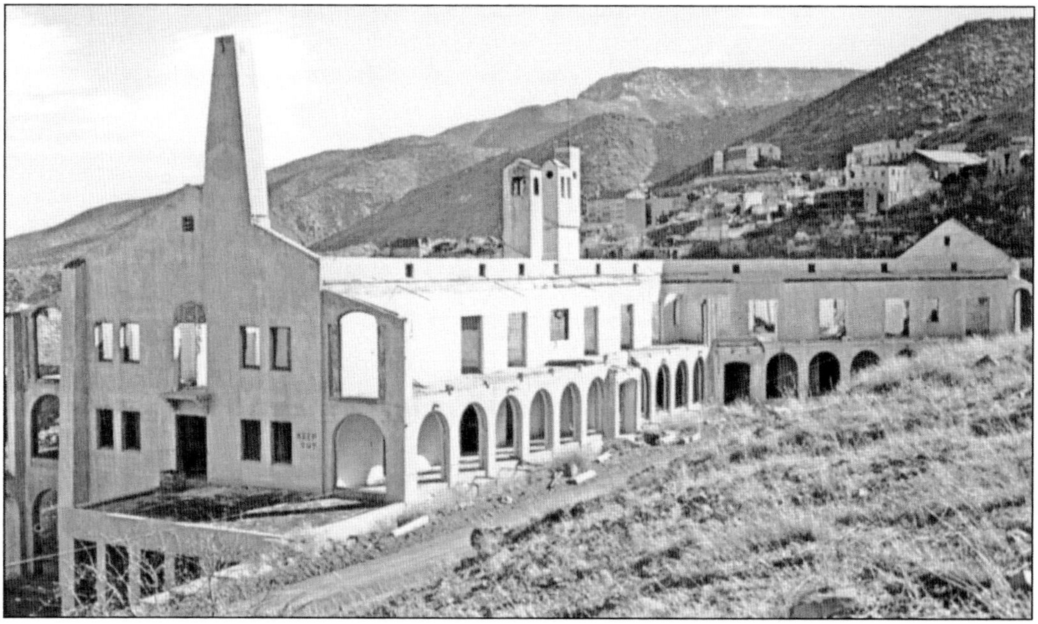

Jerome, Little Daisy Hotel, Hand Dated May 17, 1964 (Real Photo Postcard). Now a private residence, the Little Daisy Hotel was named after one of the original mines in Jerome. Built in 1919 as a dormitory for miners, it allowed miners to sleep while the next shift worked. When that shift ended, the miners had to give up their room so the other shift's miners could sleep. (Published and photograph by Bob Bradshaw.)

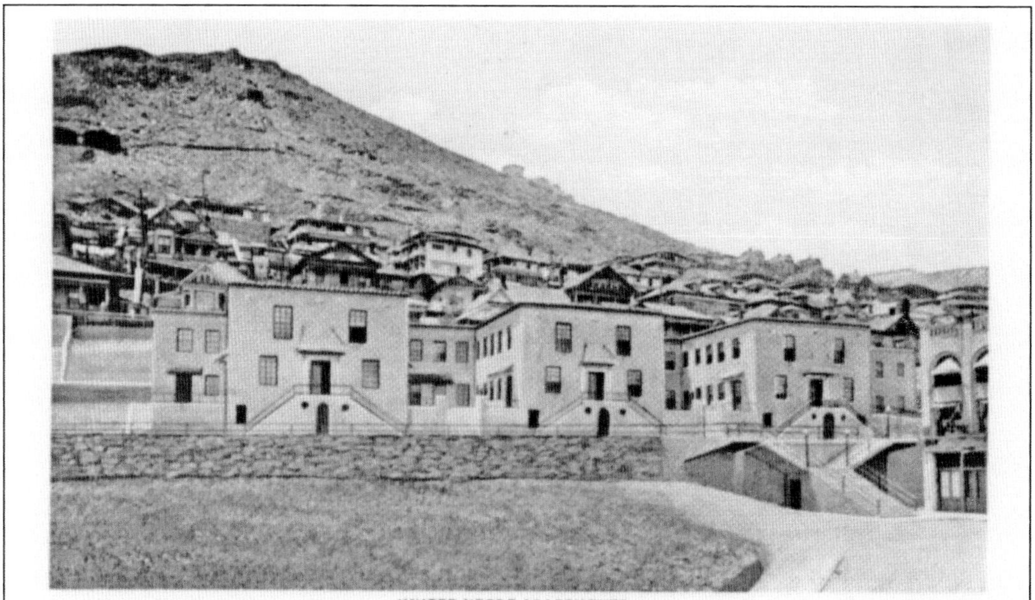

Jerome, United Verde Apartments, c. 1930s (Souvenir Folder Postcard). With its restored apartments, the old building is now a mix of housing, art studios, restaurants and retail shops. The two/three-story art deco apartment buildings, like most of Jerome, were built in the early 1900s to house local miners. The apartment complex remained abandoned from the 1950s until the 1990s, when it was restored to its present-day condition.

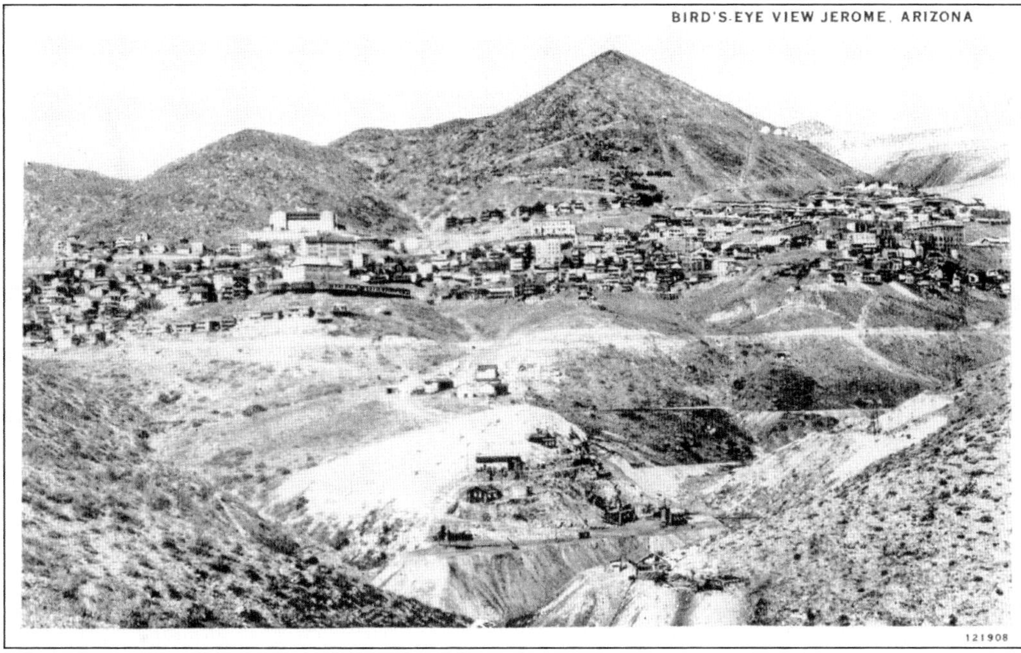

JEROME, TOWN VIEW, POSTMARKED MARCH 17, 1929 (CURT TEICH POSTCARD). In a period of just five short years, Jerome saw four disastrous fires. The first was in 1894, when the commercial district burned down. Only three years later in 1897, after rebuilding the business district, tragedy struck again as the entire business area burned once again. In 1898, again the business district burned to the ground. The last was in 1899, when a number of restaurants and saloons went up in flames. The last fire caused the citizens to finally act, and the city of Jerome was incorporated. With the incorporation, the Jerome fire district was formed. (Published by D.T. Mallonee.)

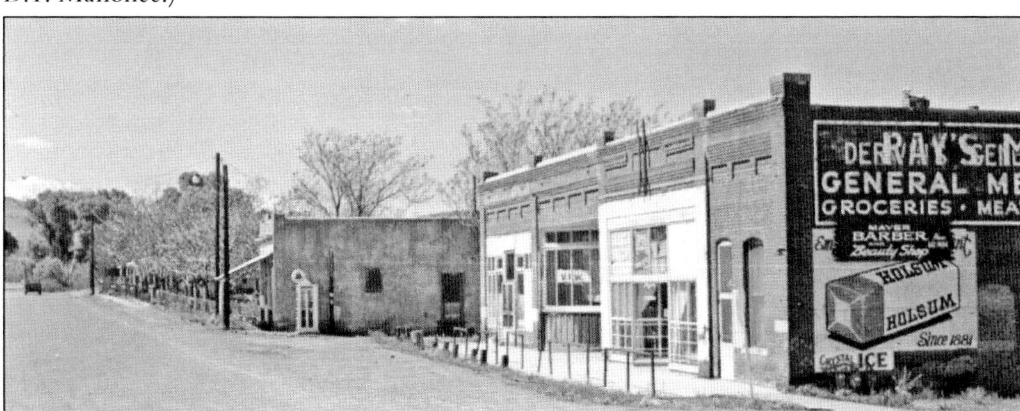

MAYER, C. 1960 (REAL PHOTO POSTCARD). The town was named after Joe Mayer, who purchased the stage station and set up a saloon and store in the late 1880s. It soon became a center for trade for local miners and farmers. In one of the darkest moments in American history, it was involved in the internment of Japanese Americans. For two months in 1942, May and June, Japanese Americans from Maricopa County and Arizona towns were confined to Mayer's Assembly Center. Approximately 245 citizens from 69 families were held there until transferred to the Poston concentration camp in southwest Arizona. (Published by Royal Pictures, photograph by Merie Porter.)

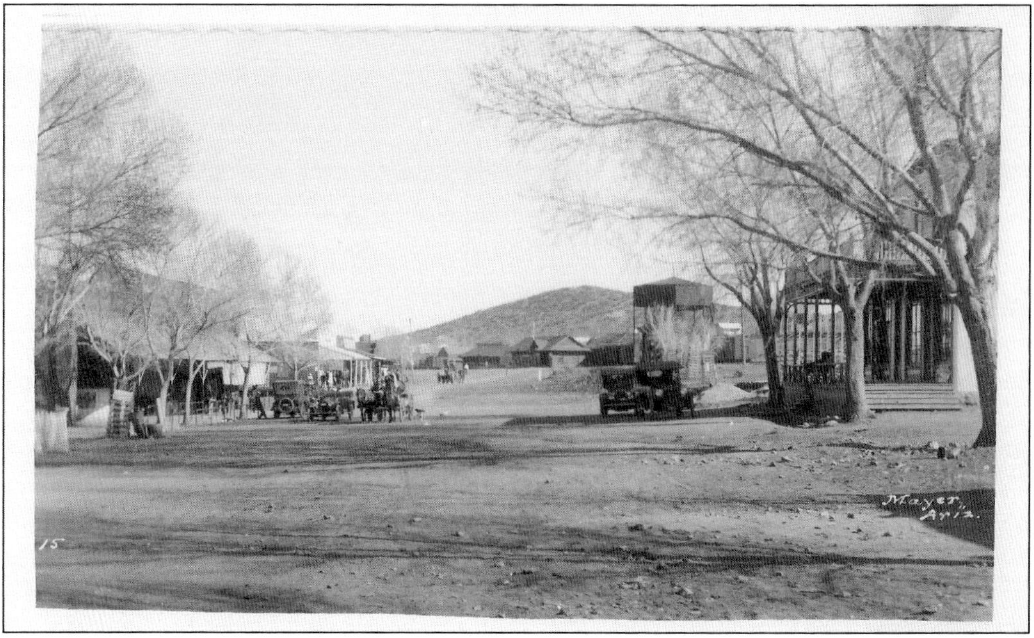

MAYER, DOWNTOWN, C. 1920 (REAL PHOTO POSTCARD). On July 13, 1882, Joe Mayer purchased the Big Bug Station, now Mayer, along with the surrounding 160 acres, for $1,200 in gold. Downtown Mayer is pictured, looking toward the Prescott & Eastern Railroad Depot with the railroads water tower on the right. The Mayer Business Block, beginning with the first building on the left, was built in four phases and was completed in 1904. Joe Mayer transplanted the cottonwood trees from Big Bug Creek. (Courtesy Nancy Burgess.)

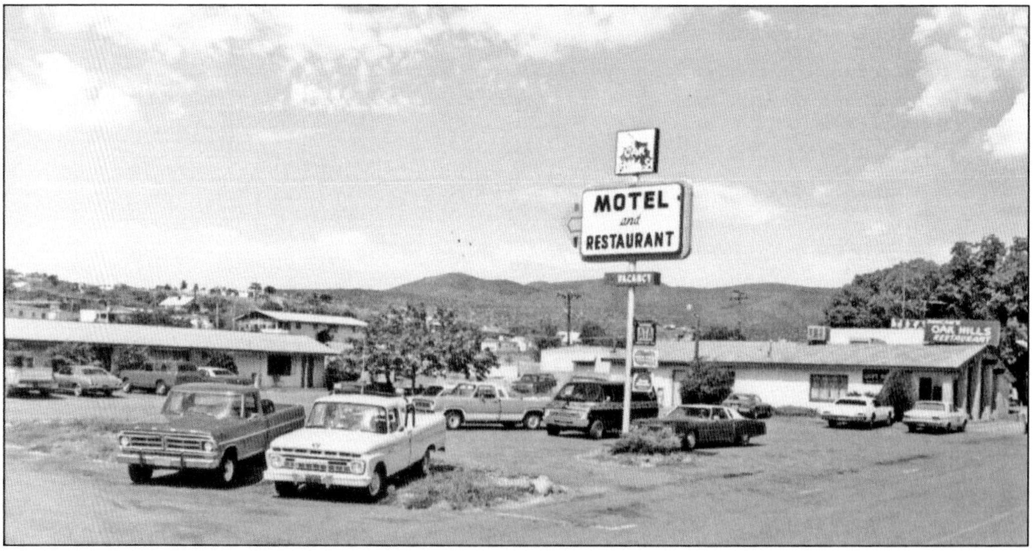

MAYER, DUNCAN'S OAK HILLS MOTEL, C. 1970S (ADVERTISING POSTCARD). Purchased by the Teskys in 1992, the Oak Hills Motel and Restaurant ran successfully until about 2000, when the hotel was bought and sold twice but ended up back in the Teskys' hands. By that time, the hotel had been so run down that it cost too much to renovate, and the hotel portion remains closed to this day. After a six-month renovation, the restaurant was reopened as Tesky's. It remains a popular local eating establishment. (Published and photograph by Charles Kendall.)

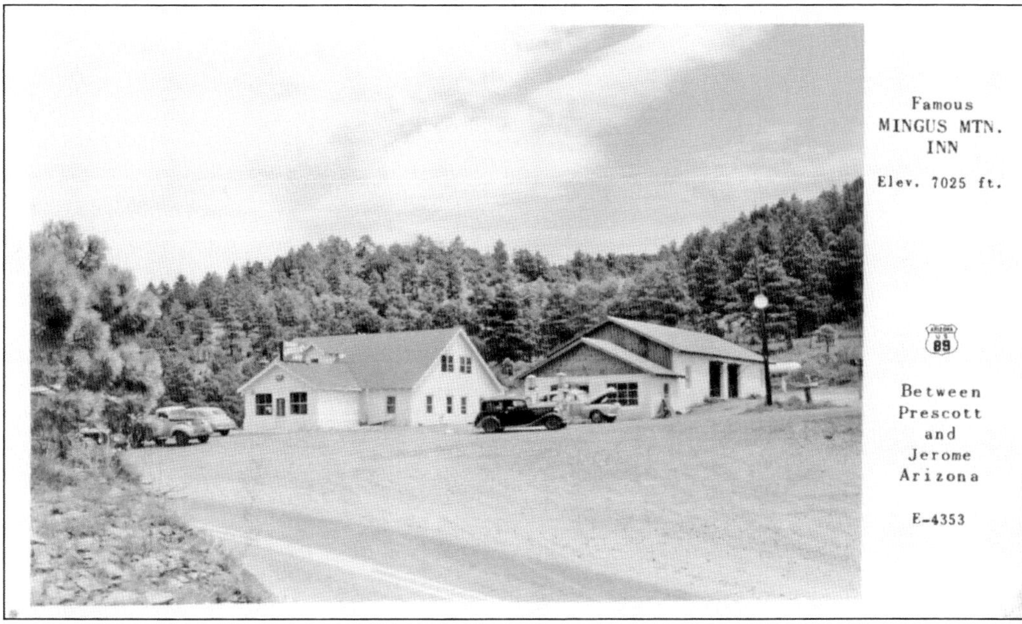

BOTH: MINGUS MOUNTAIN INN, C. 1940S (REAL PHOTO POSTCARDS). Now a parking lot at the summit of Mingus Mountain on Highway 89A between Prescott and Jerome, the Mingus Mountain Inn opened for business around 1930. In 1941, the highway changed numbers from 79 to 89A. Until the early 1970s, the inn still had the old-fashioned glass-bowl gas pumps. The inn closed around 1980. (Above, published by Frashers, Inc., courtesy Tony Meager; below, published by Frashers, Inc., courtesy Nancy Burgess.)

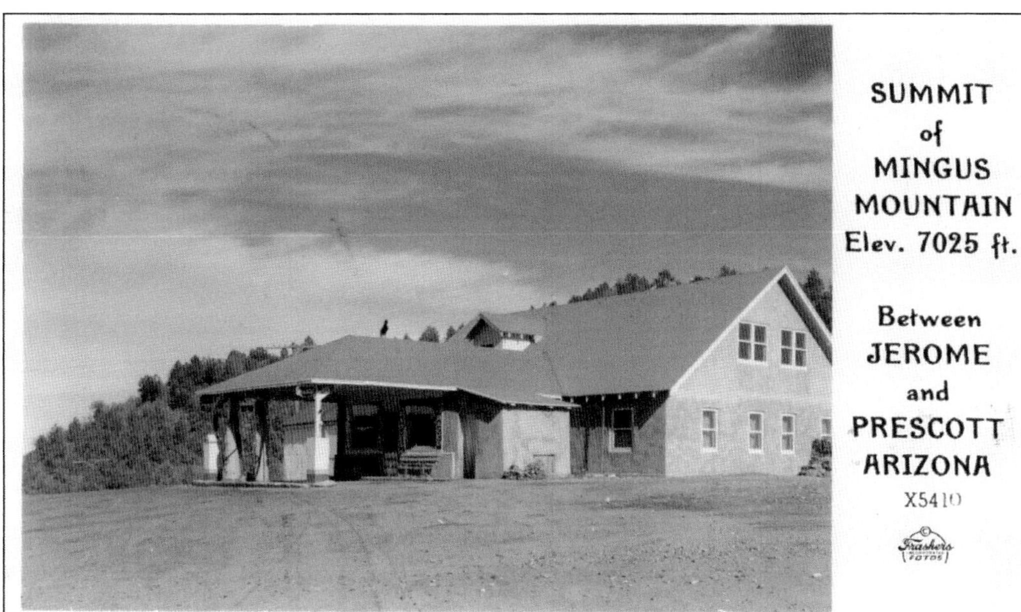

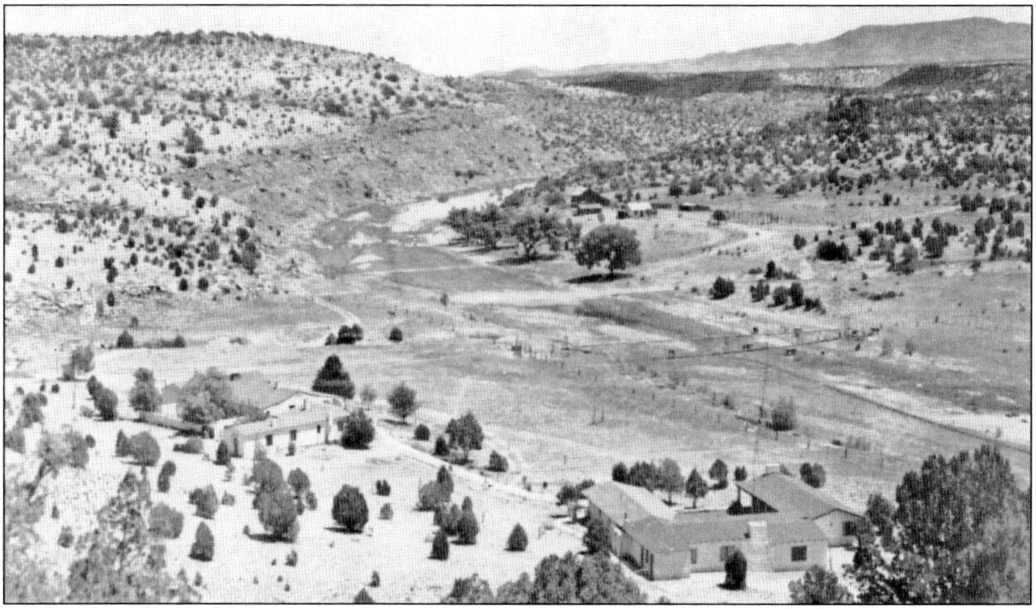

PAULDEN, VERDE CATTLE RANCH, C. 1947 (REAL PHOTO POSTCARD). Nestled along the banks of the Verde River outside of Paulden, the Verde Cattle and Guest Ranch, like many dude ranches throughout Yavapai County from the 1930s through the 1950s, hosted city slickers for a week of ranch-style living. For $35 to $50 a week, a person received living quarters, access to horses, and even shooting lessons. The ranch still looks pretty much as it did over 60 years ago, but it is now a private cattle ranch.

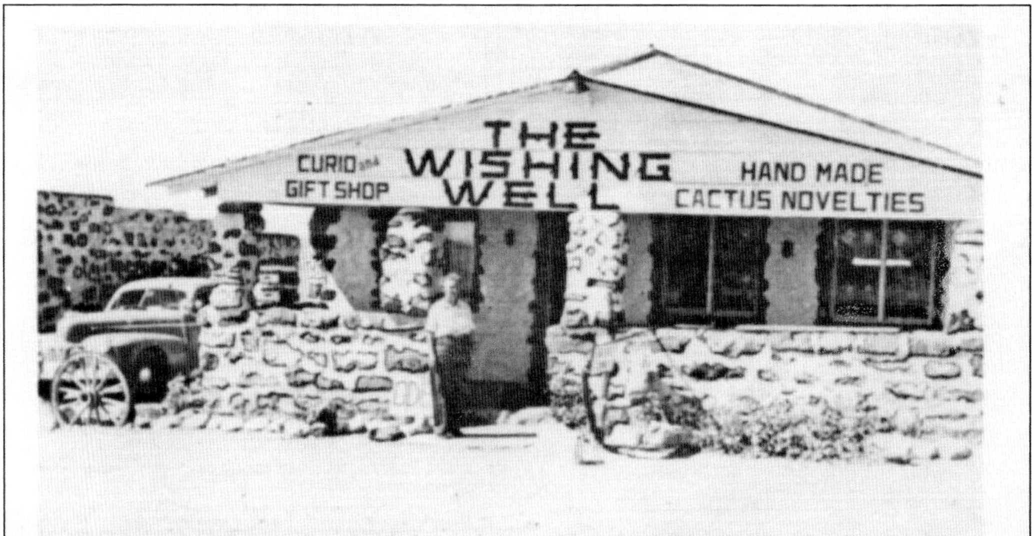

THE WISHING WELL - U.S. 89 NEAR PAULDEN, ARIZONA

PAULDEN, THE WISHING WELL, C. 1940S (ADVERTISING POSTCARD). Located just north of Paulden on Highway 89, the Wishing Well closed its doors around 2012. Possibly once a private residence, the building has seen many uses over the years. Sometime before the early 1970s, the building was turned into the Wishing Well Tavern. In 1981, the building was expanded to include a restaurant and room for outdoor concerts. (Courtesy Tony Meager.)

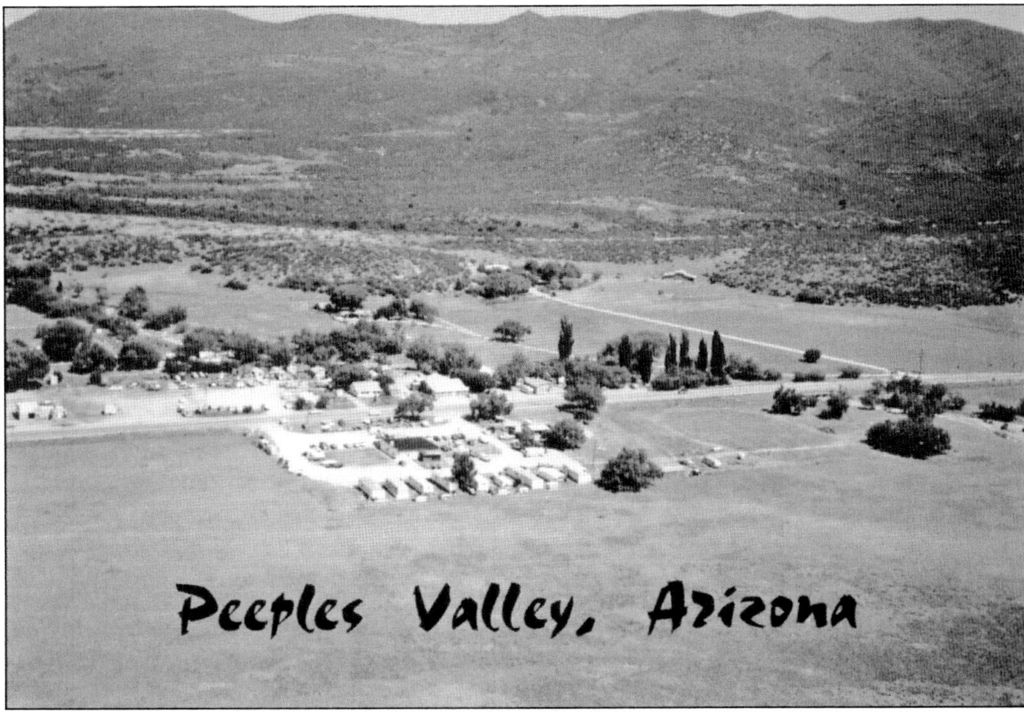

Peeples Valley, c. 1970s (Real Photo Postcard). Located just a few miles from Yarnell, Peeples Valley is a small farm and ranching community along Highway 89. The town was named after A.H. Peeples, who led a group of prospectors who discovered Gold Hill near Weaver, Arizona, in 1863. The back of the card reads, "The valley was first settled by Charley and Ida Genung and their family in the mid-1860s. Using Indian workers Genung constructed the first road from Peeples Valley to Wickenburg in 1872." (Produced by Woody Barnes.)

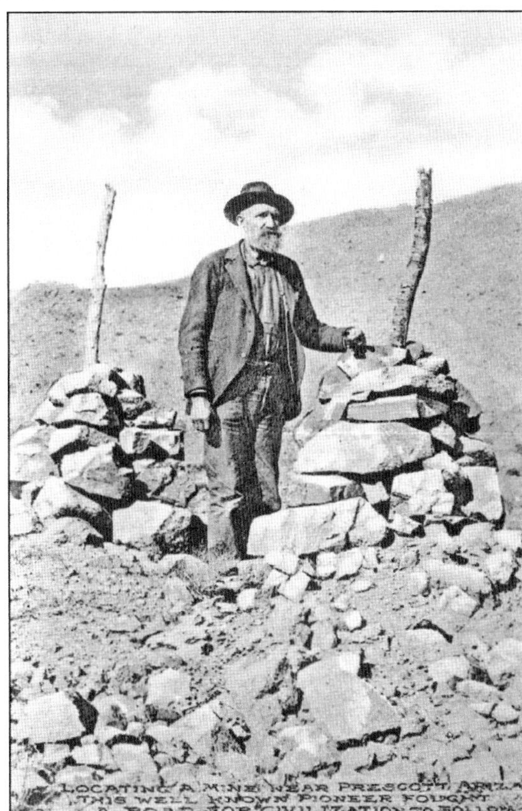

Peeples Valley, Charles Genung, c. 1910 (Albertype Postcard). Written on the front of the postcard is the following: "Locating a mine near Prescott, Ariz. This well known pioneer fought a road for civilization to follow." Born in New York in 1838, Charles was one of Arizona's pioneers, arriving in July 1863. He moved to Peeples Valley and set up ranching in 1870. Genung died in 1916 and is buried at the Citizens Cemetery in Prescott. (Produced by Brisley Drug Co., courtesy Skull Valley Historical Society.)

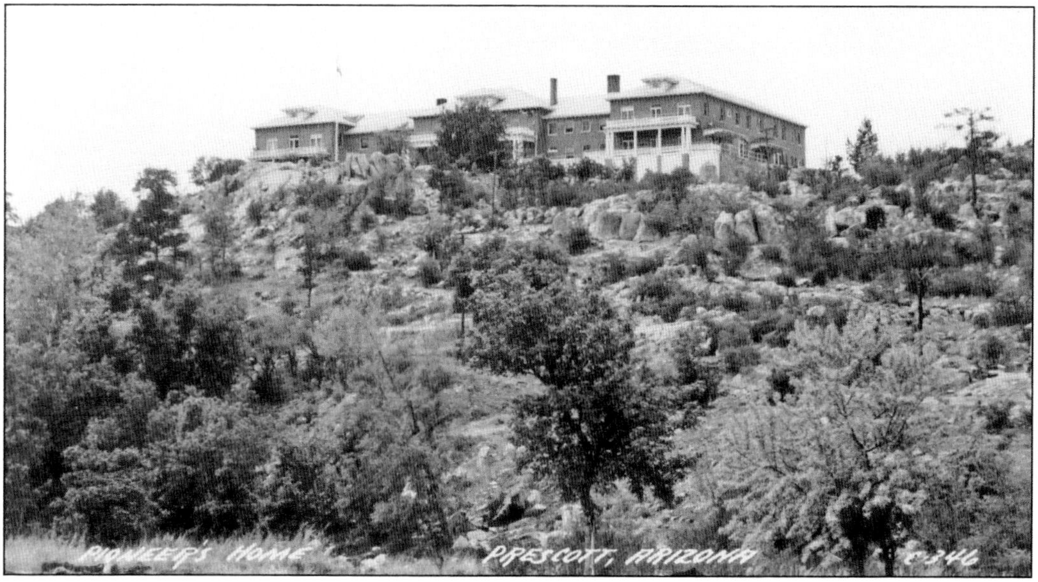

PRESCOTT, PIONEERS' HOME, c. 1940 (REAL PHOTO POSTCARD). Looking down over the town of Prescott, the three-story Pioneer's Home opened its doors in 1911. Originally it was built to house 40 men who were over the age of 60 and had lived in Arizona for at least 25 years. In 1916, it admitted 20 women, and in 1927, it was allowed to house disabled miners. One of the home's most famous residents was Mary Katherine Horony, who most people knew as Big Nose Kate. Kate was the common-law wife of Doc Holliday.

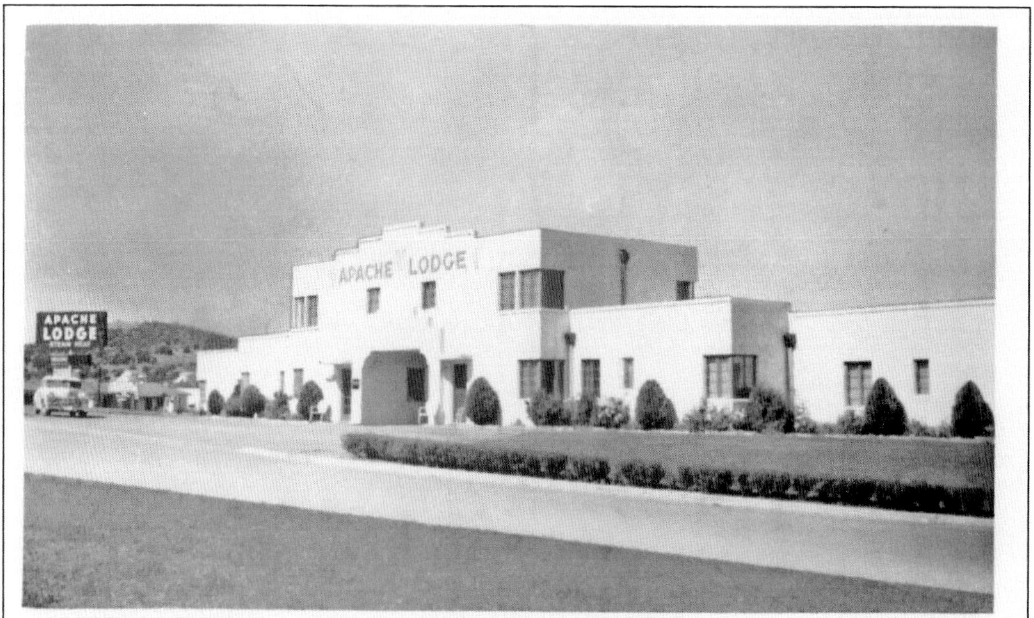

PRESCOTT, APACHE LODGE, c. 1950 (ADVERTISING POSTCARD). Opening in 1947 on East Gurley Street, the Apache Lodge boasted that its 26 rooms were carpeted and had both tubs and showers, circulating heat, and Beautyrest beds. It was approved by AAA, Best Western Motels, and Duncan Hines. Still in operation today, the Apache Lodge has been updated through the years but still has that old art deco feel. (Published by Newton Manufacturing Company.)

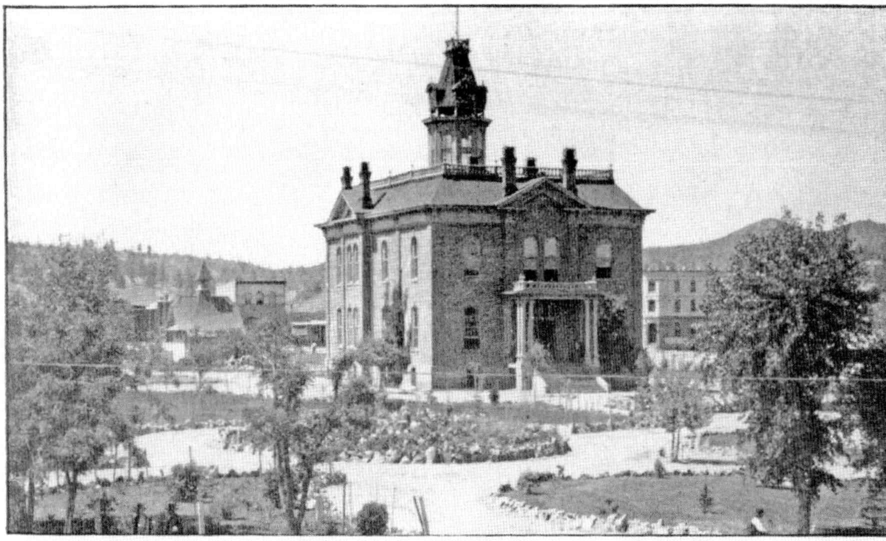

COURT HOUSE.

PRESCOTT, COURTHOUSE, C. 1910 (SOUVENIR POSTCARD FOLDER). The first county courthouse and jail, built in 1867, was a wood-framed building located on North Cortez Street. The second courthouse, built in 1878, was constructed on the same site on which the current courthouse now stands. It was torn down in 1916 to make way for the new courthouse. The only thing left of the courthouse is the old 600-pound bell that now rests in the courthouse bell tower. (Published by P.C. Armitage, Prescott.)

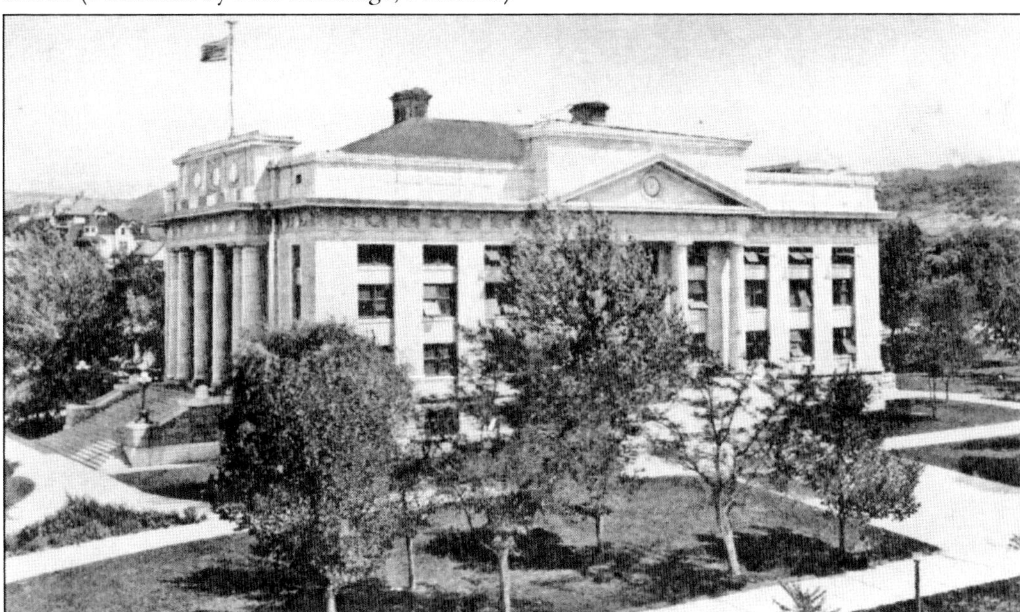

PRESCOTT, COURTHOUSE, POSTMARKED JULY 2, 1948 (ALBERTYPE HAND-COLORED POSTCARD). The current courthouse, completed in 1918, replaced a smaller brick Victorian-style courthouse built in 1878. Over many years, a number of upgrades have been done to the courthouse, but none so extensive as when a $2.4-million restoration project was started in 2012. (Published by Albertype.)

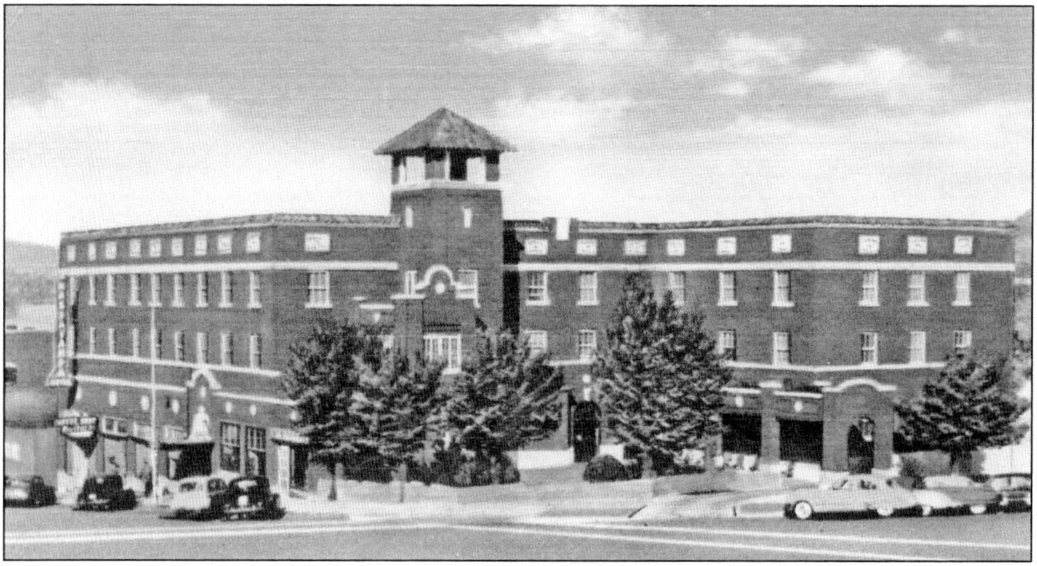

PRESCOTT, HASSAYAMPA HOTEL, C. 1940S (ADVERTISING LINEN POSTCARD). The Hassayampa is still as elegant as when it opened in 1927 on East Gurley and Marina Streets. The 78-room Hassayampa filled the need for a first-class hotel when it was built and continues as one of the finest in Prescott. According to lore, the Hassayampa is haunted by at least three sprits: one is a young woman who was jilted by her husband on their wedding night; another is a man in Western clothing; and lastly, a young boy of about six haunts the laundry room. (Published by MWM Company.)

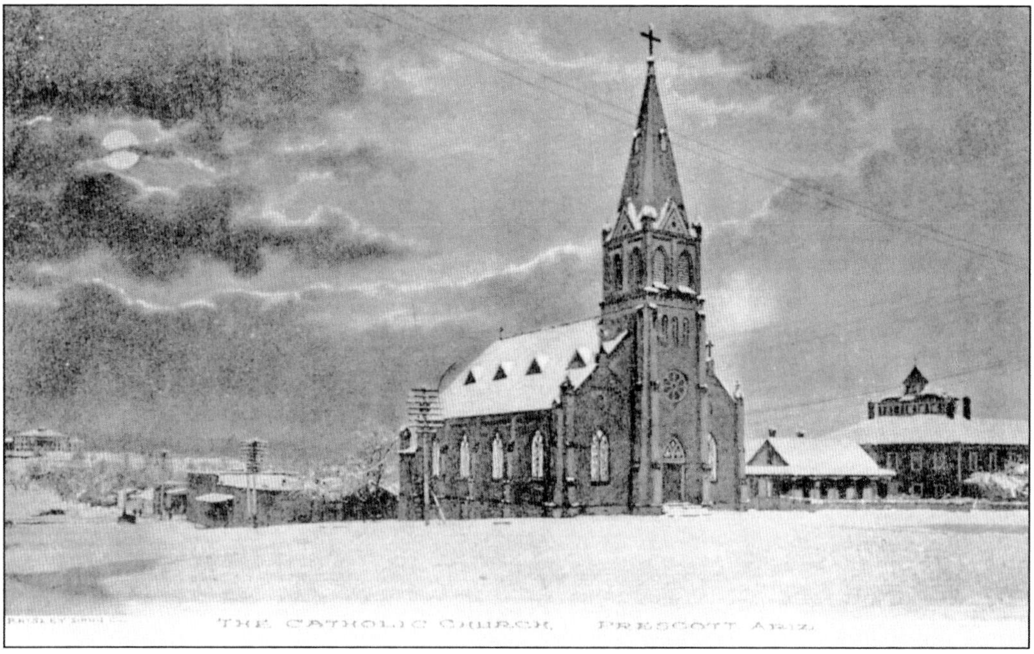

PRESCOTT, THE CATHOLIC CHURCH, C. 1910 (ALBERTYPE HAND-COLORED POSTCARD). The building of Sacred Heart Catholic Church on North Marina Street started in 1891, with the first service being held on February 17, 1895. In 1930, the church's 115-foot steeple was struck by lightning and had to be removed. (Published by Albertype.)

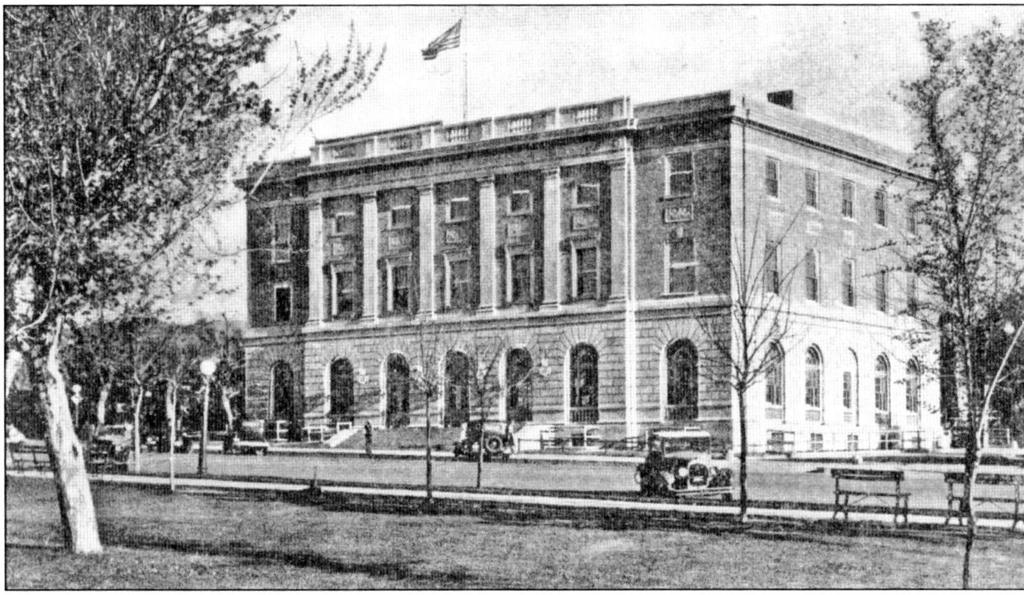

PRESCOTT, POST OFFICE, POSTMARKED AUGUST 23, 1930 (ALBERTYPE POSTCARD). Located on Goodwin and Cortez Streets, the post office is still in use today. When the building originally opened in 1931, it was both a US Post Office and a federal courthouse. While the main floor housed the post office, the two upper floors were used by the US District Court, the US Marshals Service, and the US attorney's office. In 1985, the building was listed in the National Register of Historic Places. (Published by Albertype.)

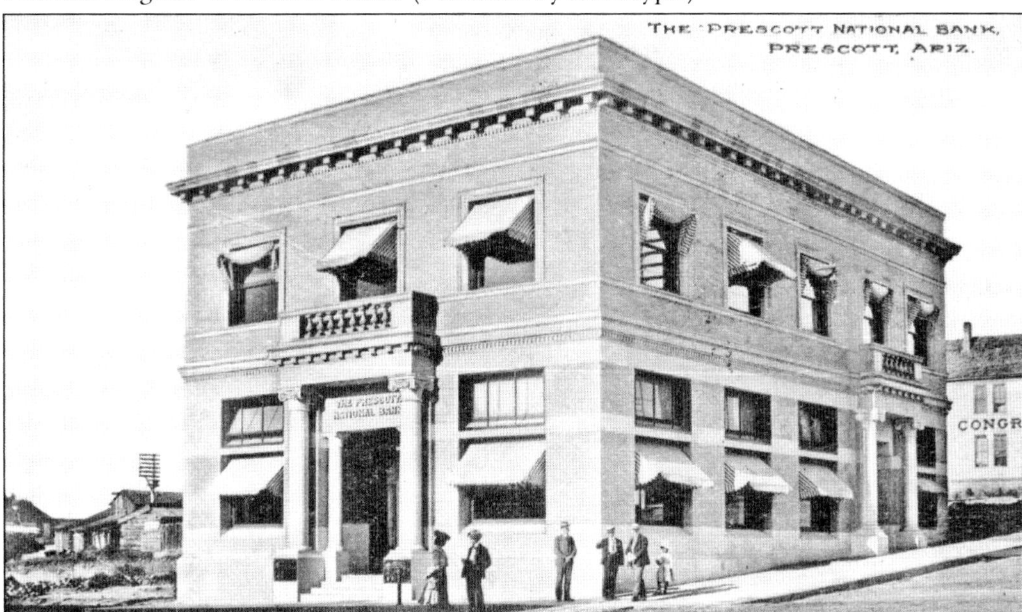

PRESCOTT, PRESCOTT NATIONAL BANK, POSTMARKED NOVEMBER 29, 1913 (ALBERTYPE POSTCARD). Construction began in 1900 at the corner of Gurley and Cortez Streets and finished in 1902. The bank closed its doors on November 15, 1920. Valley Bank moved into the building in 1922. The building was remodeled and converted into retail and professional offices after the bank moved in the 1960s. (Published by Corbin and Bork.)

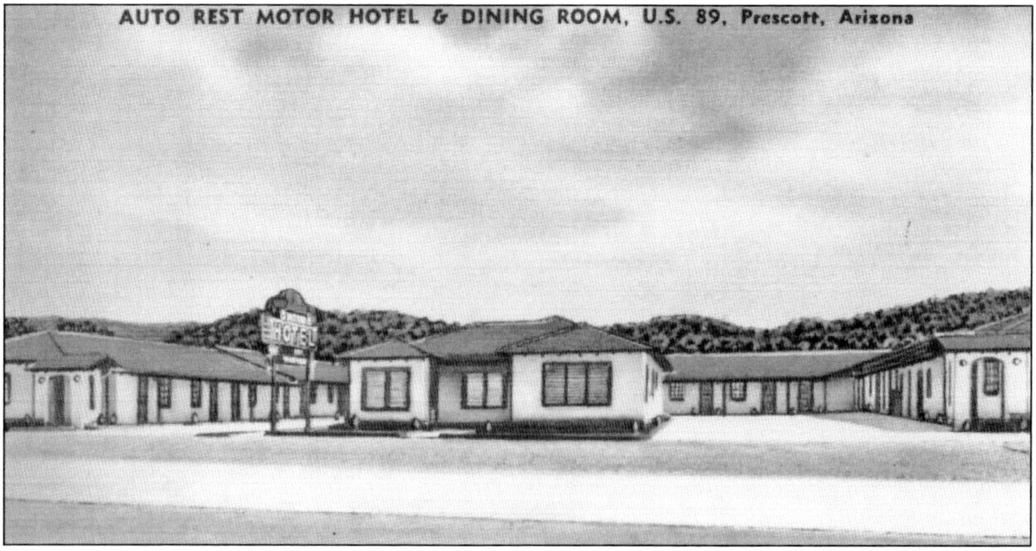

PRESCOTT, AUTO REST MOTOR HOTEL AND DINING ROOM, POSTMARKED JULY 3, 1952 (ADVERTISING LINEN POSTCARD). Opening in 1948, the Auto Rest Motor Hotel boasted of a "new 21 unit Motor Hotel, elegantly furnished, 'roomy' with full tile showers, and room telephones insulated, carpeted wall to wall, steam heat and paved parking lot." The location is currently the Senator Inn Motel. (Published by Newton MFG.)

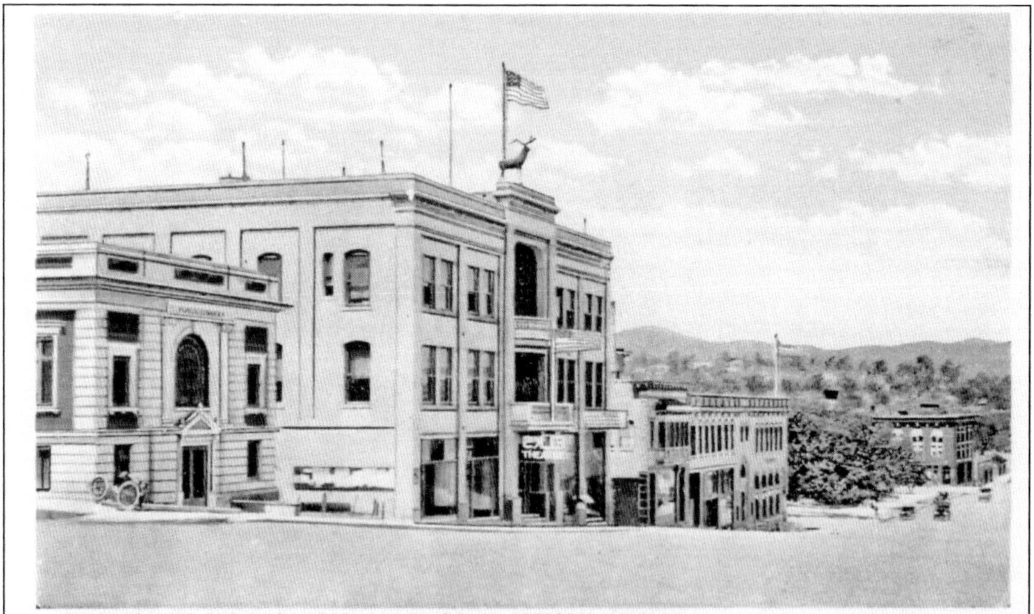

PRESCOTT, ELKS THEATER AND CARNEGIE LIBRARY, C. 1917 (CURT TEICH HAND-COLORED POSTCARD). Actress Florence Roberts preformed in the play *Mata of the Lowlands* on opening night, February 20, 1905. Tickets were $2.50 for general admission and $20 for box seats. In 2009, the interior of the theater went through a major renovation, bringing back its original beauty. In June 1899, Julia Goldwater, a Prescott resident, wrote to Andrew Carnegie, pleading for his help in securing a library for Prescott. The library opened in 1903 and served until a new library opened in 1974. (Published by C.T. American.)

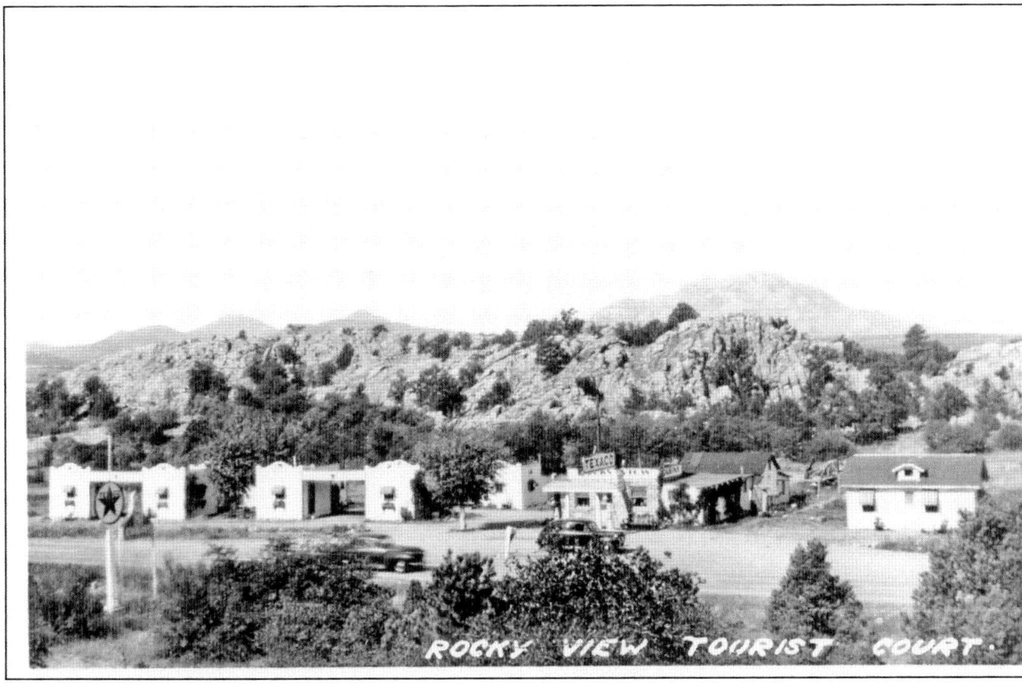

PRESCOTT, ROCKY VIEW TOURIST COURT, C. 1940S (ADVERTISING POSTCARD). A 1939 newspaper ad read, "4 miles north of Prescott on highway 89 near Granite Dells, modern cabins, groceries, gas, soft drinks." The old court was on Highway 89 about a quarter-mile north of Willow Lake Road, near where the Granite Dells Lodge now stands. (Published by Frashers, Inc.)

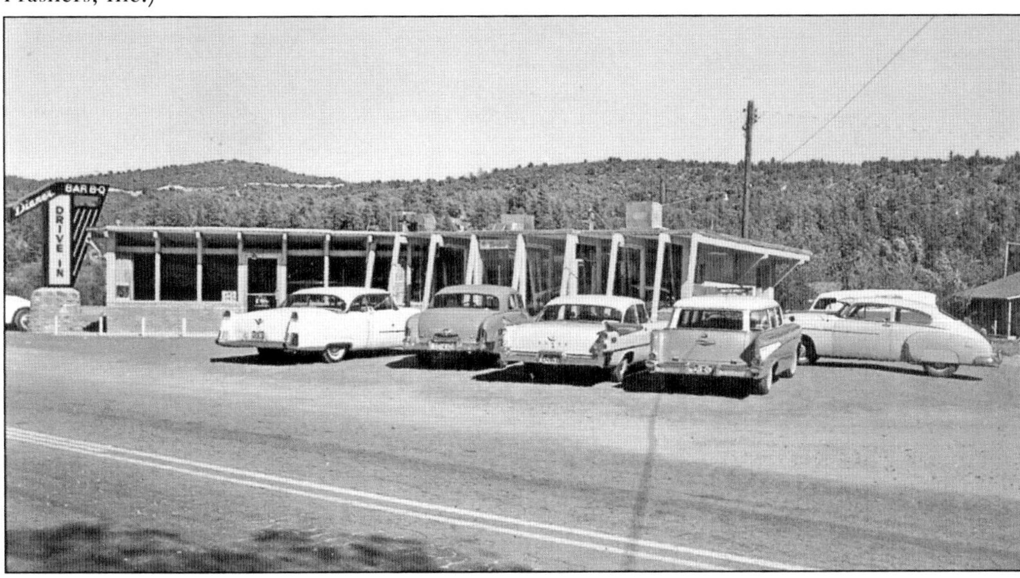

PRESCOTT, DIANE'S BAR-B-Q DRIVE-IN, C. 1960S (ADVERTISING POSTCARD). There is no sign of the old diner along Highway 89 where it once stood. An ad from the May 2, 1963, issue of the *Copper News* reads as follows: "Diane's Bar-B-Q Drive-In, window and dining room service, real pit Bar-B-Q, ice cold beer. 719 White Spar Road, on Highway U.S. 89, Prescott." (Published by Phoenix Spec. Adv. Co., photograph by Tom Reed.)

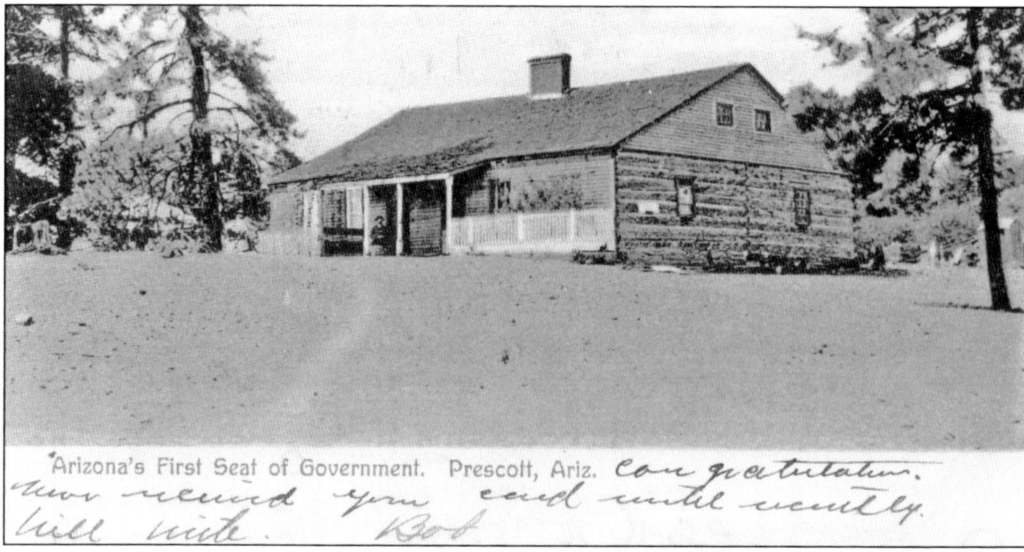

PRESCOTT, ARIZONA'S FIRST SEAT OF GOVERNMENT, C. 1905 (HAND-COLORED POSTCARD). Now safely protected within the fences of the Sharlot Hall Museum, Arizona's first governor's mansion sits exactly where it did when built in 1864. The first governor, John Goodwin, and the first secretary of the territory, Richard McCormick, pooled their own money to have the mansion built. The log cabin was built from local ponderosa pines. (Published by Brisley Drug Co.)

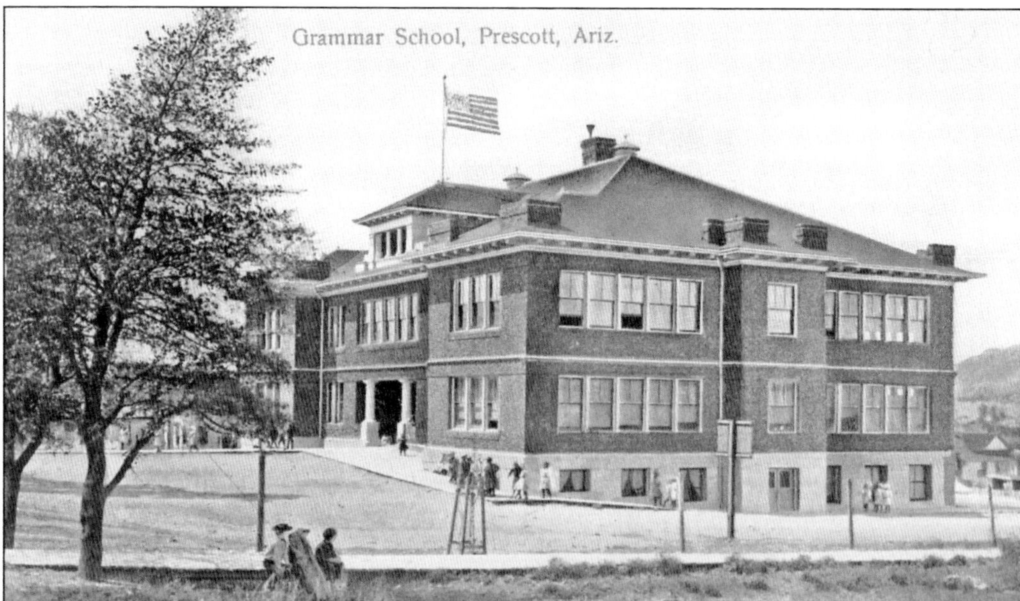

PRESCOTT, WASHINGTON SCHOOL, C. 1910 (HAND-COLORED POSTCARD). Opening in September 1903, the Washington School originally taught kindergarten through eighth grade. It wasn't until 1930, when a new junior/senior high school was constructed, that the school ended at sixth grade. Vowing to reduce its budget due to lower student enrollment, the Prescott Unified School District closed the school before the 2015 school year. (Published by M. Reider Publ.)

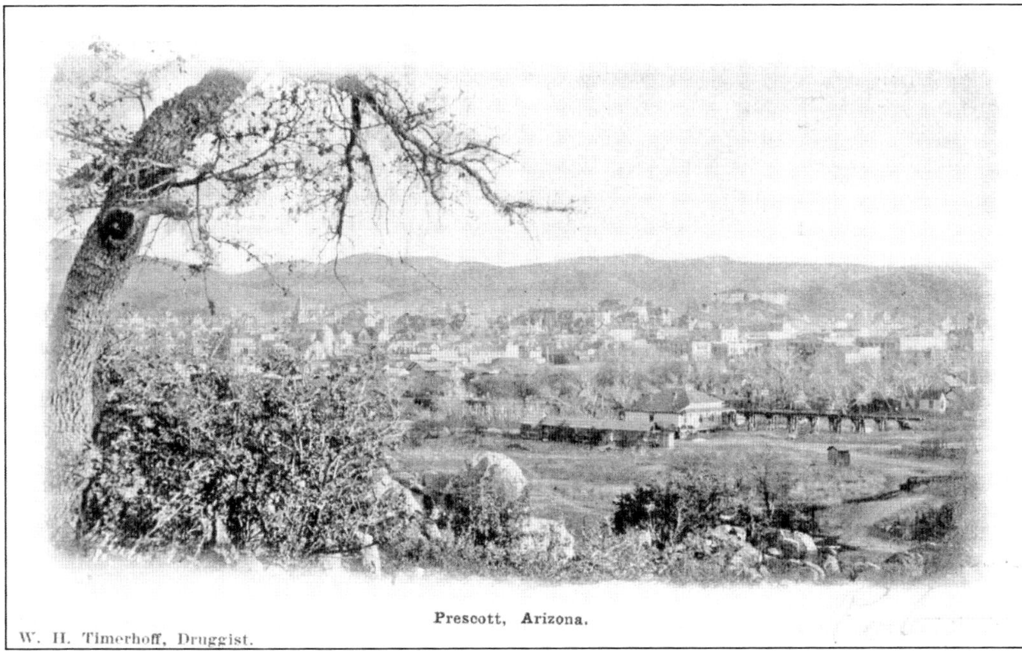

Above: Prescott, Town View, Postmarked June 8, 1905 (Undivided Back Postcard); Below: Prescott, General View, Postmarked April 4, 1908 (Hand-Colored Postcard). Names for many of the streets and roads in Prescott came from explorers, miners, guides, military officers, and local pioneers. A number of them never set foot in Prescott, including its namesake, historian William Hickling Prescott, who died in 1859. One road is named after Joseph Walker, an early pioneer to the area. Other roads, such as Carleton, Whipple, and Willis, were named after Army officers. Early pioneers such as John Goodwin, Richard C. McCormick, James Sheldon, and George Lount also have streets named after them. (Above, published by W.H. Timerhoff, Druggist; below, published by Brisley Drug Co.)

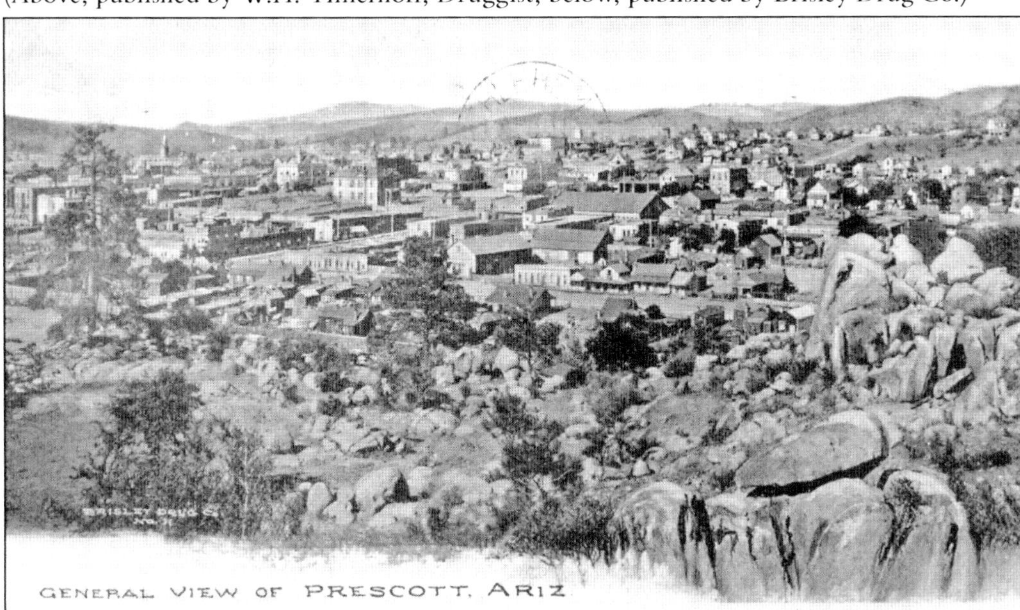

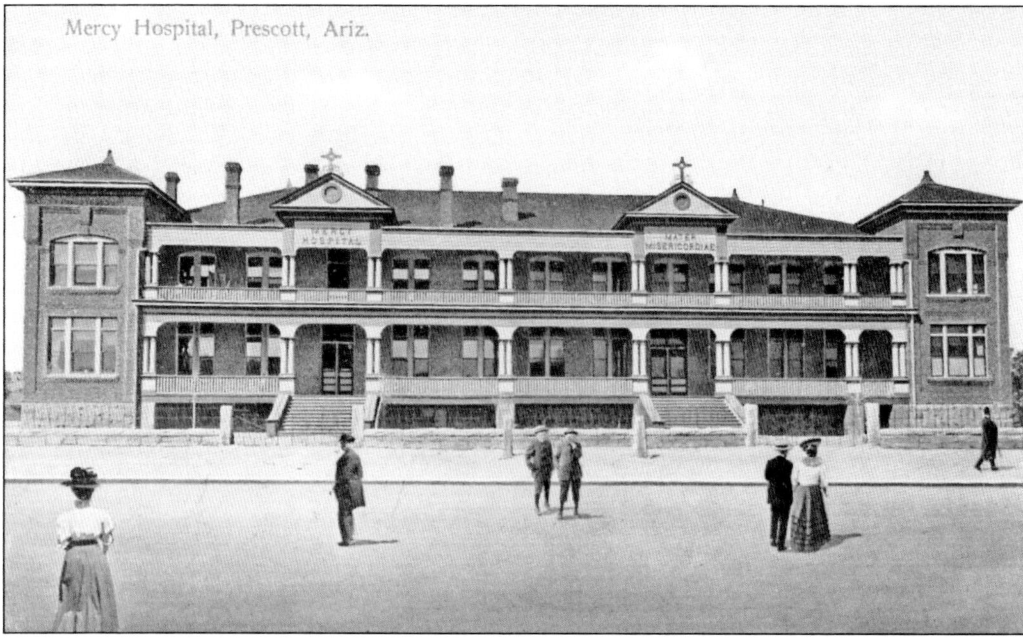

PRESCOTT, MERCY HOSPITAL, C. 1910 (HAND-COLORED POSTCARD). Operated by the Sisters of St. Joseph from its inception in the late 1870s, Mercy Hospital moved from its original location on North Marina Street to Grove Avenue in 1898. On June 8, 1940, Mercy Hospital burned to the ground. An annex to the hospital that was constructed sometime after the hospital moved in 1898 survived the fire, later to become Prescott College in 1975. (Published by M. Reider Publ.)

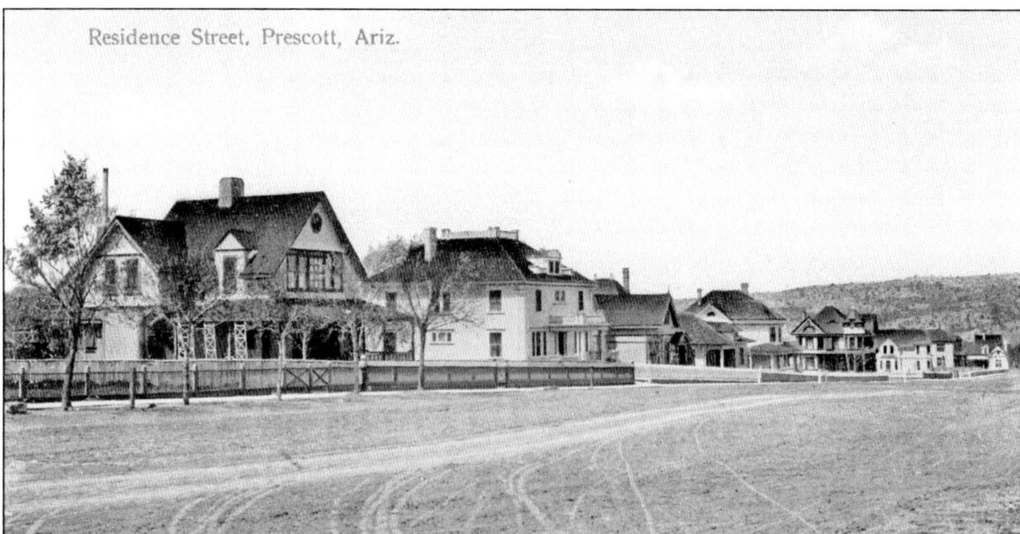

PRESCOTT, RESIDENCE STREET, C. 1910 (HAND-COLORED POSTCARD). Appearing much like most of the streets of early Prescott where homes were built in the late 1800s and early 1900s, this portion of Mount Vernon Avenue between Gurley and Willis Streets has remained mostly intact. The first two-story house on the left is now the location of the Mount Vernon Church of Christ, while the home on the near corner is now the Chapel Inn. (Published by M. Reider Publ.)

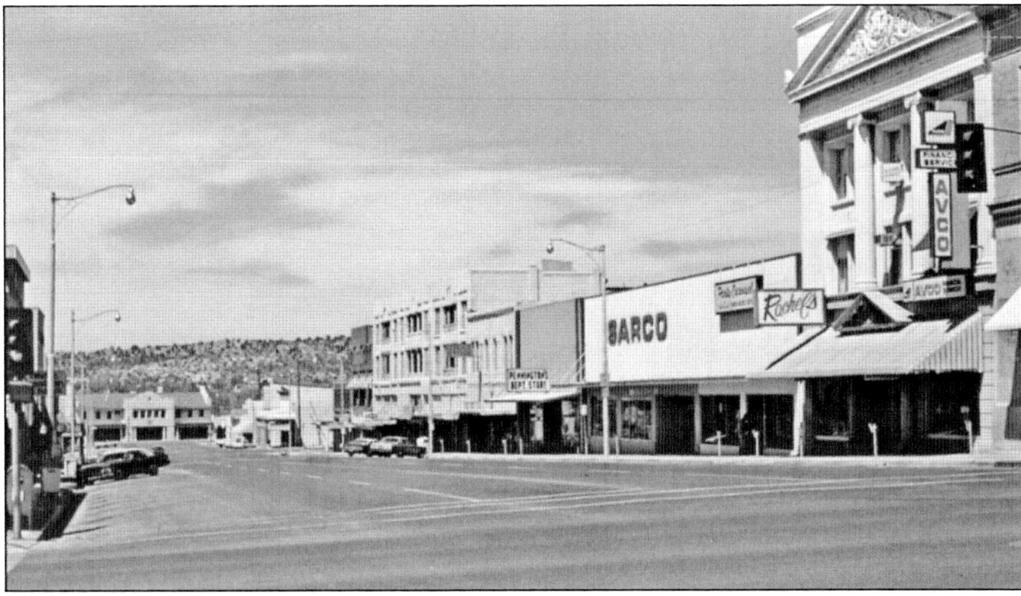

PRESCOTT, CORTEZ STREET, C. 1960S (REAL PHOTO POSTCARD). On the first map of Prescott, Cortez Street was spelled "Cortes." The name Cortez came from a book published by the city's namesake, historian W.H. Prescott. In addition to Cortez Street, two other names are mentioned in his book that appear in Prescott: Montezuma Street and Marina Street. (Published by Burmeister Ent.)

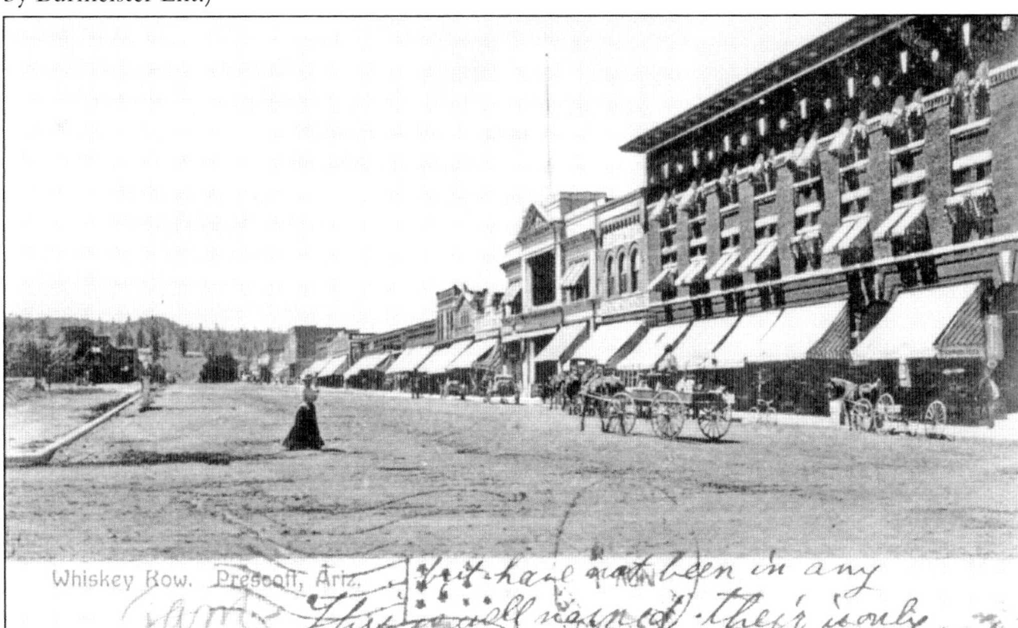

PRESCOTT, WHISKEY ROW, POSTMARKED OCTOBER 18, 1907 (HAND-COLORED POSTCARD). Construction on the Hotel St. Michael (foreground) was started almost immediately after the July 1900 fire that decimated downtown Prescott. Opening as the Burke Hotel on June 1, 1901, the brick Renaissance Revival–style hotel is said to be haunted by more than one spirit. In 1907, the ownership changed hands, and the name was changed to the St. Michael. This photograph was taken in 1902. (Published by Brisley Drug Co.)

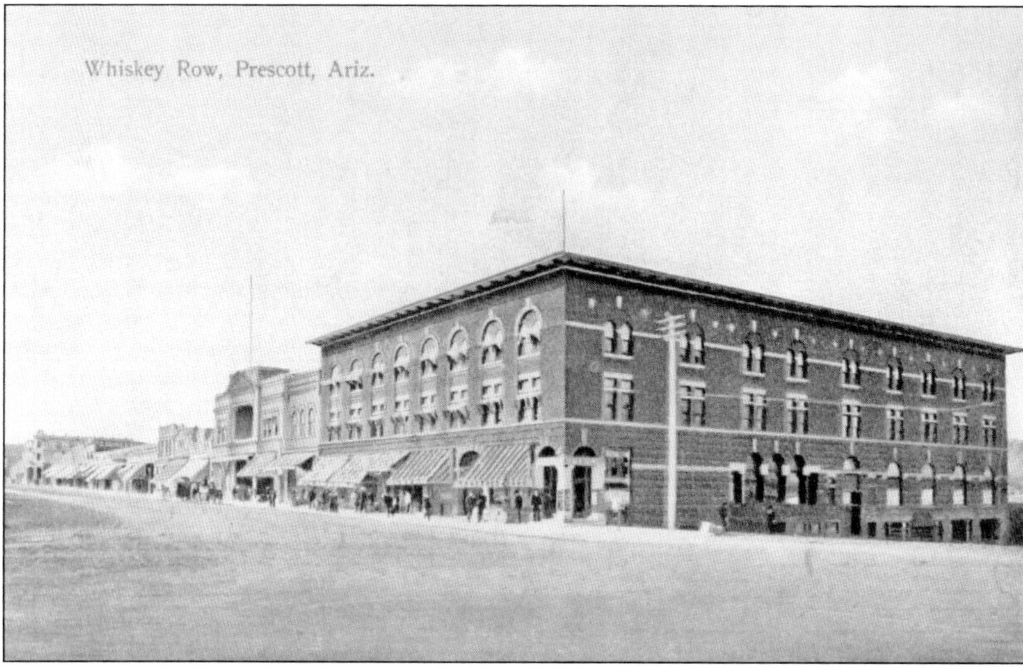

PRESCOTT, WHISKEY ROW, C. 1910S (HAND-COLORED POSTCARD). Dating well back into the late 1800s, Whiskey Row, famous for its 40 saloons, encompassed Montezuma Street from the old train station near Sheldon to well past Goodwin. It also included portions of Gurley and Cortez Streets. On July 14, 1900, a fire raged through Montezuma Street between Gurley and Goodwin Streets, failing to spare a single building. At the Palace Saloon, the patrons rescued the prized bar and carried it across the street to the Plaza, where drinks continued to be poured. (Published by M. Reider, Publ.)

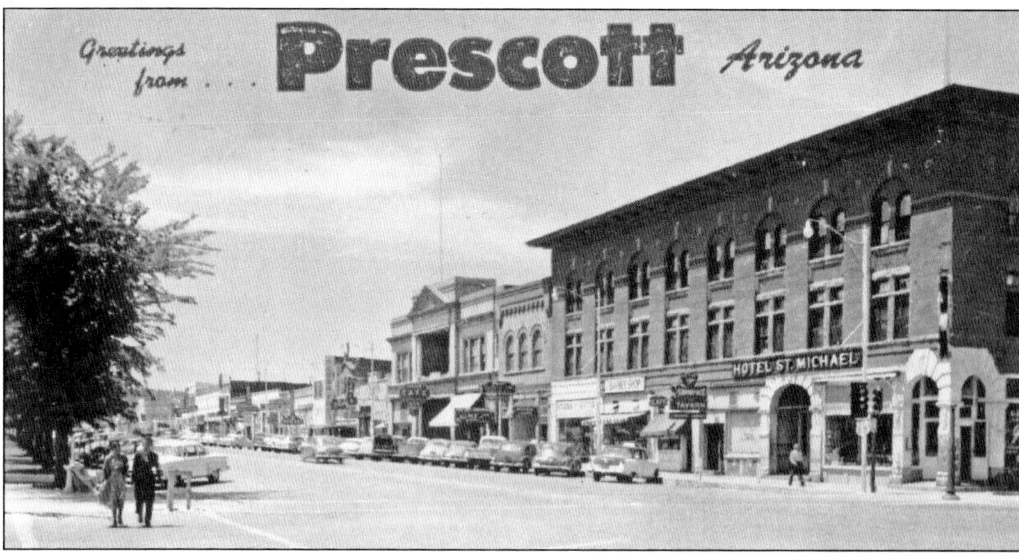

PRESCOTT, WHISKEY ROW, C. 1950S (REAL PHOTO POSTCARD). All of the buildings on Montezuma Street were rebuilt after the 1900 fire and continue to have that old-time charm. There are no longer 40 saloons along Montezuma Street and Whiskey Row, but there are still enough to keep up the moniker of Whiskey Row. (Published by Bob Petley.)

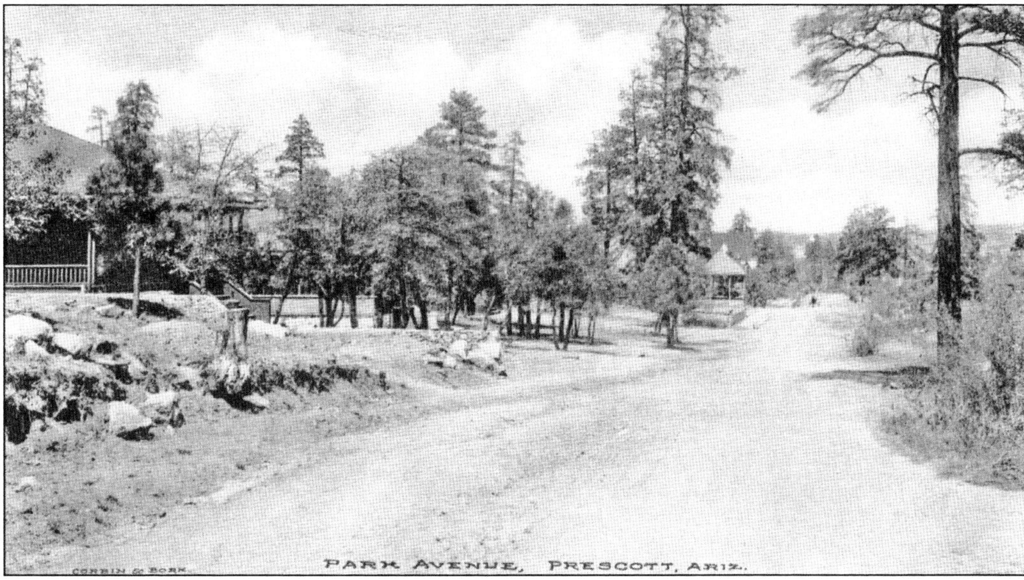

PRESCOTT, PARK AVENUE, C. 1920S (ALBERTYPE POSTCARD). Park Avenue was a quiet residential street running between Gurley Street and Copper Basin. One of the oldest schools in the city, Lincoln Elementary School, was constructed on Park Avenue in 1909. Over 100 years later, Lincoln has gone through some modifications and additions but still proudly serves students of Prescott. (Published by Corbin and Bork.)

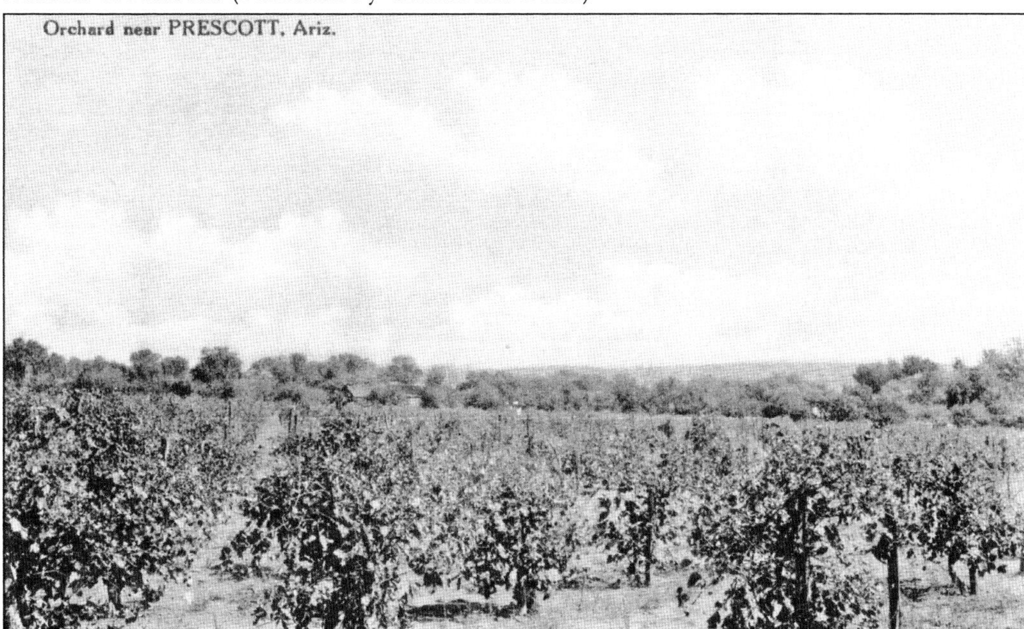

PRESCOTT, ORCHARD, C. 1920S (ALBERTYPE POSTCARD). Peaches, apples, and other fruits were planted by Alfred Clough, who purchased the property just north of the Granite Dells in 1877. He died in 1908, and the property was purchased by John Bianconi. At one time, Bianconi had the largest orchard in the state of Arizona, comprising nearly 34 acres. In 1939, the peach orchard developed peach mosaic and was destroyed by the US government to prevent the disease from spreading. (Published by Brisley Drug Co.)

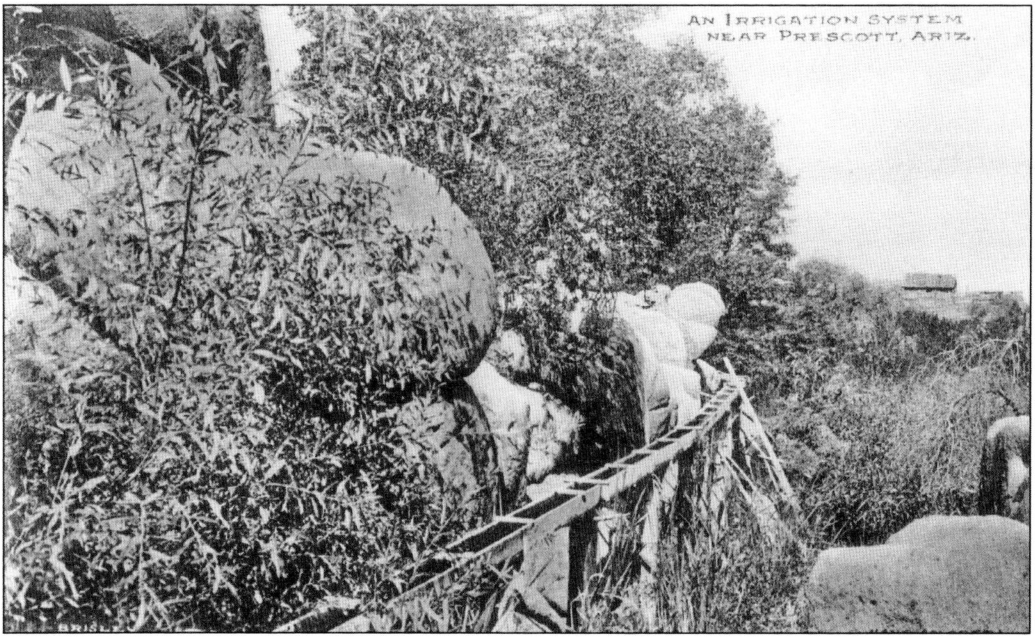

PRESCOTT, IRRIGATION SYSTEM, C. 1915 (ALBERTYPE POSTCARD). Part of the original flume, built sometime prior to 1911, carried water from Willow Creek to the Bianconi Ranch to water the ranch's orchards and crops. Part of the old flume is still visible today on the trail along Willow Creek below Watson Dam. (Courtesy Andy Christenson.)

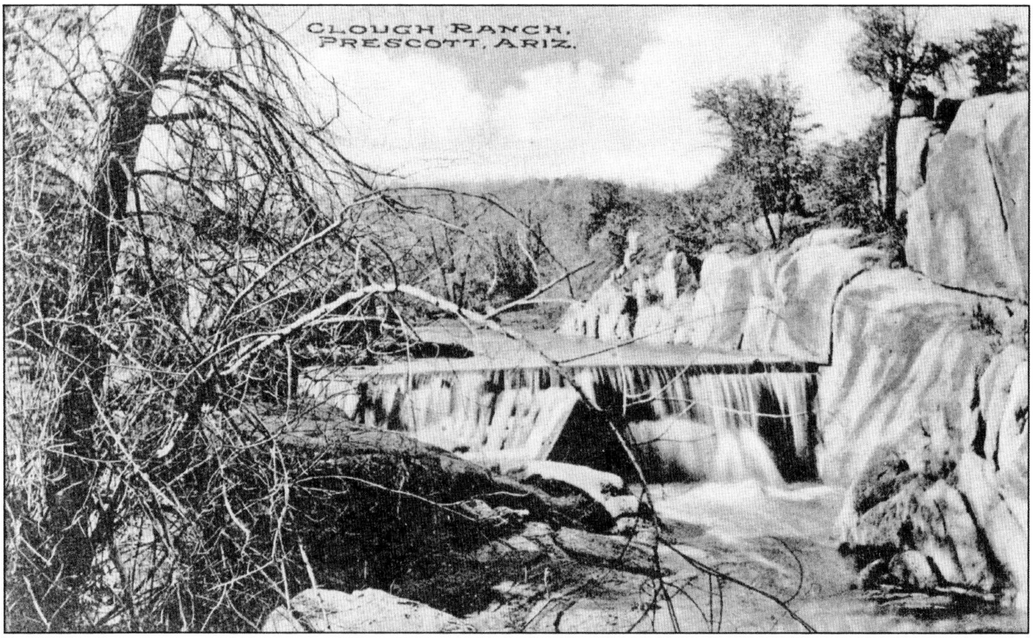

PRESCOTT, CLOUGH RANCH, POSTMARKED OCTOBER 22, 1912 (ALBERTYPE POSTCARD). Arriving in Prescott in 1864, Alfred Clough purchased what became known as the Clough Ranch in 1877 from Alfred Curtis. Soon after Clough died at the ranch at 72 in 1908, the property was sold to John Bianconi. After the devastating loss of the orchard in 1939, John sold the ranch in 1941 and moved to town. (Published by W.H. Timerhoff, Druggist.)

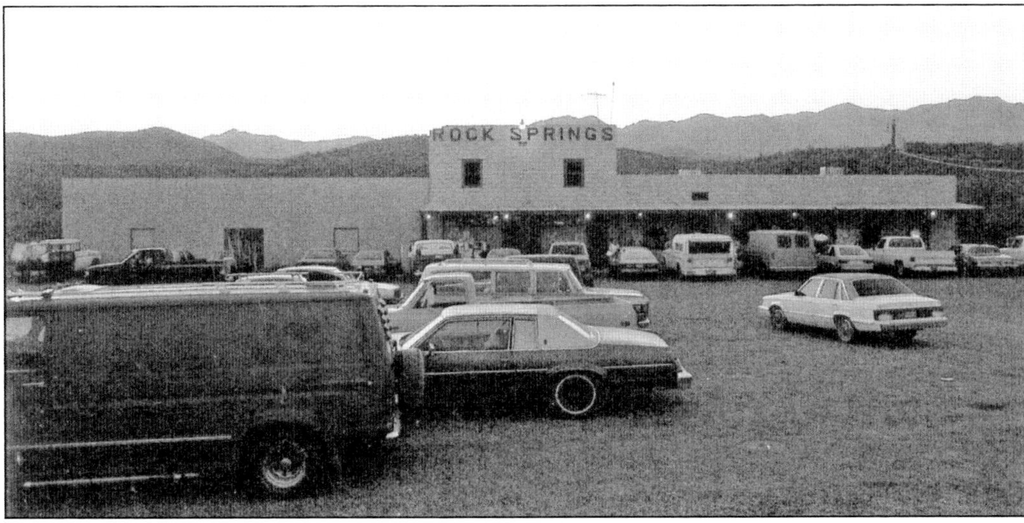

ROCK SPRINGS, ROCK SPRINGS STAGE STOP, C. 1970S (ADVERTISING POSTCARD). An early encampment for the Yavapai Indians, Rock Springs later became a military bivouac site, a water stop for miners and cattle drives, and eventually a stage stop between Phoenix and Prescott. When the last stage stopped in 1917, a young man by the name of Ben Warner opened a hotel and general store. Today, Rock Springs is still a popular stop along Highway 17 for its food and especially its famous pies. (Published by James Davis Mktg., photograph by Jim Davis.)

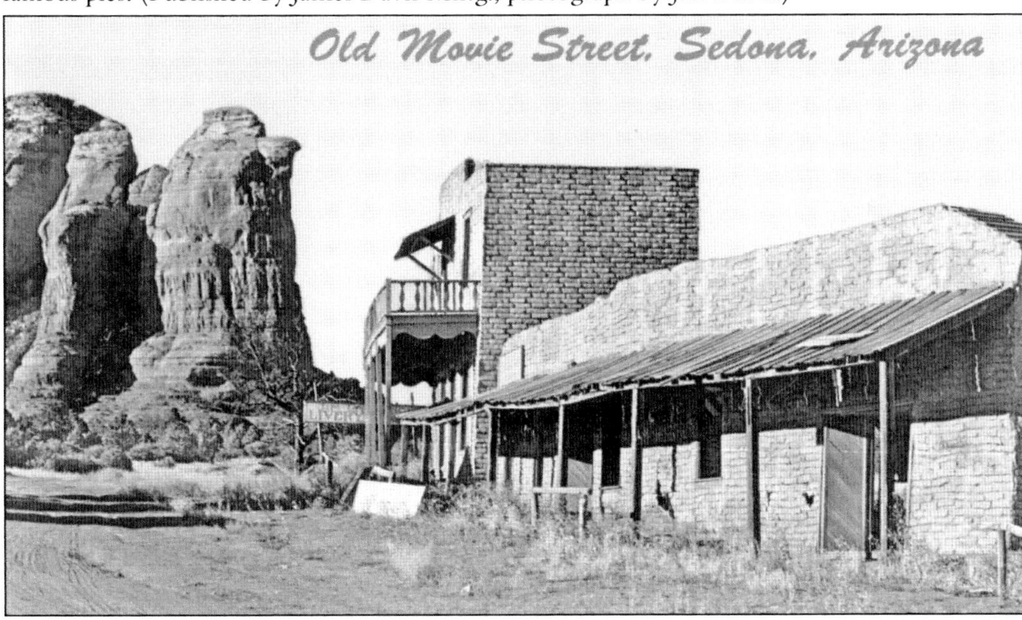

SEDONA, OLD MOVIE SET, C. 1960 (REAL PHOTO POSTCARD). Once known as the Bradshaw Ranch, the old movie set was purchased by the US Forest Service in 2003. In 1960, Bob Bradshaw purchased the 140-acre ranch near Hartwell Canyon and Loy Canyon and built a Western set that would be used in numerous movies, two television series, and a number of commercials and photo shoots. The first movie filmed on the set was *Stay Away Joe*, starring Elvis Presley, in 1967. The movie was set in a town named Bitter Creek, which was also used in later movies. The town was burned down in 1986 when Wells Fargo used it for a commercial. (Published by Petley Studios.)

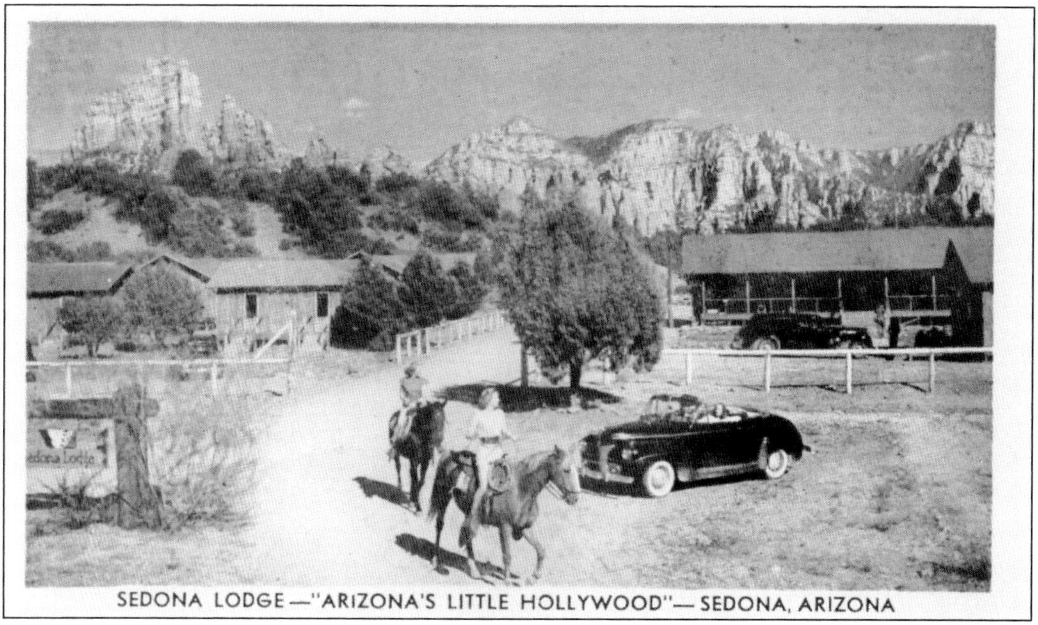

SEDONA, SEDONA LODGE, C. 1950S (REAL PHOTO POSTCARD). Written on the reverse side is the following: "Sedona Lodge, In the heart of Arizona's famous Oak Creek Canyon on Alternate Route 89, 30 miles south of International Highway 66 where Hollywood Movie Companies make many of their pictures." (Published by McLaughlin & Co.)

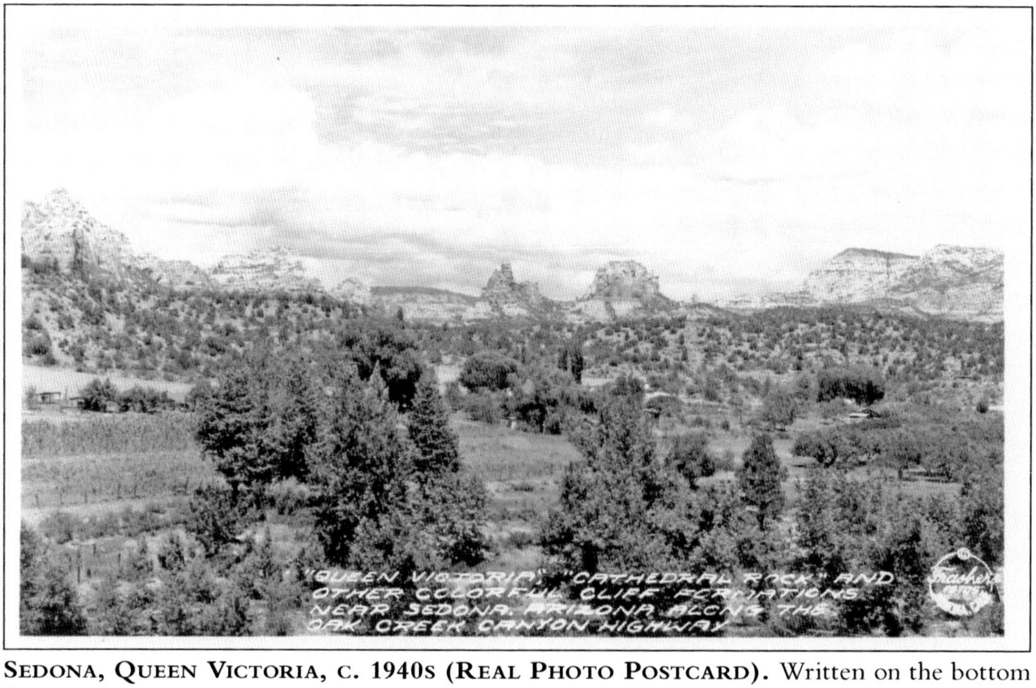

SEDONA, QUEEN VICTORIA, C. 1940S (REAL PHOTO POSTCARD). Written on the bottom front is "Queen Victoria, Cathedral Rock and other colorful cliff formations near Sedona Arizona along the Oak Creek Canyon Highway." Before Sedona became a tourist haven, small farms dotted the countryside, as indicated by the cornstalks on the left portion of the card. (Published by Frashers, Inc.)

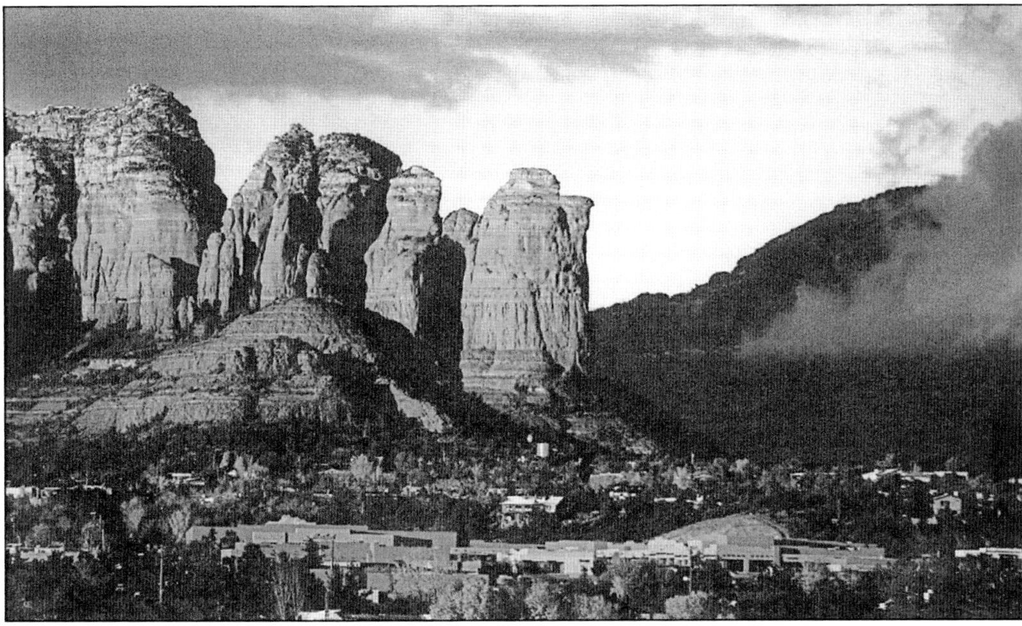

ABOVE: SEDONA, WEST SEDONA, C. 1970S (REAL PHOTO POSTCARD); BELOW: SEDONA, WEST SEDONA FROM AIRPORT, C. 1979 (REAL PHOTO POSTCARD). Sedona, named after its first postmaster's wife, Sedona Arabella Miller Schnebly, is a town straddling two counties, Yavapai and Coconino. Upper Sedona lies in Coconino County and consists mostly of the downtown area, while West Sedona rests in Yavapai County. A few settlers were living in the area in the 1870s, but the town was not founded until 1902 and was only incorporated in 1988. (Above, published by the Bradshaw Studios, courtesy of John Bradshaw and Bradshaw Color Studios; below, published by the Bradshaw Studios, photograph by Bob Bradshaw.)

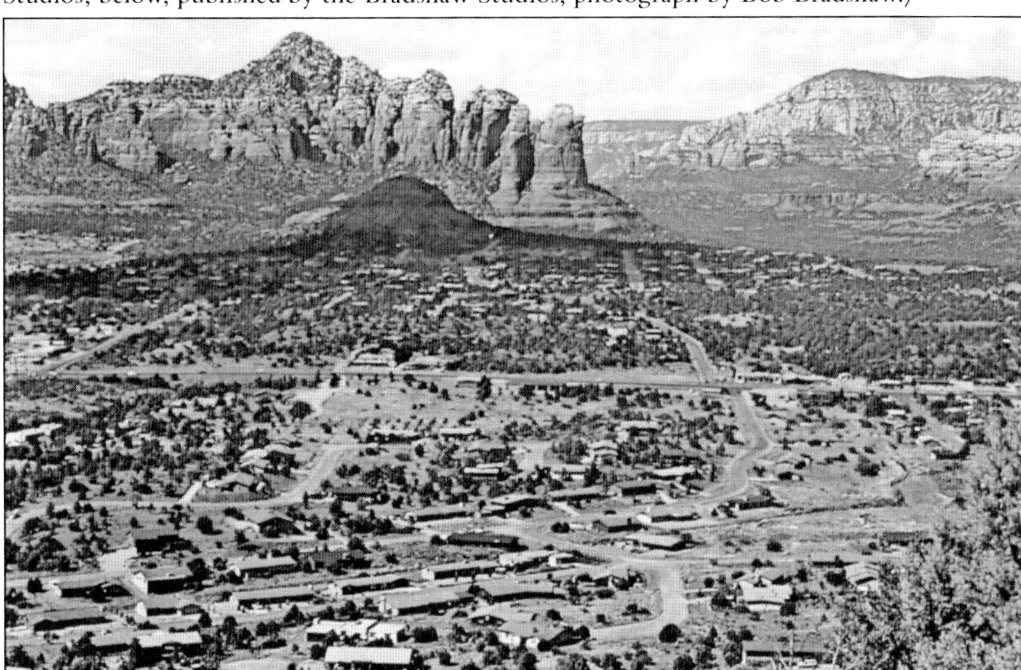

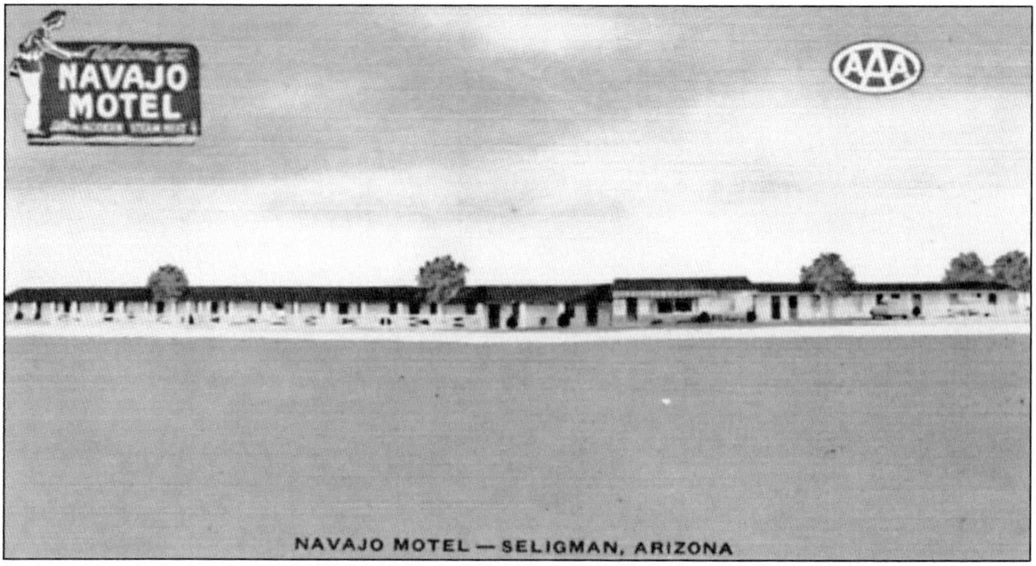

SELIGMAN, NAVAJO MOTEL, POSTMARKED MARCH 31, 1959 (ADVERTISING LINEN POSTCARD). The Navajo Hotel had "15 Deluxe Units—individually controlled heat—tiled showers." The motel changed its name many years ago to the Historic Route 66 Motel and is popular with tourists looking for that old Route 66 experience. (Published by Lynx Products.)

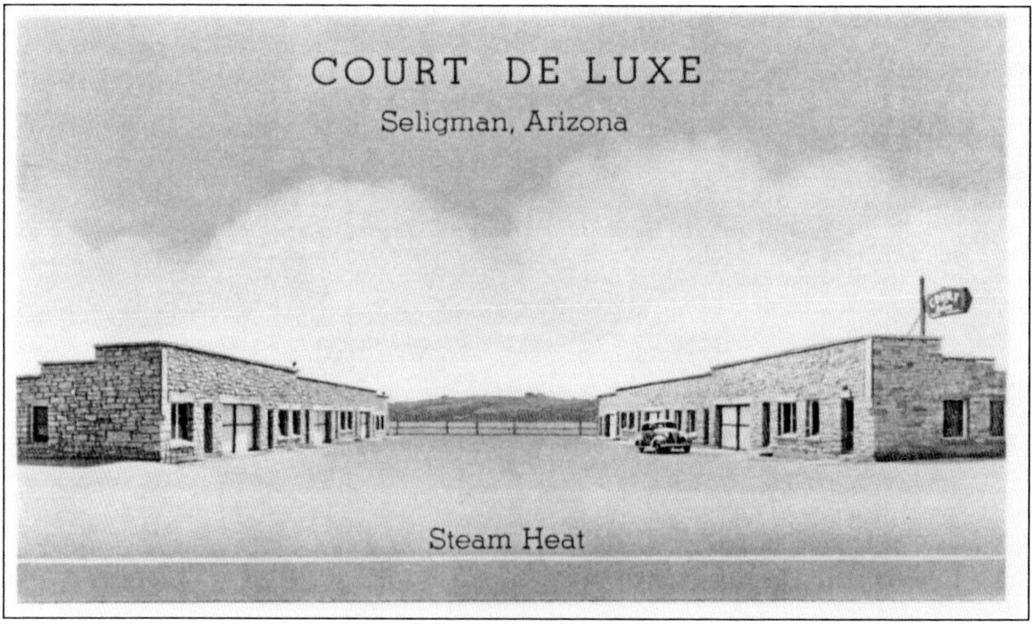

SELIGMAN, COURT DE LUXE MOTEL, C. 1950 (ADVERTISING PORTRAITONE POSTCARD). Seligman is still a popular stop for motorists wanting to experience the nostalgic Route 66. From 1926 to 1978, Seligman was on the original Route 66 until Interstate 40 was built and bypassed the town a few miles south. Built in 1932, it is now known as the Deluxe Inn Motel and is the oldest motel in town still in operation. The Court De Luxe was advertised to have "new, fireproof" rooms that were "quiet, restful, attractively furnished. Steam heated rooms with or without tub or shower baths and kitchenettes. For one or the family. Closed garages. Popular prices." (Produced by ASCO.)

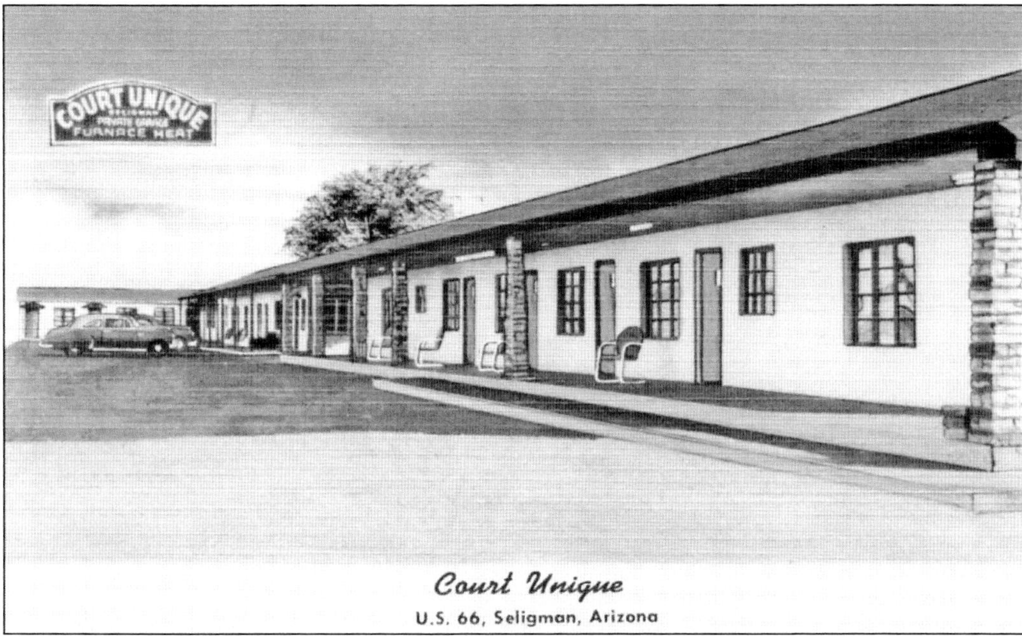

SELIGMAN, COURT UNIQUE, C. 1950 (ADVERTISING POSTCARD). The reverse of the card advertised that the hotel had "A new, modern, air-cooled, 17 unit court with furnace heat. Private locked garages. Some kitchenettes." (Published by Colourpicture Publications.)

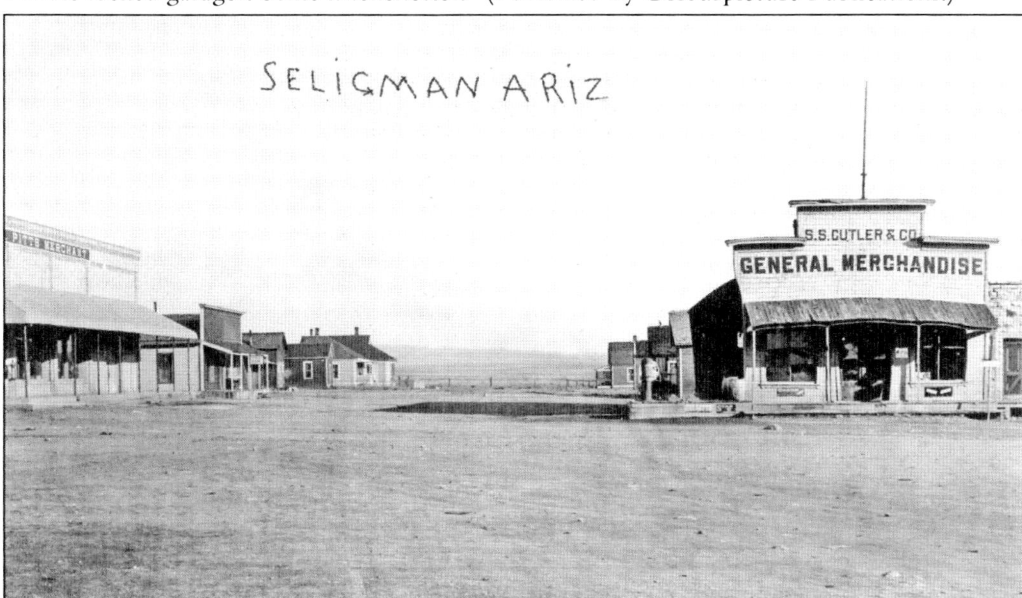

SELIGMAN, MAIN STREET, C. 1910 (UNDIVIDED BACK POSTCARD). The dirt dead-end street is now the famous Route 66 and main throughway through Seligman. The Cutler Store to the right was torn down, and in 1928, the Corner Bar and Hotel opened for business; it burned down in 1962. The lot is now a small park with a bandstand. The Pitts Merchant to the left opened in 1903 and carried everything from groceries to clothing. In 1926, it was sold and renamed Central Commercial. That closed in 1965, and the building has been used for a number of different businesses since, but like many old buildings, it now stands empty.

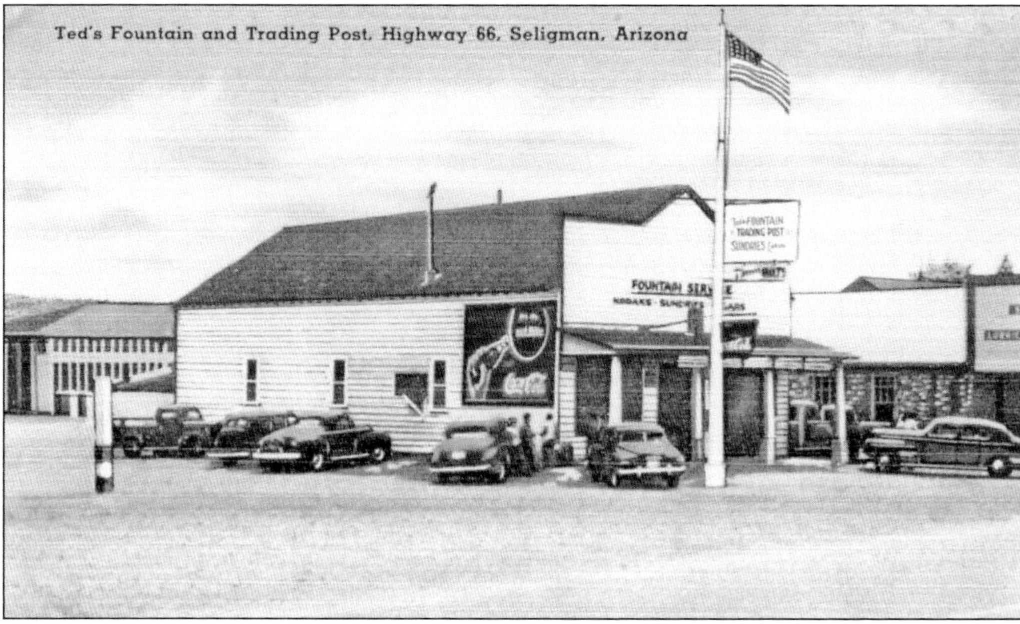

SELIGMAN, TED'S FOUNTAIN AND TRADING POST, C. 1940S (LINEN POSTCARD). Constructed in 1904, the building has seen many uses over the years. It started out as a theater, then it was a dance hall, then a trading post, and later Ted's Fountain. It is still open today as the Historic Seligman Sundries. (Published by Tichnor Bros., Inc.)

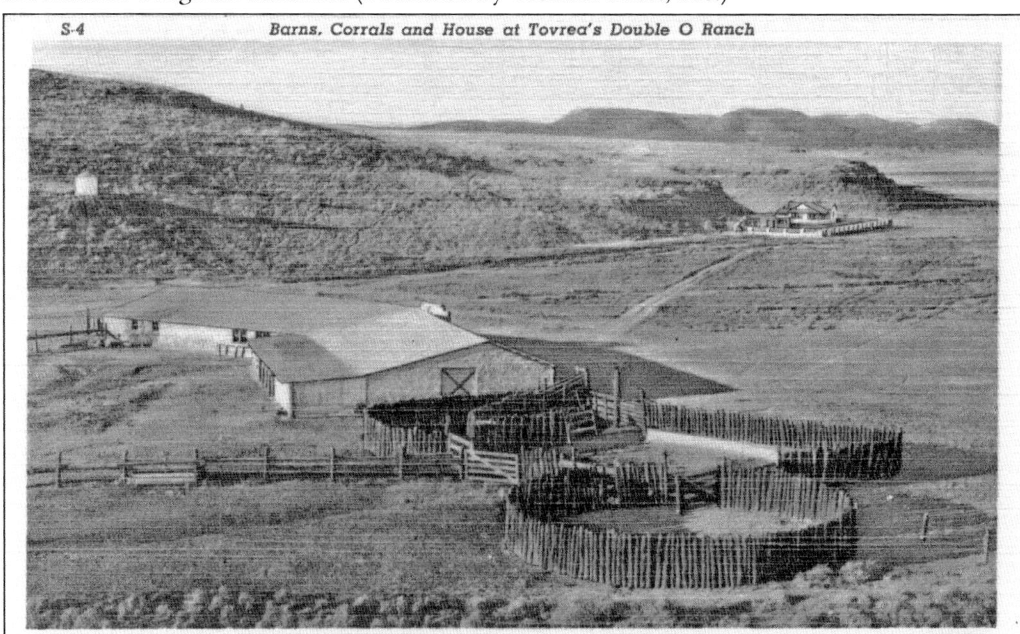

SELIGMAN, TOVREA'S DOUBLE O RANCH, C. 1942 (CURT TEICH LINEN POSTCARD). The back of the card reads, "Tovrea's Double O Ranch is one of the largest cattle ranches in the United States. It is located in Northern Arizona amidst rolling hills and rich in grass, heavy forage and timber. Tovrea's Meat Processing Company at Phoenix, Arizona operates many large ranches and feed yards in the Southwest and Pacific Coast area." (Published by C.T. Art-Colortone.)

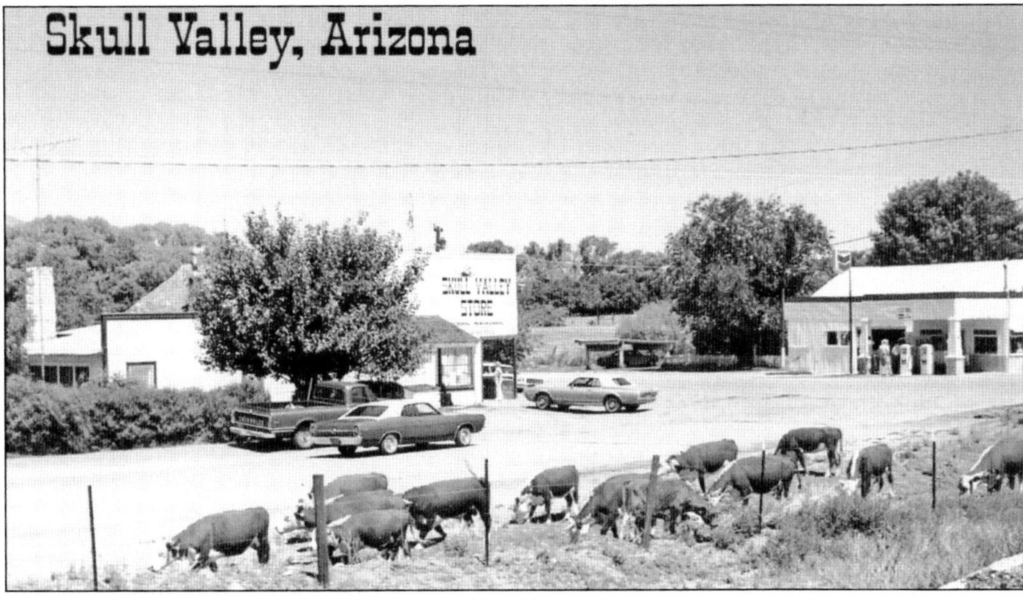

Skull Valley, General Store, c. 1960s (Real Photo Postcard). In 2014, after nearly 100 years, the Skull Valley Store closed its doors for good. E.K. Dutcher built the general store in 1916 and ran it for nine years until selling out in 1925. The store changed hands another four or five times through the years until its closure. The store housed the post office until 1983, when a devastating flood caused the post office to relocate a few blocks away. Originally the store offered gasoline sold out of barrels, and in 1923, gas pumps were installed. It was not until 1947 that Skull Valley finally saw electricity reach its community. (Photograph by Charles Kendall, courtesy Skull Valley Historical Association.)

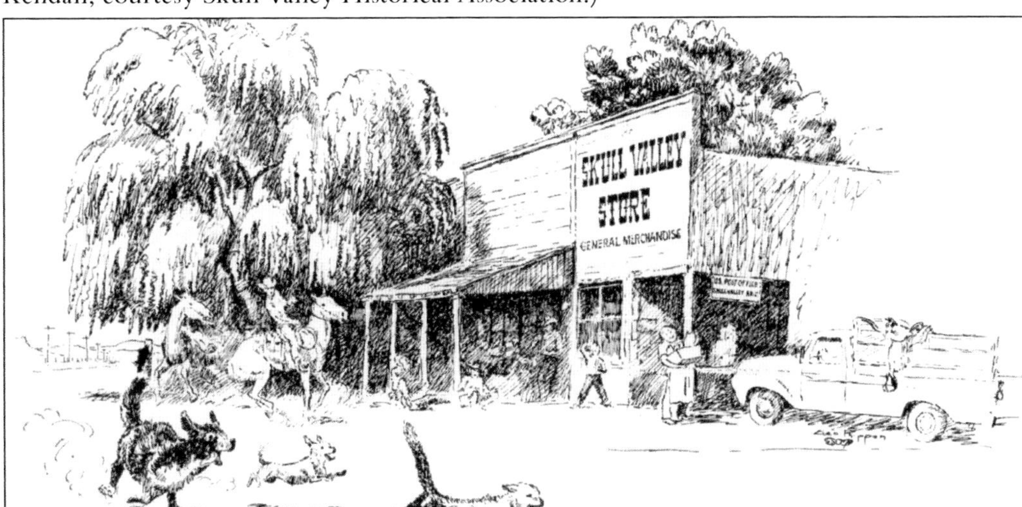

Skull Valley, General Store, 1964 (Cartoon Postcard). George Phippen was a Western artist who made his home in Skull Valley. Many of his creations are displayed at the Phippen Museum in Prescott. Renowned for his Western paintings and bronze sculptures, Phippen often displayed a sense of humor in his drawings, such as with the dogs chasing the cat in front of the Skull Valley Store. (Drawn by George Phippen, courtesy Skull Valley Historical Association.)

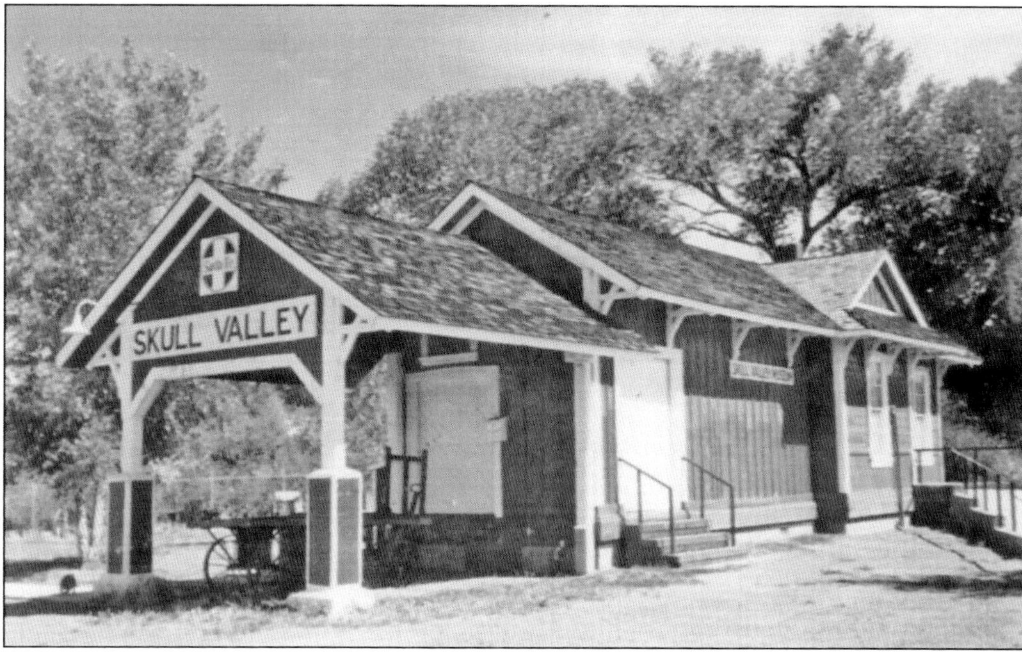

Skull Valley, Depot Museum, c. 1970s (Real Photo Postcard). As railroad traffic decreased along the old Prescott & Eastern Railroad, the old Cherry Creek Depot became obsolete. In 1926, the depot was taken apart and relocated to Skull Valley. The depot was rebuilt and used until 1969, when the last train stopped in Skull Valley. That same year, the Skull Valley Historical Society purchased the depot and, in 1970, moved it a quarter-mile north to its current location. The old historic depot is still in use today, not as a starting or ending point for train passengers but as a historical museum in which people from all over the world enjoy a peek into railroad and Skull Valley's past. (Courtesy Skull Valley Historical Association.)

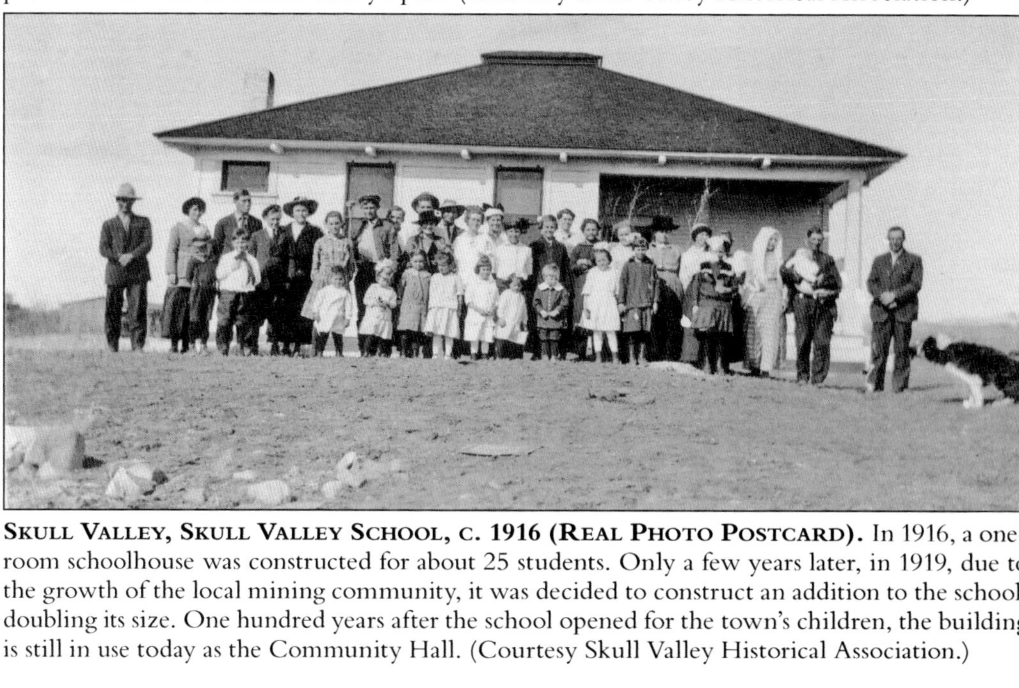

Skull Valley, Skull Valley School, c. 1916 (Real Photo Postcard). In 1916, a one-room schoolhouse was constructed for about 25 students. Only a few years later, in 1919, due to the growth of the local mining community, it was decided to construct an addition to the school, doubling its size. One hundred years after the school opened for the town's children, the building is still in use today as the Community Hall. (Courtesy Skull Valley Historical Association.)

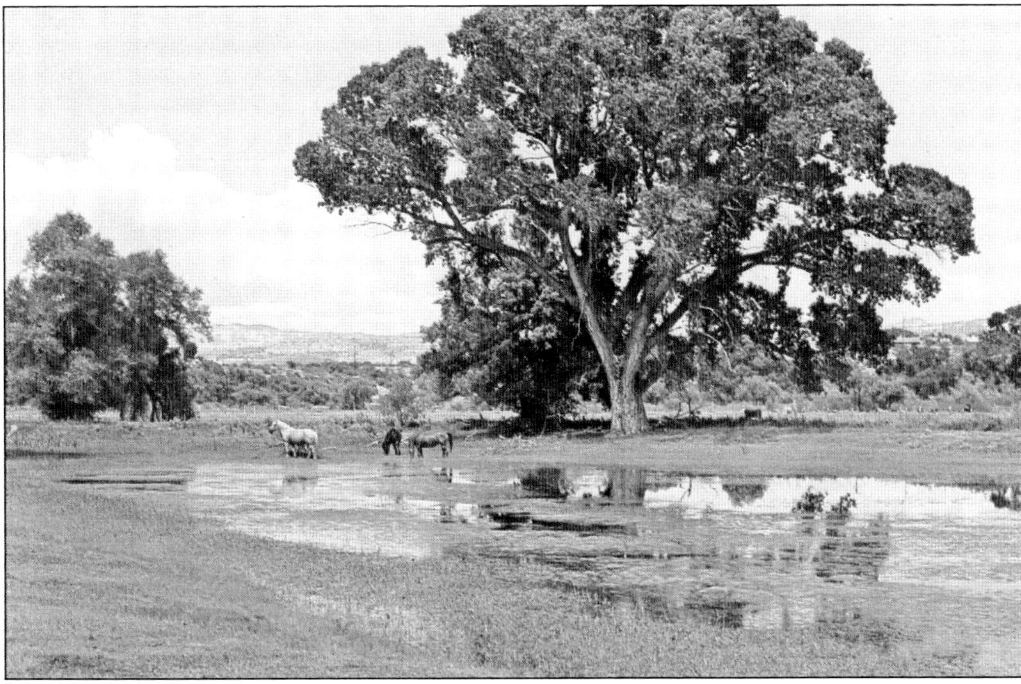

ABOVE: CAMP VERDE, VERDE VALLEY, C. 1973 (REAL PHOTO POSTCARD); BELOW: CAMP VERDE, VERDE VALLEY, C. 1970S (REAL PHOTO POSTCARD). The earliest inhabitants in the valley may have lived as far back as 1,500 years ago, with the Sinagua people living around the valley from around 600 AD to 1400 AD. The earliest recorded visit was by Spaniard Antonio de Espejo, who explored the area in 1583. (Above, published by CreARTive Productions, photograph by Bob Bradshaw; below, published and photograph by Bob Bradshaw.)

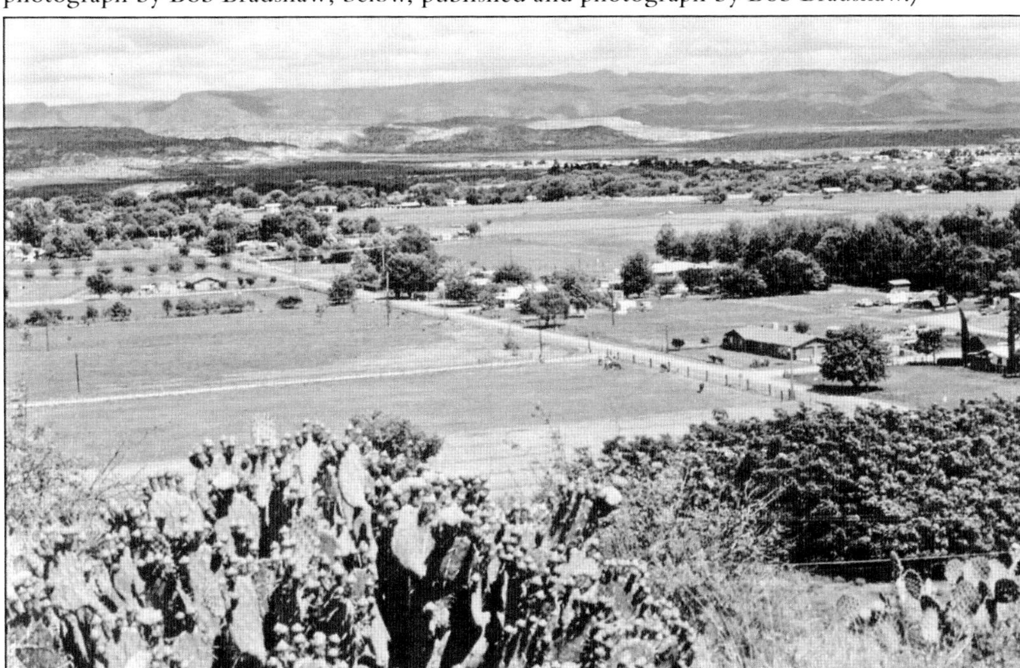

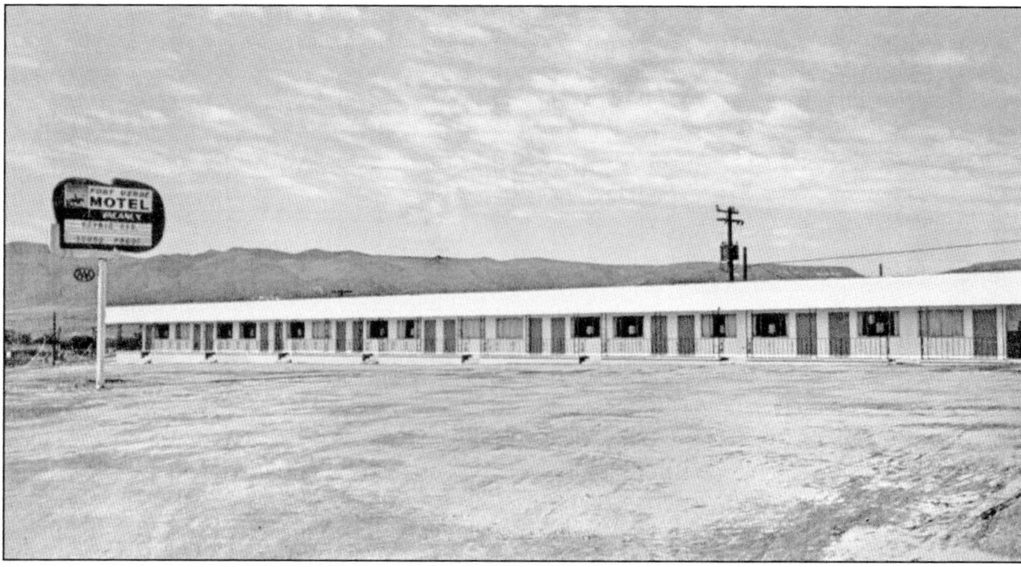

Camp Verde, Fort Verde Motel, c. 1960s (Real Photo Postcard). Located on Main Street in historic downtown Camp Verde, the Fort Verde Motel is now known as the Fort Verde Suites. In a joint venture, Herb Lovett, along with his sister Irene and her husband, George Dodge, built the Fort Verde Motel, opening in June 1963. (Published by Carlton H. Dexon, photograph by Shelton & Matthews.)

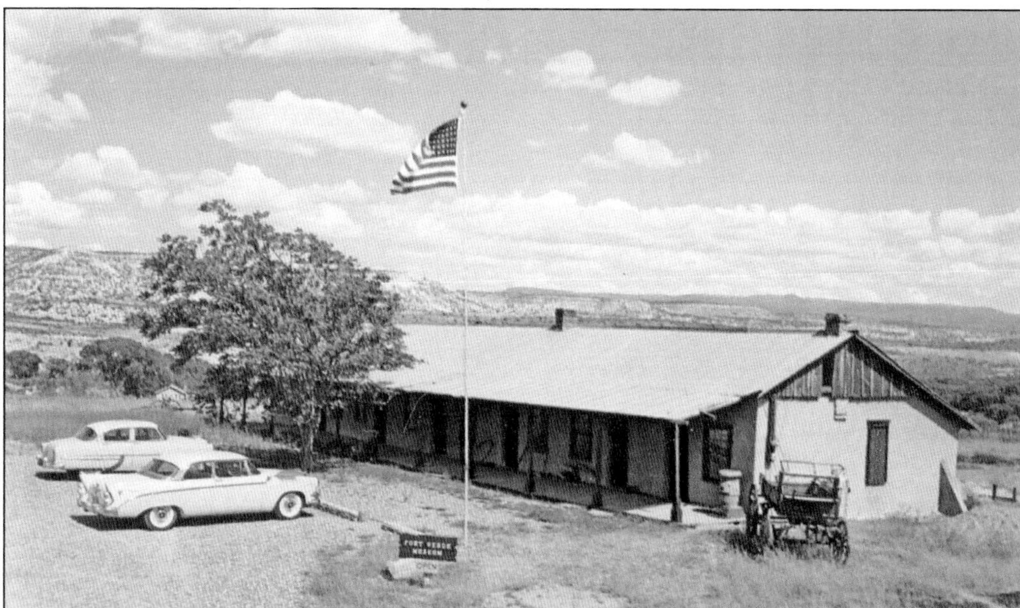

Camp Verde, Fort Verde Museum, c. 1960 (Real Photo Postcard). At the request of local settlers, farmers, and miners to protect them from the Yavapai Apaches, the US Army set up a number of forts starting in 1865. Camp Lincoln moved to the Camp Verde area in the early 1870s. The post changed its name to Fort Verde in 1879 and was abandoned in 1891. In 1899, the fort property was divided into small parcels and sold at auction. In the 1960s, the Fort Verde Museum Association was able to save what remained of the fort from destruction. On October 10, 1970, it was dedicated as a state park. (Published and photograph by Bob Bradshaw.)

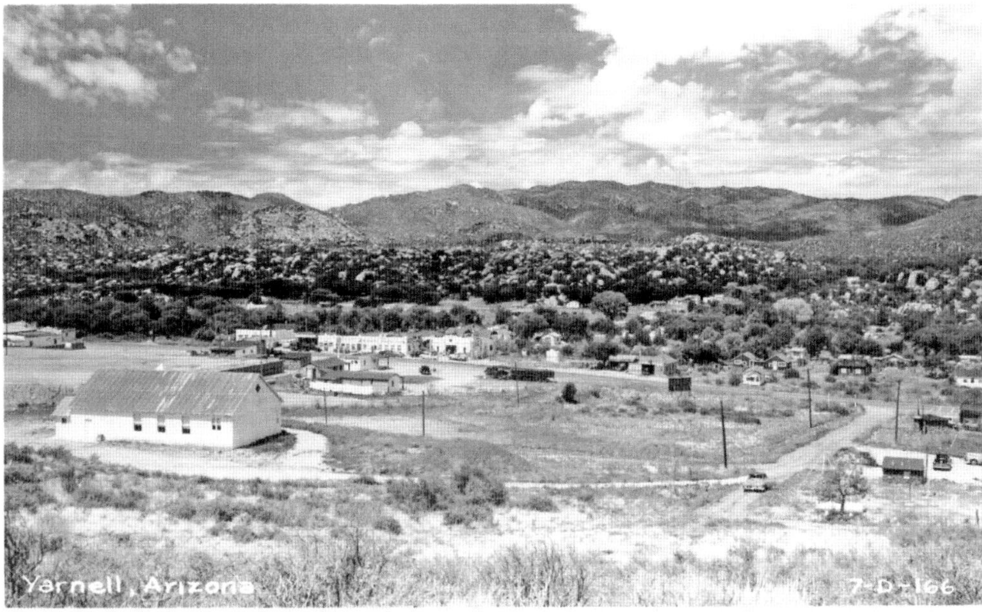

YARNELL, TOWN VIEW, C. 1950 (REAL PHOTO POSTCARD). One of the smaller communities within Yavapai County, Yarnell is a little over eight square miles in size. In 1933, according to a story in the *Arizona Republic* newspaper, Yarnell had a population of just 18 people. It reached 645 people by 2000, and by 2015 it had added four more for a total of 649 people.

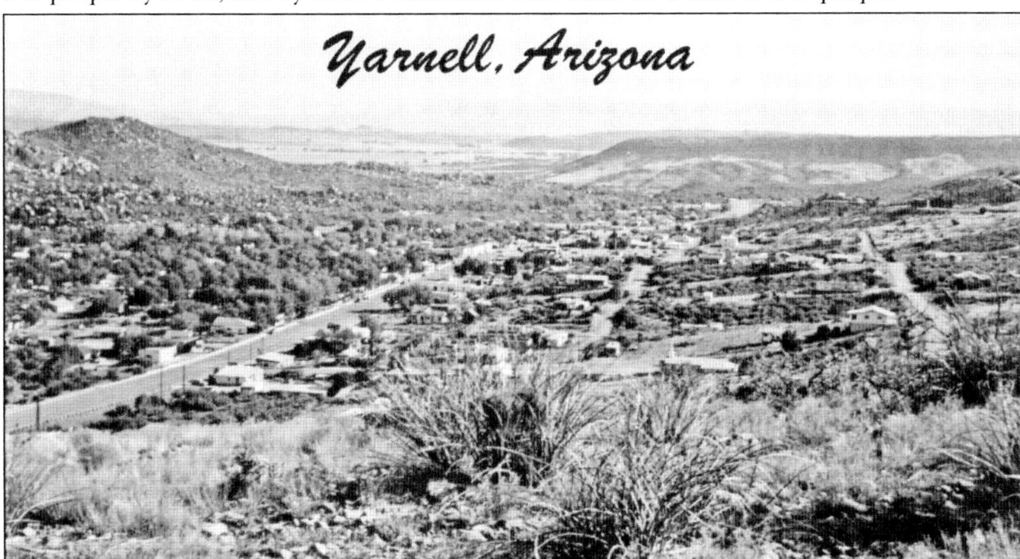

YARNELL, C. 1960S (REAL PHOTO POSTCARD). One of Yarnell's earliest inhabitants may have been Charles Genung, who discovered gold in the area around 1865. The town itself was named after Harrison Yarnell, who discovered the Yarnell mine in 1873. Probably one of the saddest days in Yarnell's history came on June 30, 2013, when a devastating fire struck the town and surrounding hills. Nearly half the town was turned to ash, and 19 Hotshot firefighters lost their lives. (Published by Kendall Photography, photograph by Charles P. Kendall.)

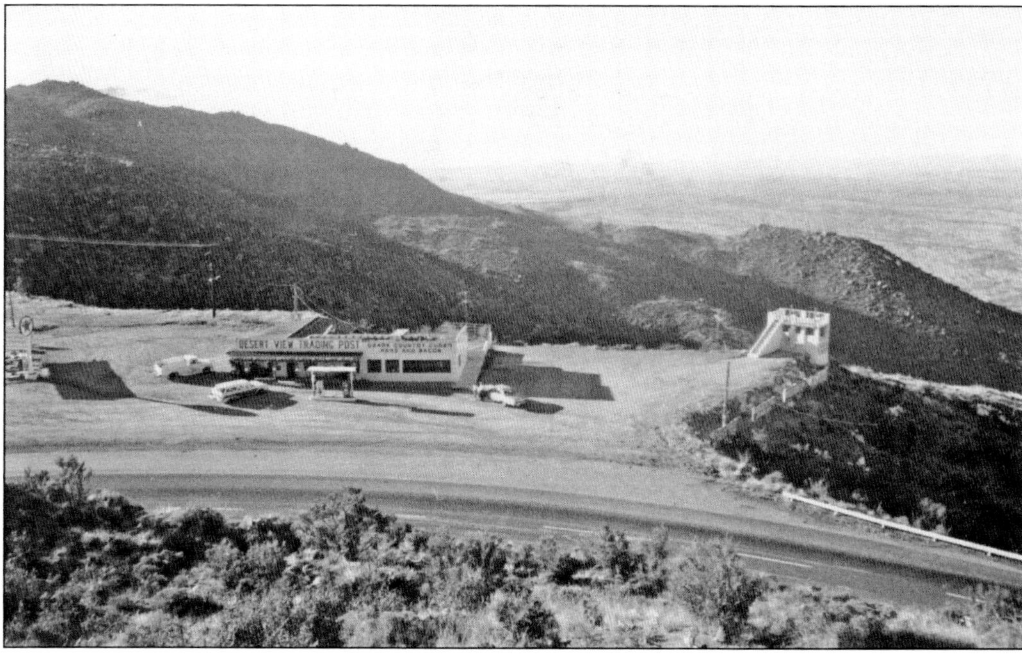

Above: Yarnell, Desert View Trading Post, Postmarked June 17, 1971 (Ektachrome Postcard); Below: Yarnell, Navahogan Post, c. 1940s (Real Photo Postcard). Now long gone, the old trading post was a popular stop for souvenirs along Highway 89 just outside of Yarnell. The card below advertises, "On Yarnell Hill and U.S. Highway 89 is one of the most attractive curio and gift shops in the west. It is a favorite stop for the Greyhound buses, and everyone who stops here is pleased with the things they find here and the friendly folks that serve them, Mr. and Mrs. Tom Tilley." (Above, published by Fronske Studio; below, published by L.L. Cook Co., courtesy Tony Meager.)

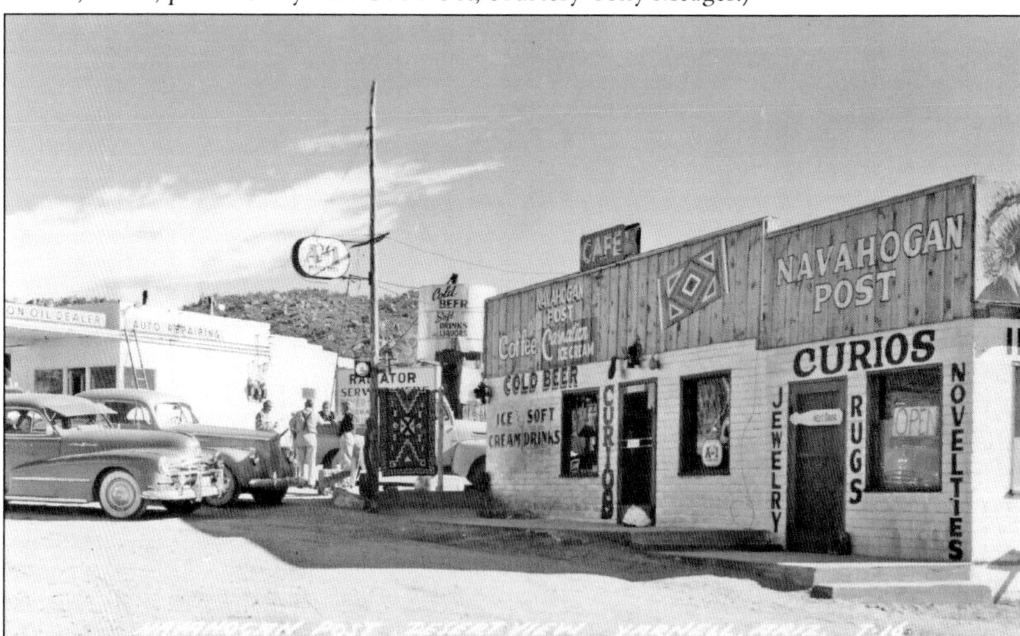

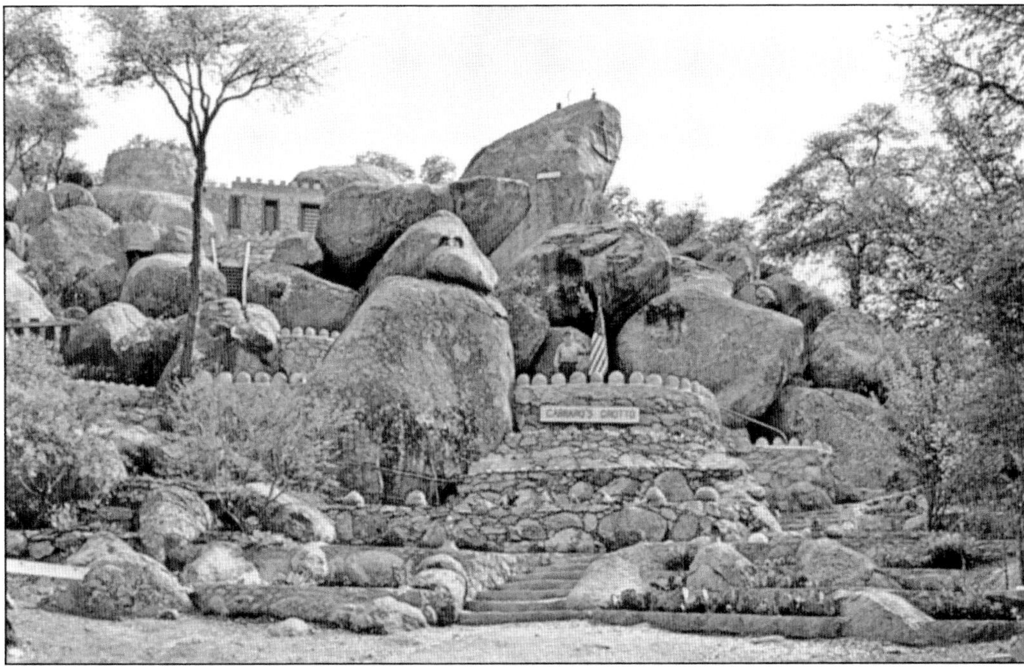

YARNELL, CARRARO'S GROTTO, C. 1960S (REAL PHOTO POSTCARD). After completing what would be known as the Tovrea Castle in Phoenix, Alessio Carraro moved to Yarnell in 1957. He immediately began building what he believed would become a tourist attraction among the boulders. His "Zoo of Rocks" was built on five acres that also included hiking trails and a small castle perched high on the hill. Carraro died in 1964, but his vision lives on in what now is known as Carraro's Grotto. (Published by Arizona Color Card Corp., photograph by Jim Sexton.)

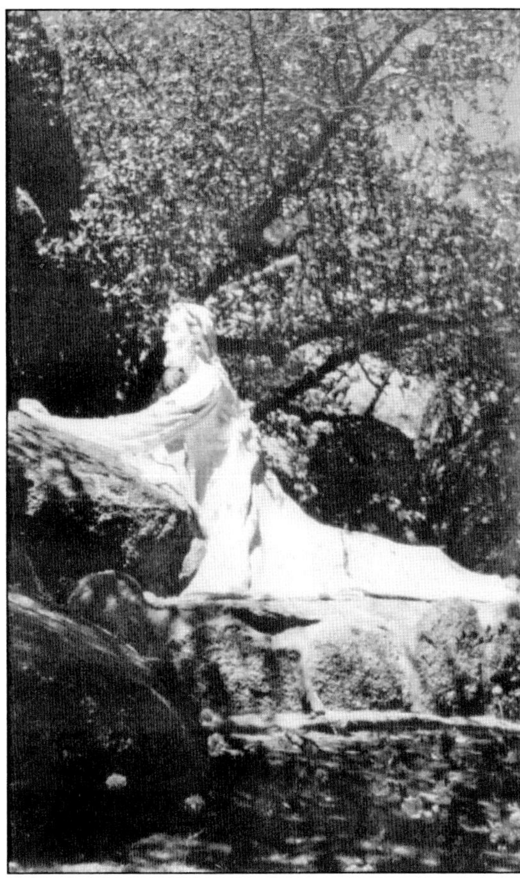

YARNELL, SHRINE OF ST. JOSEPH OF THE MOUNTAIN, C. 1970 (KODACHROME POSTCARD). Much of the retreat was lost in the Yarnell fire, including the large crucifix, gift shop, kitchen, and dormitories, just to name a few. The shrine, completed in 1939, was the creation of William and Mary Wasson. Along with nine families from Phoenix, they formed the Catholic Action League and set out to build the Shrine of St. Joseph of the Mountains among the boulders and hills of Yarnell. (Published by Bob Petley, photograph by E.A. Stein.)

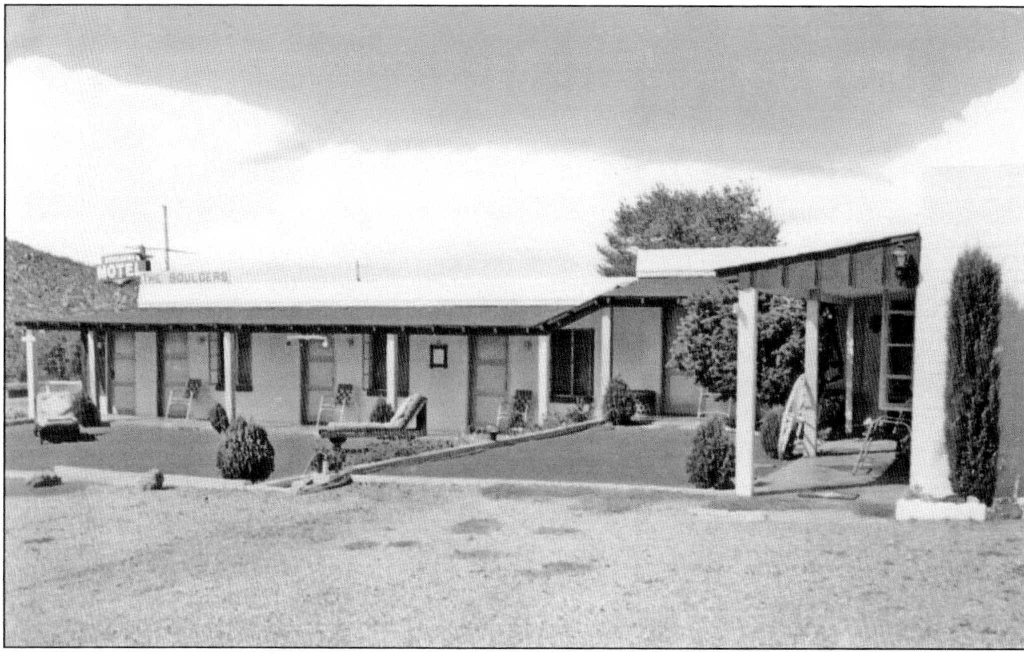

ABOVE: YARNELL, BOULDERS MOTEL, C. 1960S (ADVERTISING POSTCARD); BELOW: YARNELL, BOULDERS MOTEL, POSTMARKED MARCH 4, 1955 (ADVERTISING POSTCARD). The description on the back of the cards reads, "All modern—Private showers, The home of the Shrine of St. Joseph. Sleep in the fresh mountain breeze. Restaurants and service stations nearby." On the reverse of the card below, a guest wrote in part, "Thought I would show you a picture of our home for the night. A nice clean little place and a small bed so I am rested and ready for the final sprint." (Above, published by Dexter Press, Inc.; below, published by National Press, Inc.)

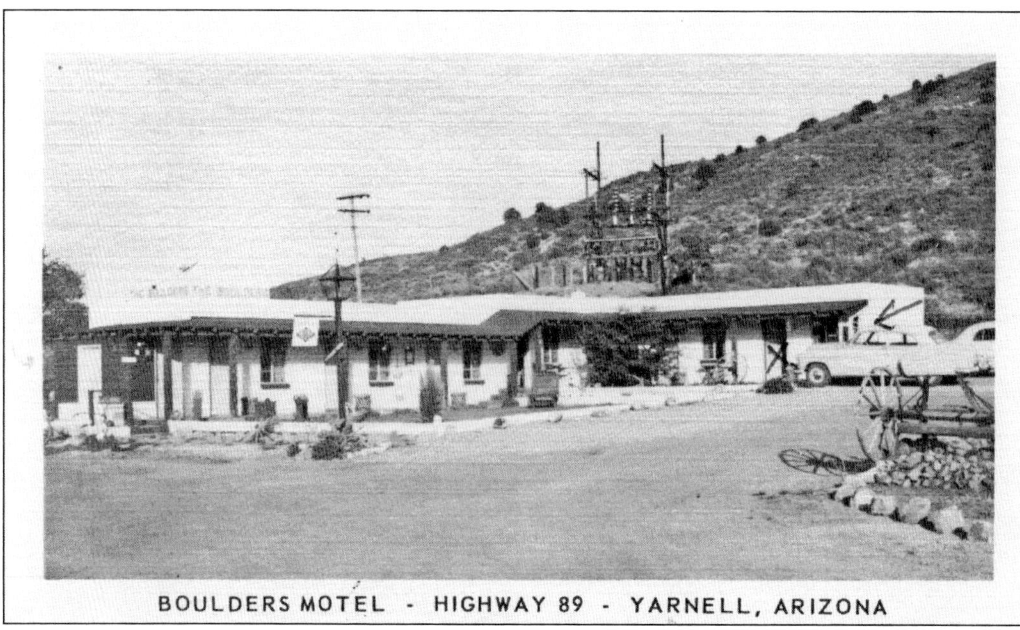

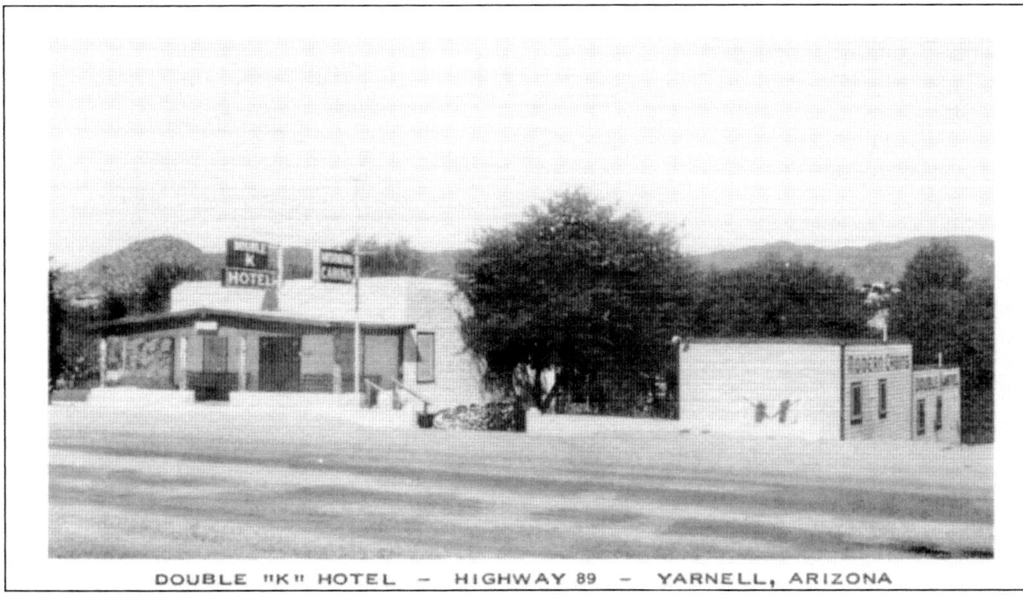

YARNELL, DOUBLE "K" HOTEL, C. 1965 (ADVERTISING POSTCARD). The back reads, "A clean, comfortable and reasonable priced place to stay. Located between Prescott and Wickenburg, Arizona on U.S. Highway 89. Modern cabins, kitchenettes, rooms, double and single units. Delightfully cool in the summer and heated with vented heaters during the colder months." (Published by National Press, Inc.)

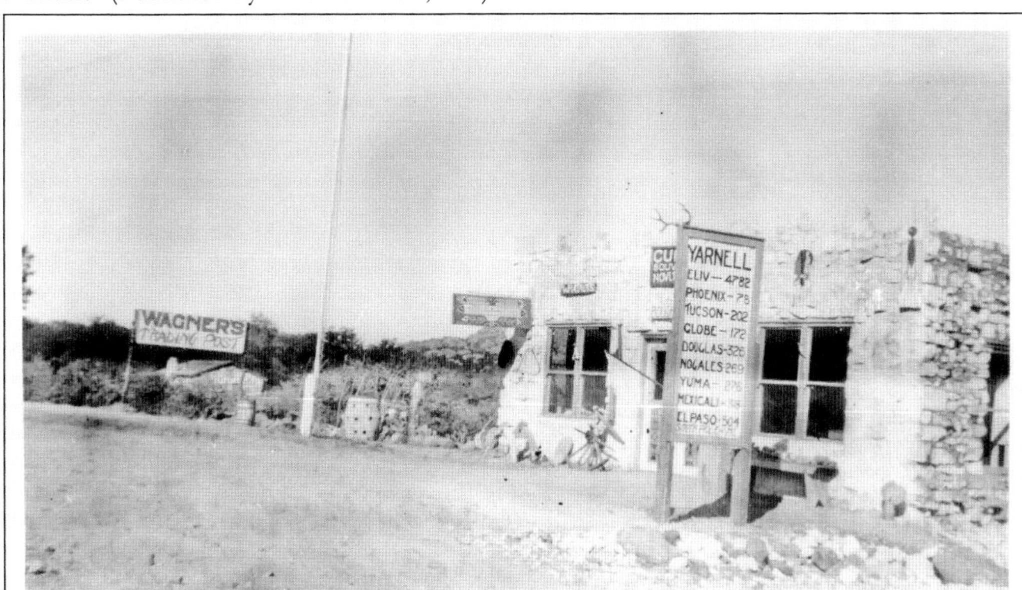

YARNELL, WAGNERS TRADING POST, C. 1940S (REAL PHOTO POSTCARD). According to the June 13, 1954, *Arizona Republic*, Ray Wagner arrived in Yarnell in the spring of 1933 and set up his first shop alongside the newly completed Highway 89. His first store consisted of four upright poles with a brush roof. His merchandise was handmade "doodads made from dried bones." Later in the 1930s, Wagner built the store seen here of tufa stone and adobe. (Published by L.L. Cook Co.)

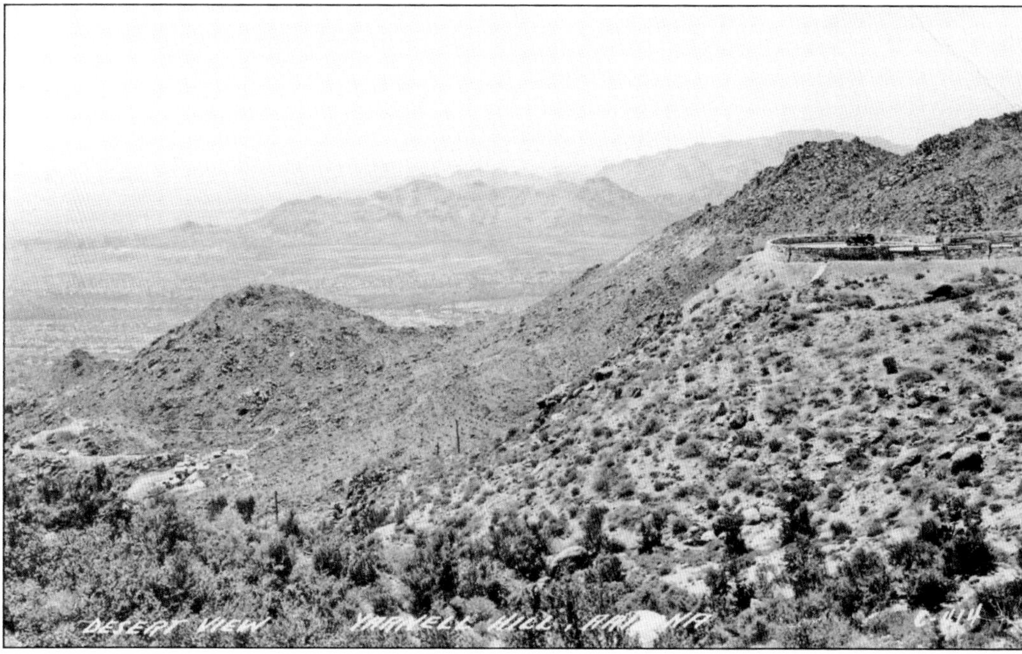

YARNELL, DESERT VIEW, C. 1940S (REAL PHOTO POSTCARD). Located just south of Yarnell on Highway 89, Desert View is a large pull-out off the road overlooking the valley. Situated above the Planet Saturn Mine, the spot affords stunning views of Congress and Wickenburg. (Published by Kodak.)

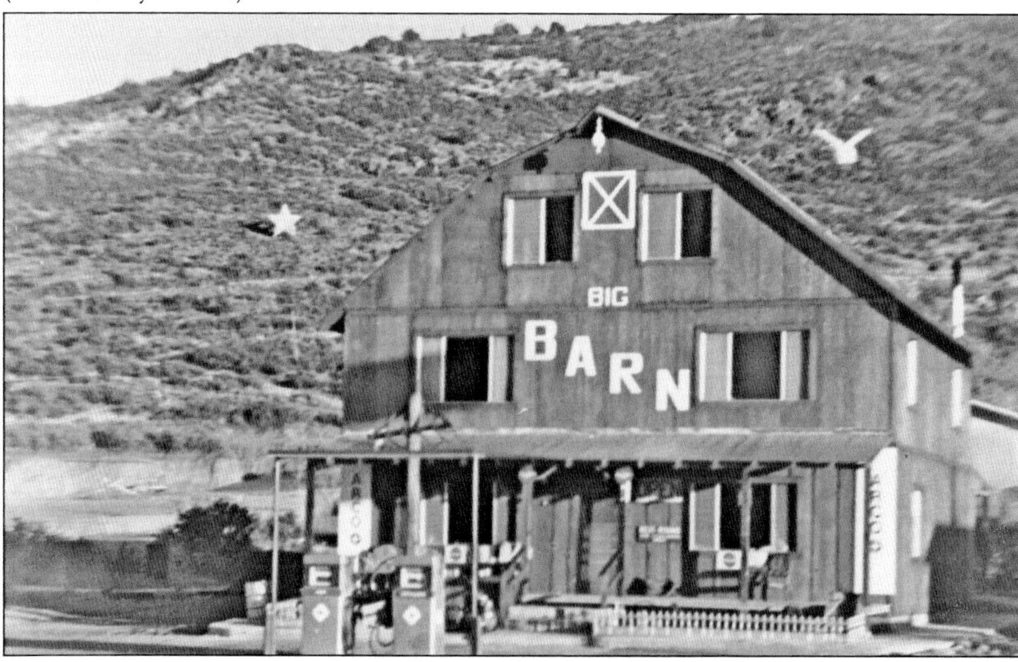

YARNELL, BIG BARN, C. 1960S (ADVERTISING POSTCARD). The back reads, "Gift shop, souvenirs, gasoline, oils. US 89 Highway links the Alaska Highway to the Pan-American Highway forming a West Coast Avenue from Fairbanks, Alaska to Puerto Montt, Chile." (Published by Petley Studios.)

Two

Recreation, Parks, and National Monuments

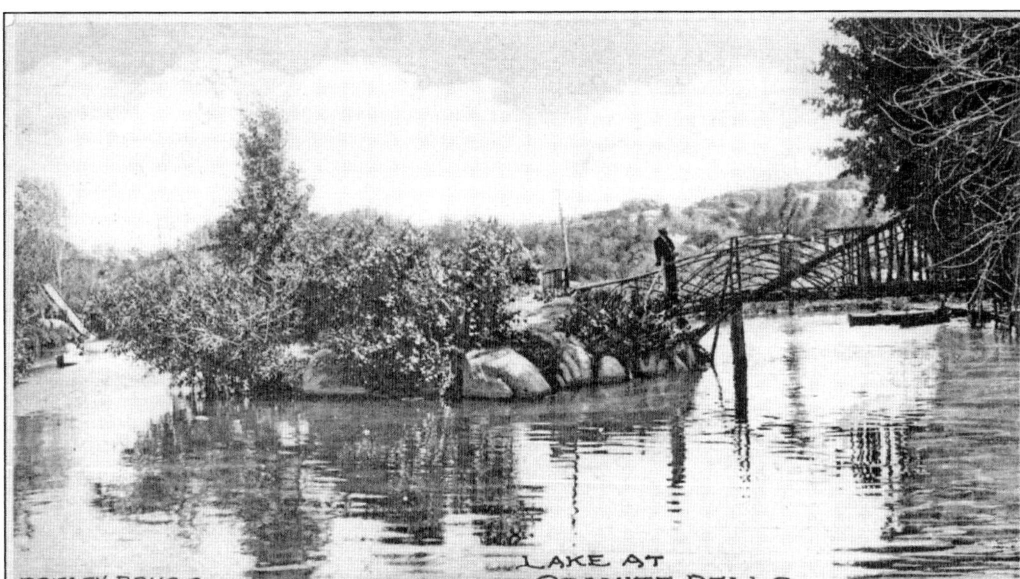

Prescott, Lake at Granite Dells, Postmarked September 3, 1906 (Undivided Back Postcard). A bridge led to a small island that featured diving boards, and as visitors walked along the lake's shore, there was a rope swing that threw them far out into the lake. During the early part of the 1900s, a special train would bring people to the resort and pick them up in the afternoon for the trip back to Prescott. The resort was not limited to just a swimming lake; it also had a dance hall, picnic area, lawn bowling, roller-skating rink, bathhouse, and two-story hotel. In 1945, the movie *Leave Her to Heaven*, starring Gene Tierney and Jeanne Crain, was filmed there. (Published by Brisley Drug Co.)

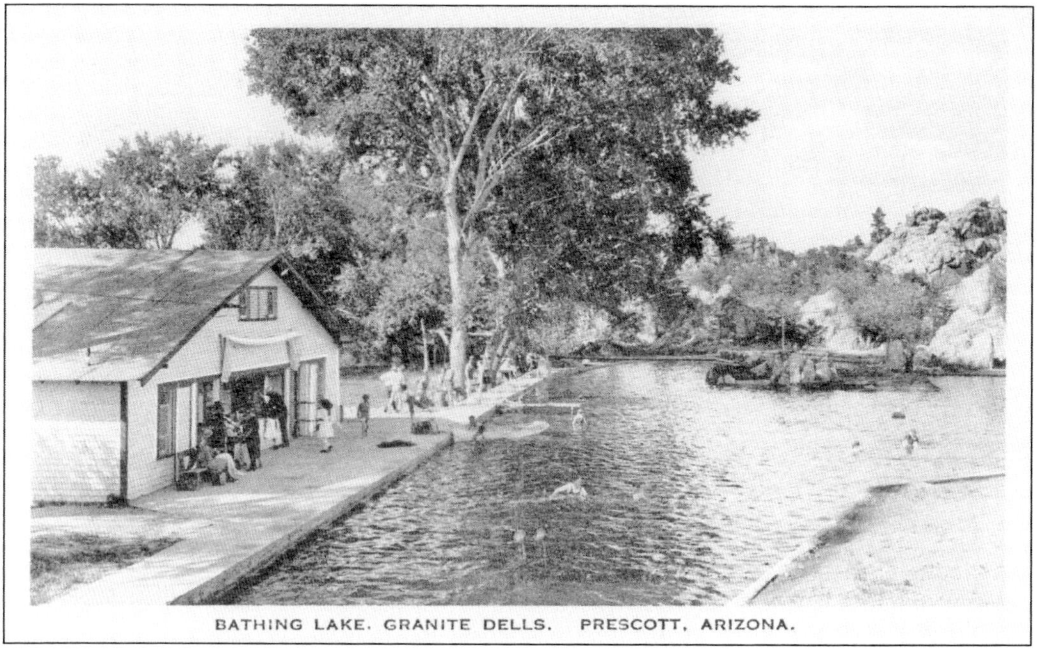

ABOVE: BATHING LAKE—GRANITE DELLS, C. 1920S (ALBERTYPE POSTCARD); BELOW: LAKE AT GRANITE DELLS, POSTMARKED SEPTEMBER 17, 1936 (ALBERTYPE POSTCARD). The lake had its beginnings in the 1880s, when James Wing built a small dam and irrigation system along Granite Creek to water his orchard and crops. Years later, a ditch was run to a pond that eventually became the Granite Dells Swimming Lake. (Both, published by Owl Drug and Candy Company.)

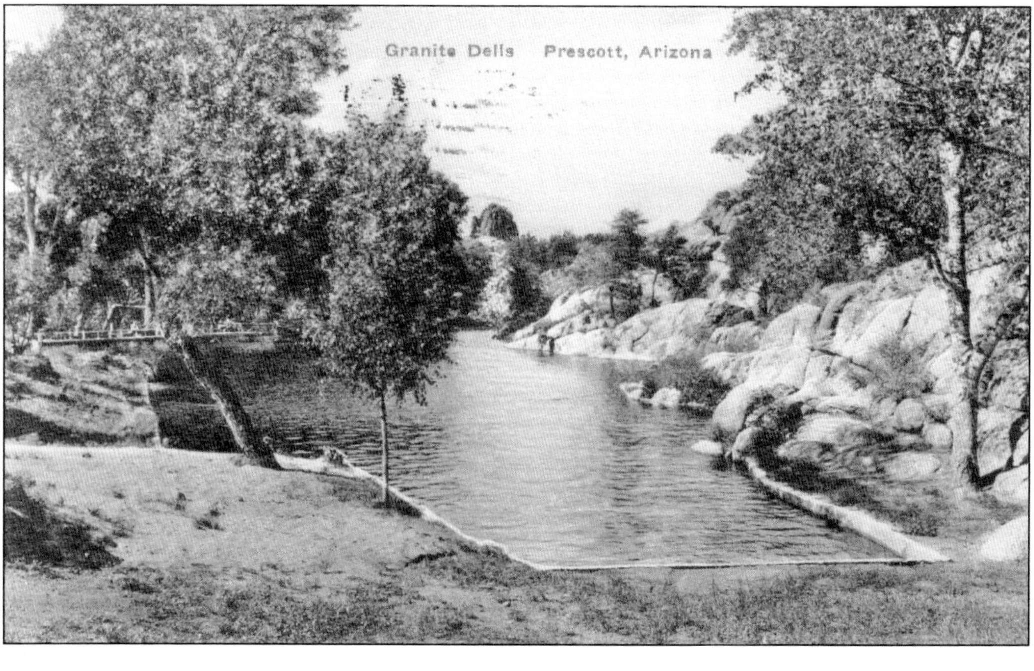

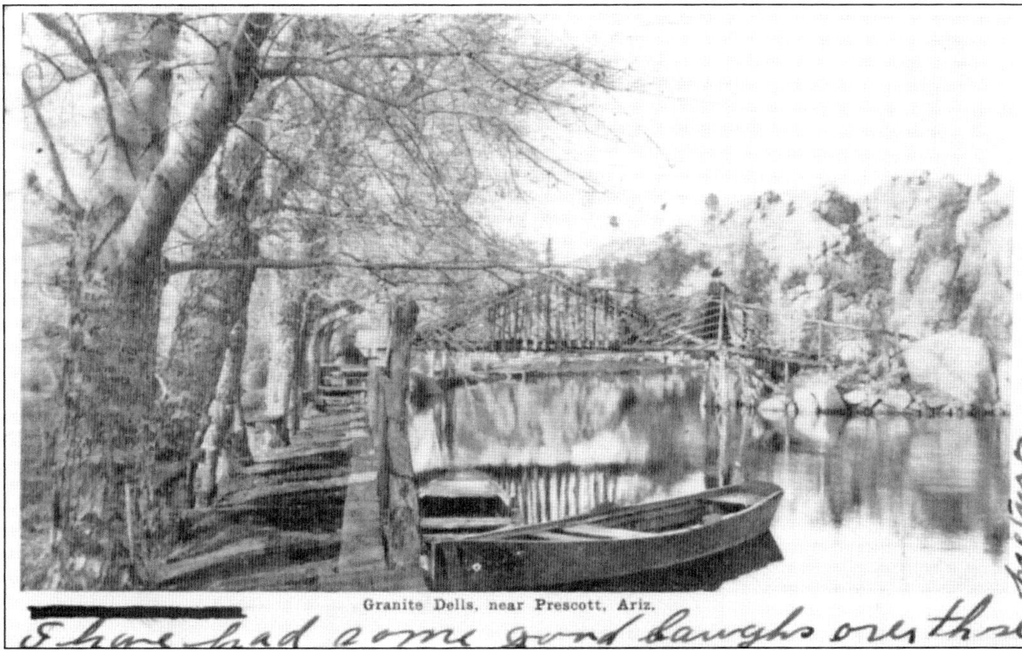

BOATING LAKE, POSTMARKED APRIL 7, 1908 (DIVIDED BACK POSTCARD). In 1922, the pond was lined with cement. Through the years, many additions were made to the resort, which became a popular destination for locals as well as the rich and famous. The resort was open from 1922 through 1971 and again briefly from 1978 to 1982. (Courtesy Skull Valley Historical Society.)

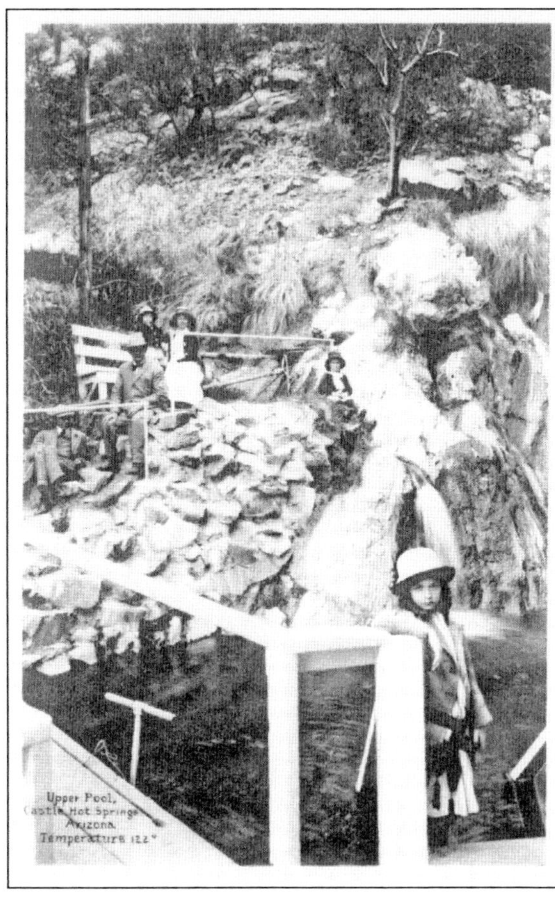

CASTLE HOT SPRINGS, UPPER POOL, C. 1910–1915 (ADVERTISING POSTCARD). Children play in the upper pool while the parents relax in the warm sun. This same pool is still in existence and has not changed much over the years. In 2014, the hot springs, along with its 210 acres, sold for $1.95 million. The new owners are looking at different options for the property. (Produced by the Fairman Co.)

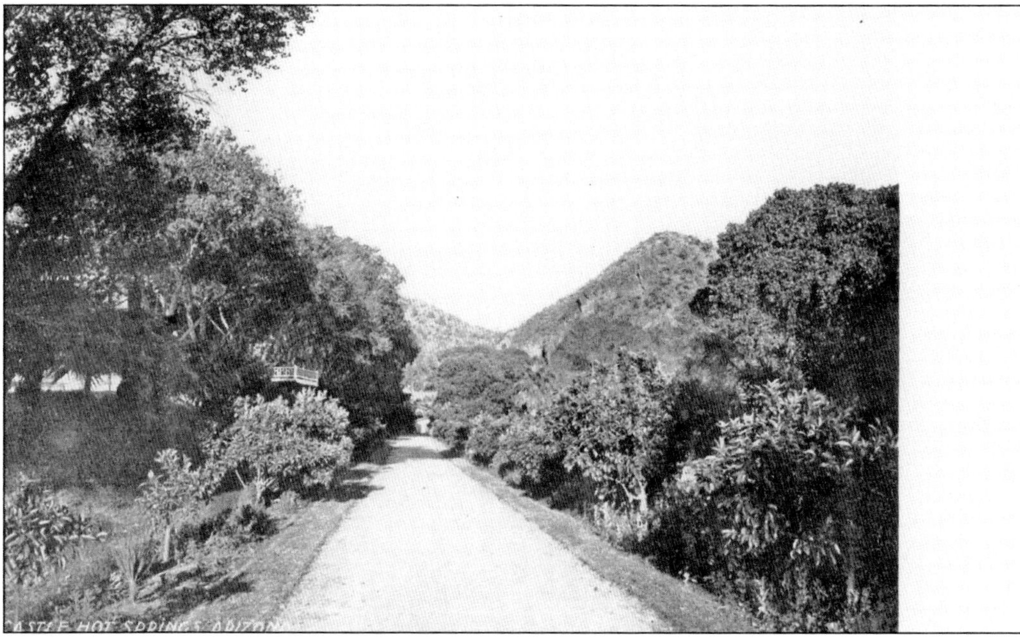

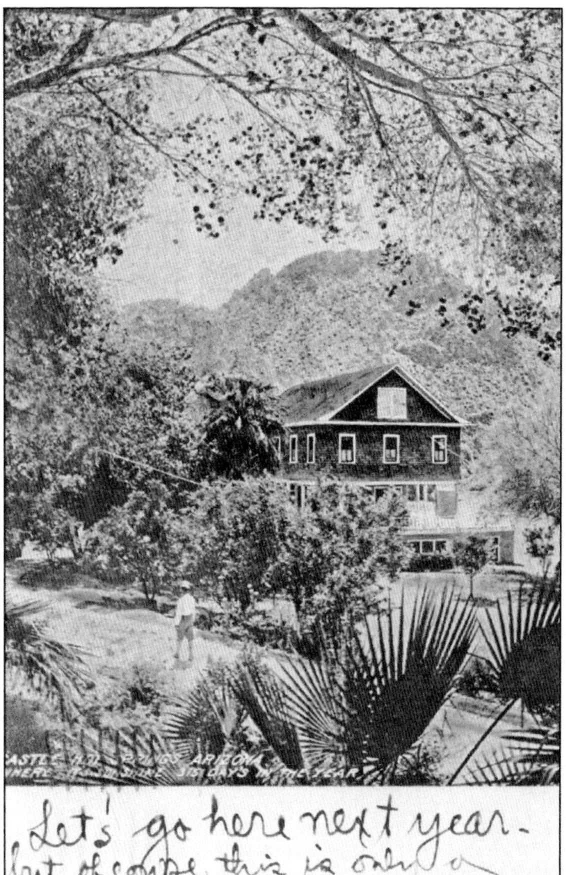

ABOVE: CASTLE HOT SPRINGS, ROAD TO THE SPRINGS, C. 1910S (DIVIDED BACK POSTCARD); LEFT: CASTLE HOT SPRINGS HOTEL, POSTMARKED NOVEMBER 15, 1907 (DIVIDED BACK POSTCARD). There is only one road leading to the resort. Starting near Lake Pleasant, the road winds behind the lake and through the rugged Bradshaw Mountains. Due to the ruggedness of the area, the springs weren't discovered until 1867, when the US Cavalry led by Col. Charles Craig chased a raiding party of Apaches through the mountains. When he came upon the springs, he named them Castle Hot Springs after the surrounding mountains, which resembled castles.

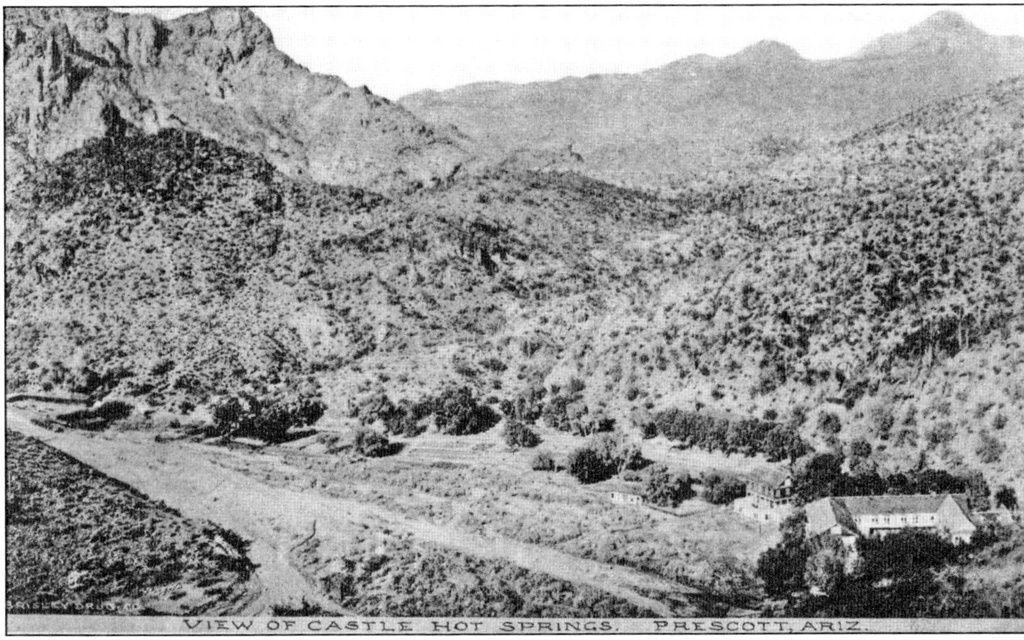

Castle Hot Springs, View of Castle Hot Springs, Postmarked March 14, 1908 (Divided Back Postcard). The resort had only been open about eight years when this photograph was taken. The photograph shows the remoteness of the resort and why the Apache Indians held this land to be so sacred. (Published by Brisley Drug Co., courtesy Skull Valley Historical Association.)

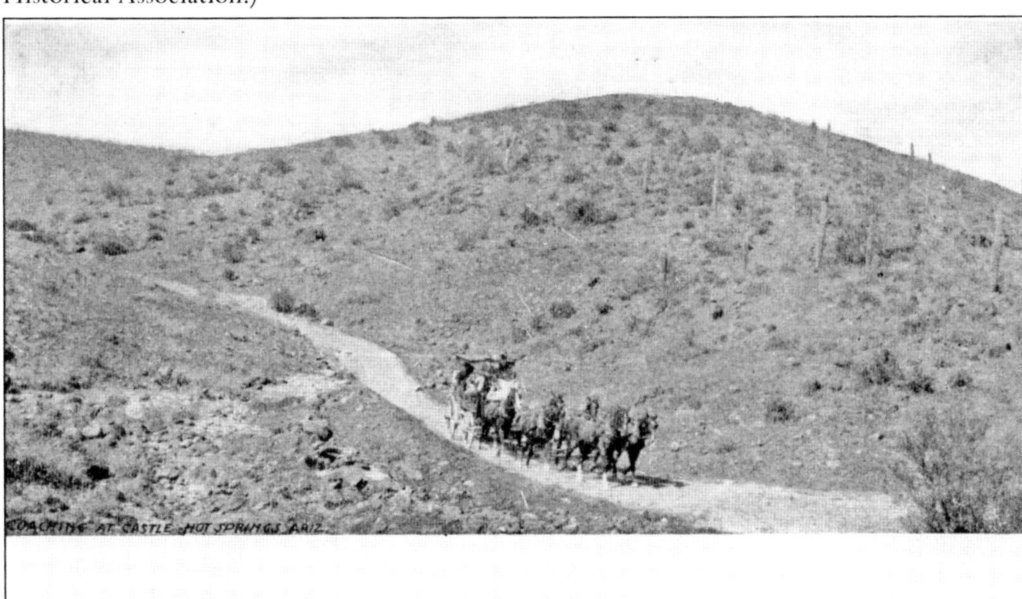

Castle Hot Springs, Coaching, c. 1910 (Divided Back Postcard). In the early days of Castle Hot Springs, the only way to get there was to take the train to Hot Springs Junction, between Phoenix and Wickenburg, and catch the coach for the 20-mile, five-hour ride over a rough wagon road to the hot springs. The photograph itself was taken closer to 1900. Vehicles started using the road to the springs in 1913. (Courtesy Nancy Burgess.)

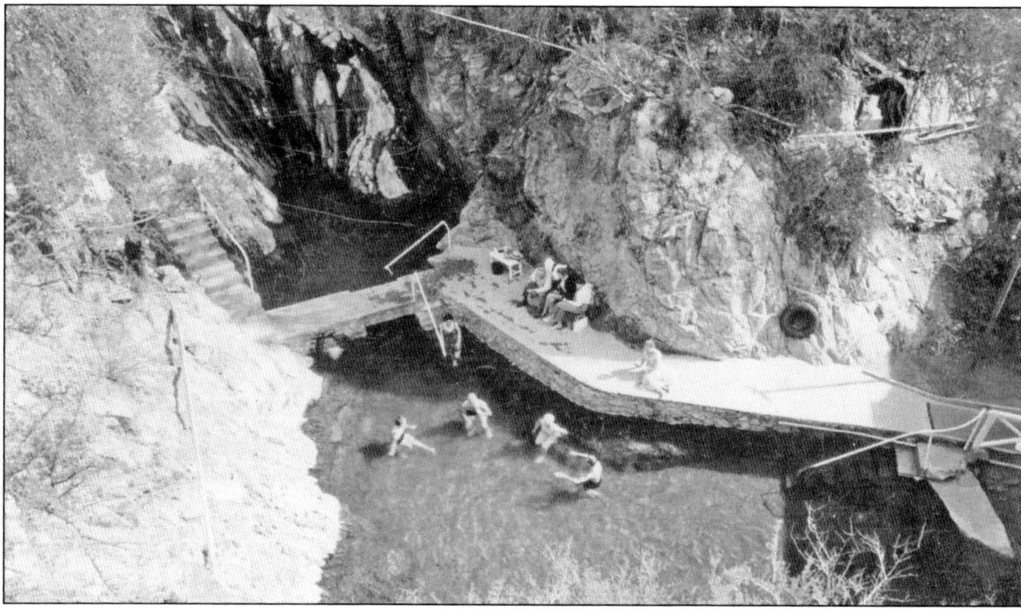

ABOVE: CASTLE HOT SPRINGS, CASTLE HOT SPRINGS HOTEL, C. 1960 (ADVERTISING POSTCARD); BELOW: CASTLE HOT SPRINGS, C. 1930S (REAL PHOTO POSTCARD). Pictured are two of the resort's hot pools. Naturally hot mineral waters flow from the rocks at a rate of 400,000 gallons a day. Pool temperatures range from 90 to 125 degrees. The resort's main building burned down in 1976. Since that time, only groundskeepers have lived on the property.

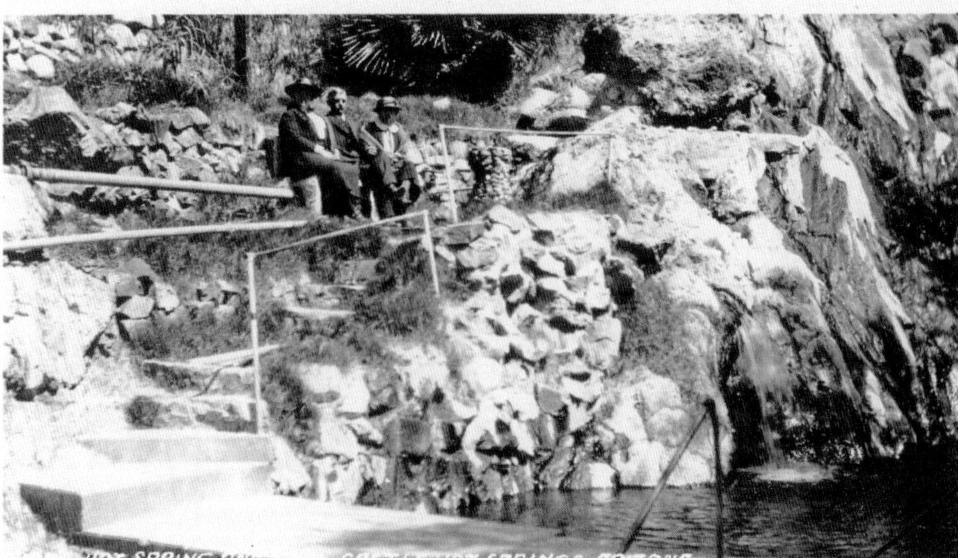

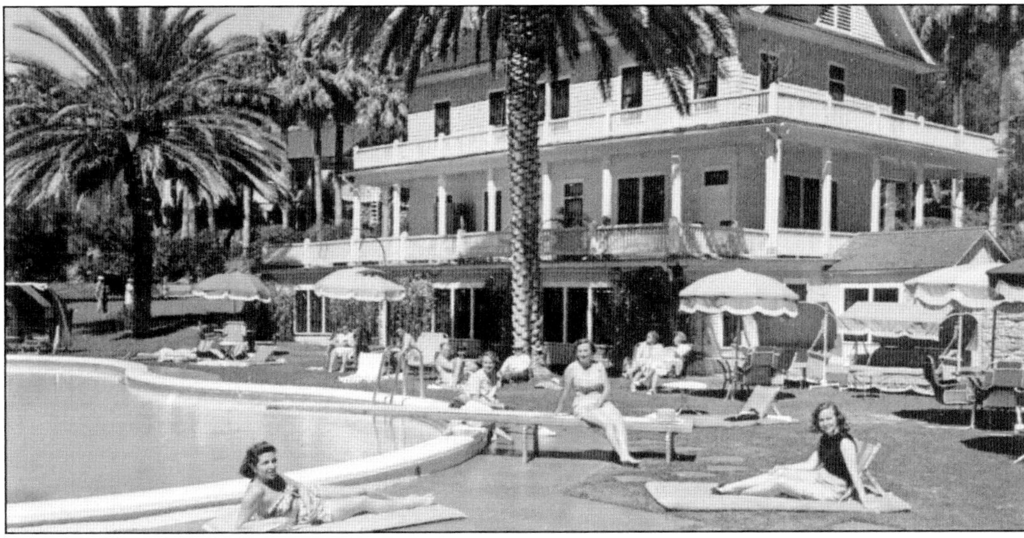

ABOVE: CASTLE HOT SPRINGS, CASTLE HOT SPRINGS HOTEL, C. 1960 (REAL PHOTO POSTCARD); BELOW: CASTLE HOT SPRINGS, ORANGE GROVE, POSTMARKED DECEMBER 26, 1942 (LINEN POSTCARD). Although the springs had been known for some time, development was delayed until the 1890s due to local Indian wars. Frank Murphy purchased the property and began building his health resort. In 1896, Castle Hot Springs opened for business. Over the years, Castle Hot Springs hosted many celebrities, such as Zane Grey, Vanderbilts, Carnegies, Astors, and Rockefellers. During a portion of World War II, the US military used Castle Hot Springs as a rehabilitation center. Future president John F. Kennedy spent three months recuperating from injuries he sustained when his PT boat was sunk. (Above, produced by Dexter Press, photograph by Bob Bradshaw.)

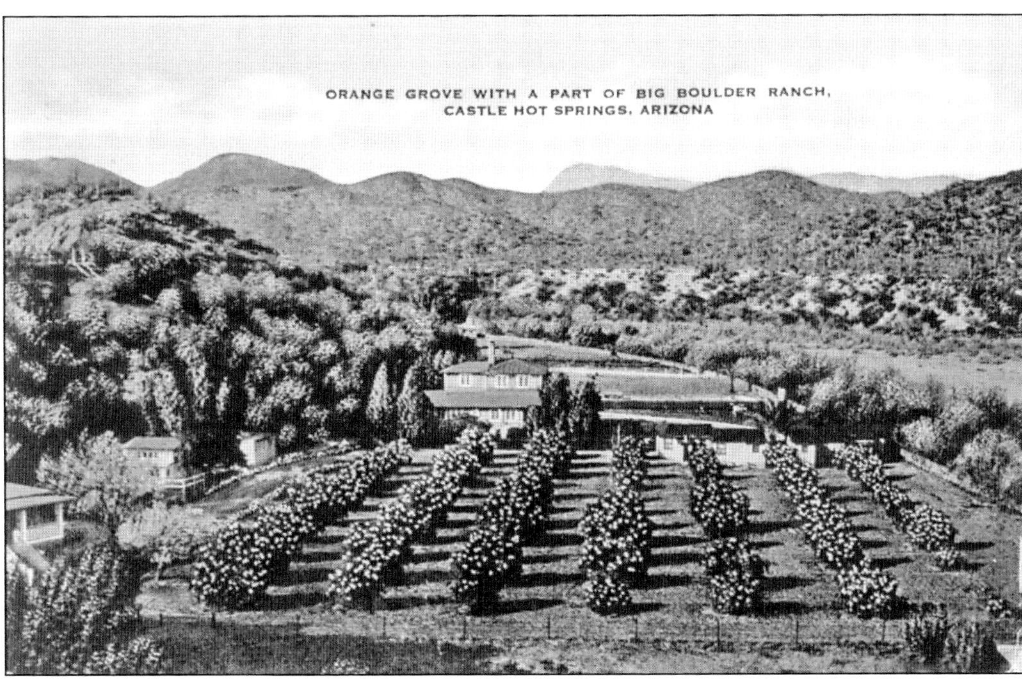

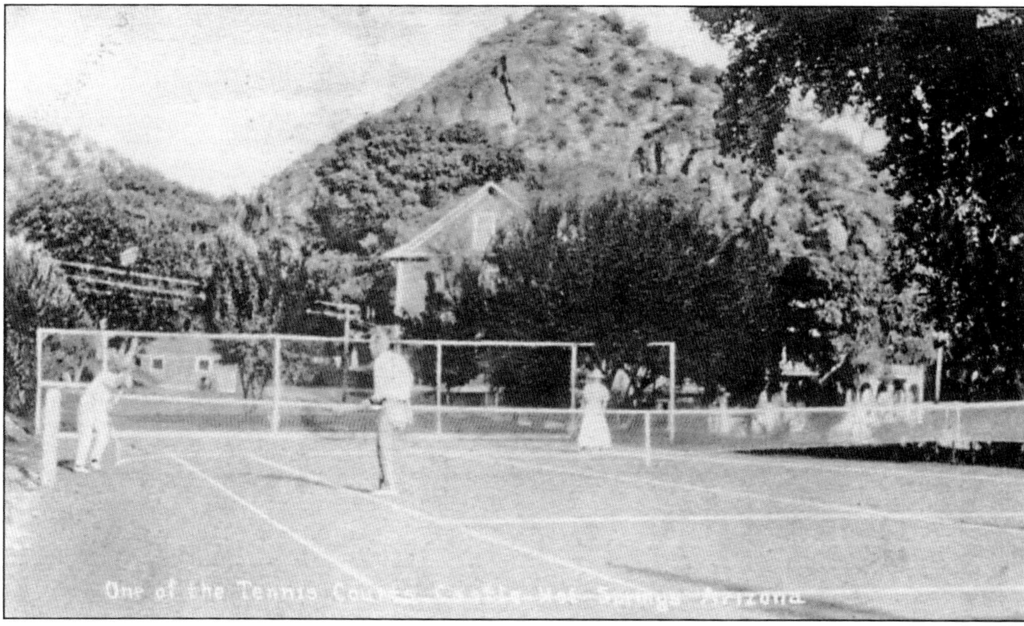

CASTLE HOT SPRINGS, TENNIS COURTS, C. 1910–1915 (DIVIDED BACK POSTCARD). The hot springs were originally believed to have therapeutic properties that could heal blood disorders, rheumatism, kidney disease, and a list of other ailments. In addition to the tennis courts, the hot springs' 210 acres included a 125,000-gallon swimming pool fed with spring water, and an 18-hole golf course. (Produced by the Fairman Co.)

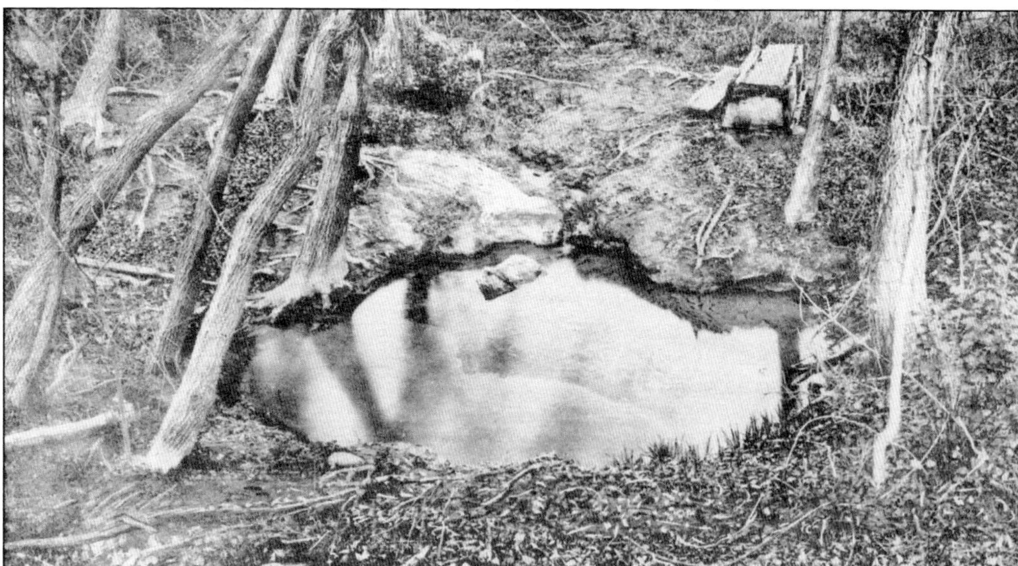

SODA SPRINGS, FINNIE'S RANCH. PRESCOTT, ARIZONA.

SODA SPRINGS, FINNIE'S RANCH, C. 1925 (ALBERTYPE POSTCARD). In 1876, William Clift settled his family along Beaver Creek near Rimrock and used the water from Soda Springs to irrigate his garden. In 1883, Robert Finnie bought the land and began planting fruit and planning his ranch. Eventually, due to the popularity of the springs, the Finnies built a guest ranch on their property. Later, in 1928, the Rimrock Dude Ranch opened for business. (Produced by Owl and Candy Co., printed by Albertype.)

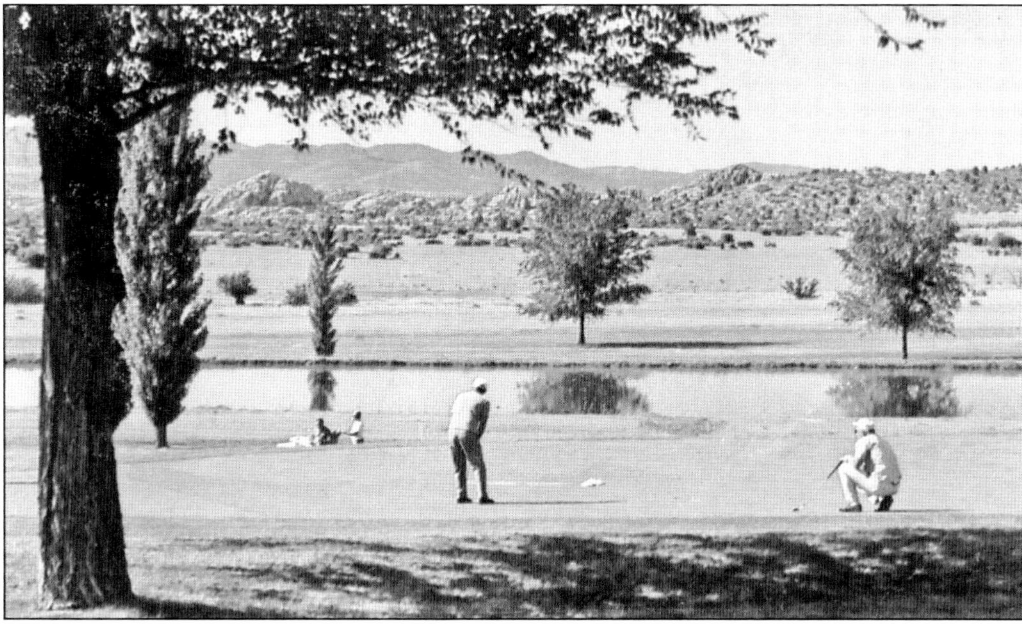

ANTELOPE HILLS GOLF COURSE, C. 1970S (ADVERTISING POSTCARD). On land donated to the city of Prescott by the US Navy, Antelope Hills Golf Course has 36 holes of golf spread over two courses. The older course, now known as the North Course, opened in 1956, while the second 18 holes, known as the South Course, opened in 1992. (Published by Classic Printers, Prescott.)

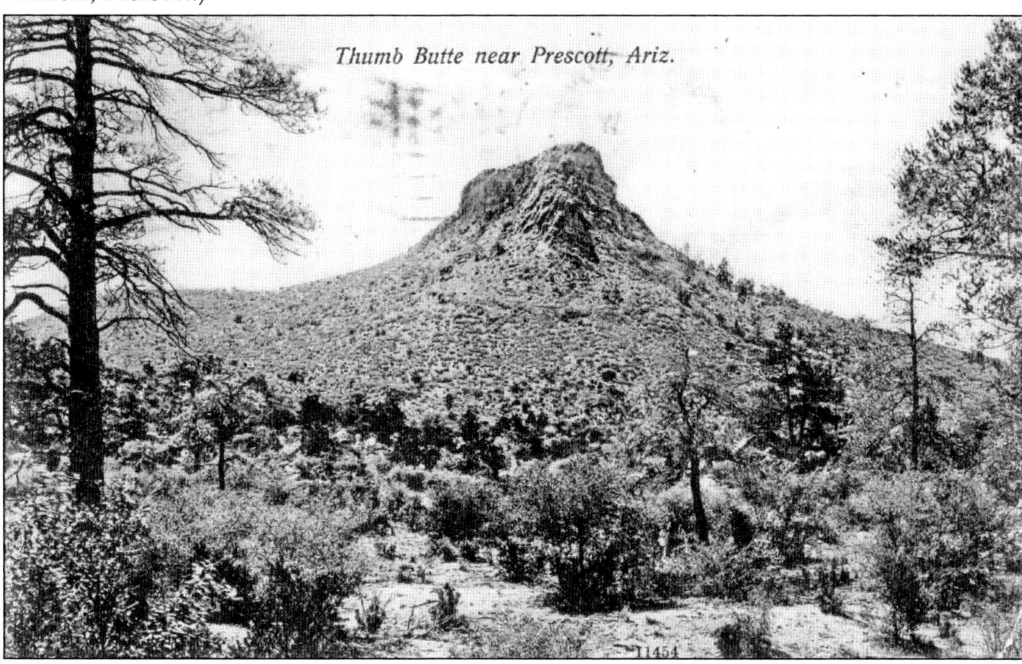

THUMB BUTTE, POSTMARKED MAY 31, 1910 (DIVIDED BACK POSTCARD). Two versions of this card exist, one by Albertype that was hand colored from the 1920s and this earlier black-and-white version by Souvenir Post Card Co. According to the National Park Service, there are approximately 18 miles of maintained hiking trails around Thumb Butte.

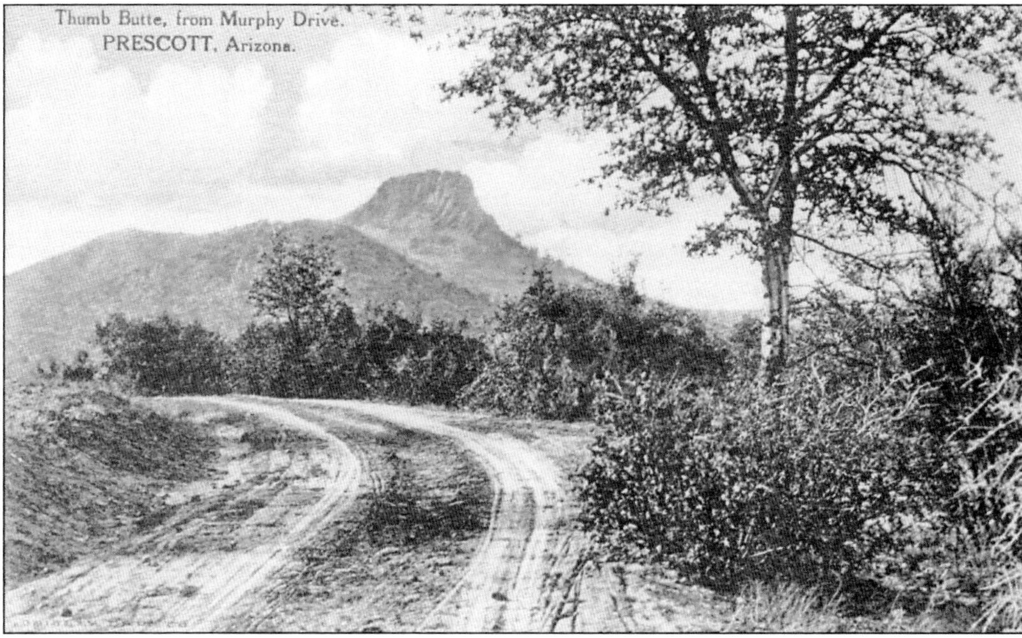

THUMB BUTTE, FROM MURPHY DRIVE, C. 1910 (ALBERTYPE POSTCARD). There are at least two versions of this card, both made by Albertype. One was published by Heil Drug Store and is labeled "Thumb Butte, Prescott Arizona," while the second card is unsponsored and is labeled "Thumb Butte from Murphy Drive, Prescott Arizona." The name of Murphy Drive has since been changed Thumb Butte Road.

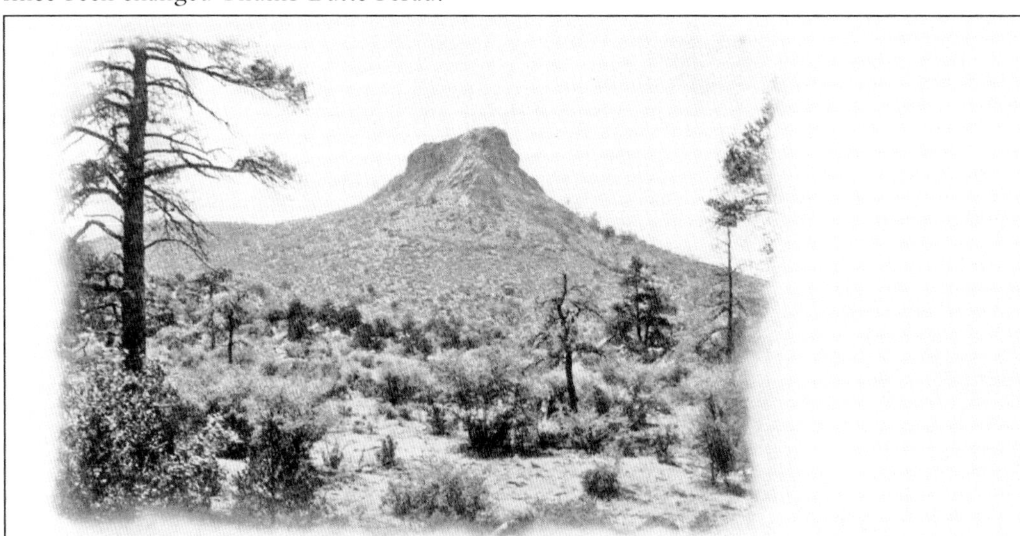

THUMB BUTTE, C. 1905 (UNDIVIDED BACK POSTCARD). At 6,514 feet, Thumb Butte rises 1,200 feet above downtown Prescott. For years, Thumb Butte was thought to be a volcanic plug. A volcanic plug is the hardened center of a volcano that has eroded over millions of years. But more recently, Thumb Butte is believed to be a basalt flow, which is simply a tall lava flow. (Published by W.H. Timerhoff, Druggist.)

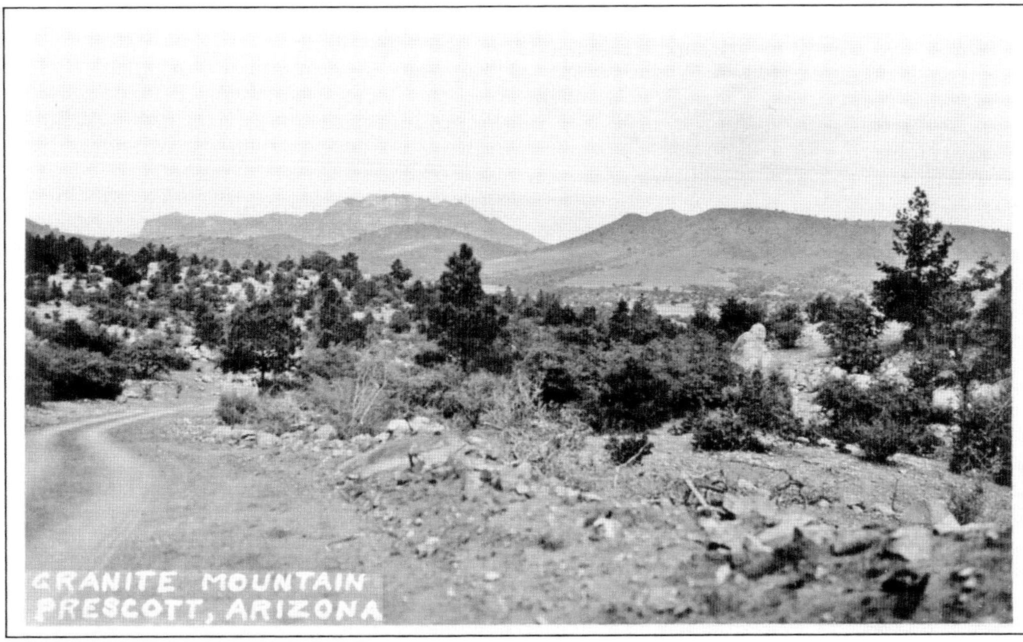

ABOVE: GRANITE MOUNTAIN, C. 1940S (REAL PHOTO POSTCARD); BELOW: GRANITE MOUNTAIN, C. 1940S (REAL PHOTO POSTCARD). Once named Mount Gurley, after the first territorial governor, John A. Gurley, Granite Mountain stands 7,626 feet and covers 12 square miles. Located in the Granite Mountain Wilderness, which is part of the Prescott National Forest, Granite Mountain is popular among hikers and rock climbers. There are approximately 41 miles over 15 trails open to hikers. Within the park and protected by the National Park Service are sites known only to a few, such as petroglyphs left by the area's first inhabitants and the nation's largest alligator juniper. It is estimated that the 46-foot-high juniper is 1,400 years old.

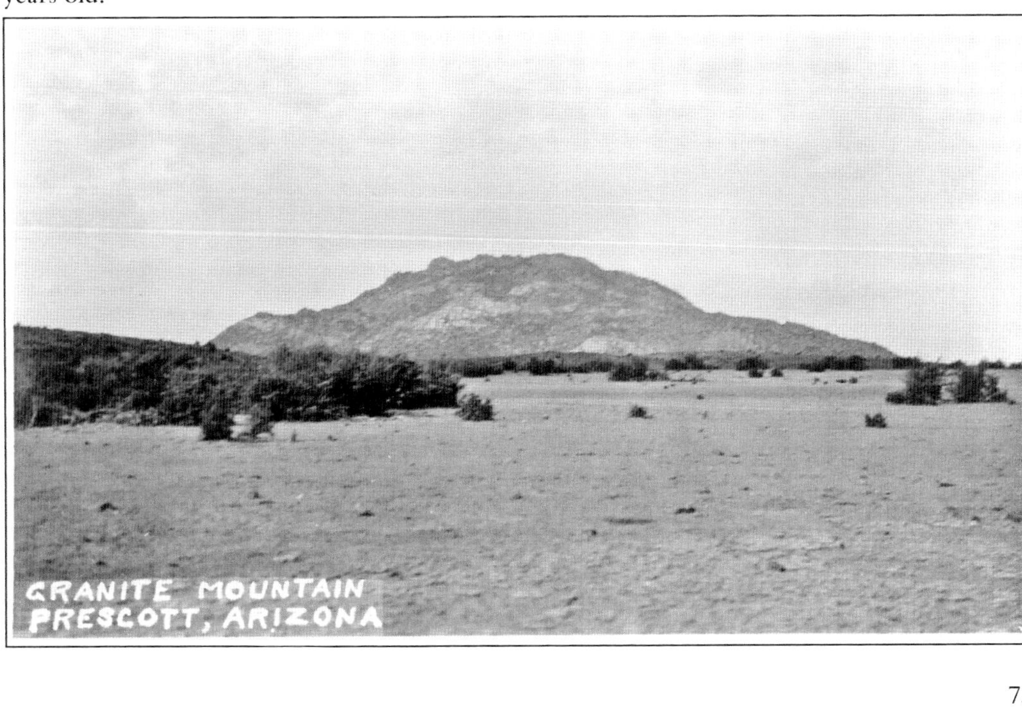

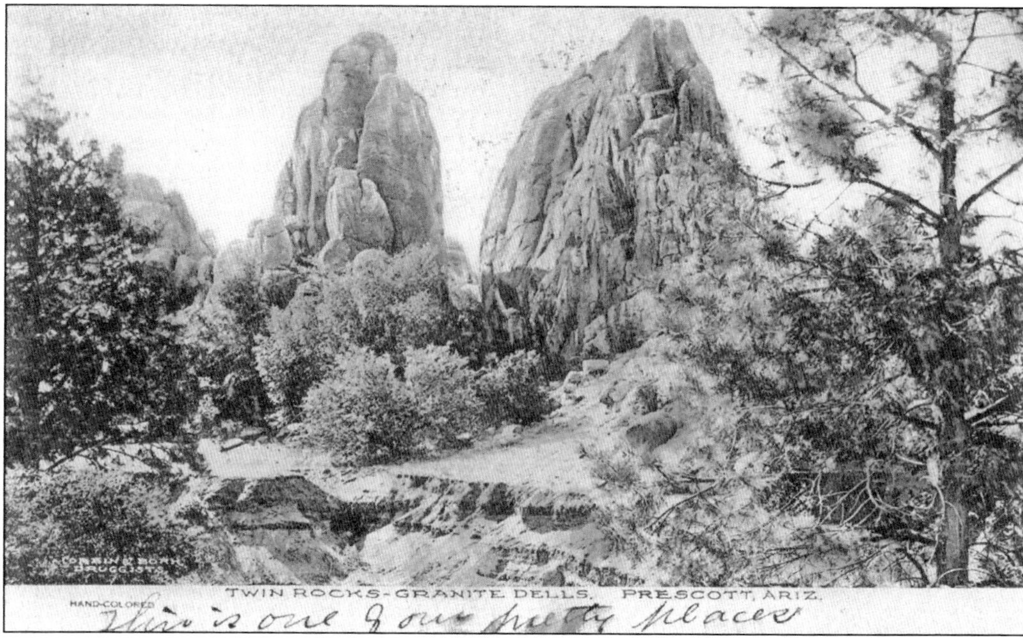

ABOVE: GRANITE DELLS, TWIN ROCKS, POSTMARKED NOVEMBER 3, 1907 (HAND-COLORED POSTCARD); BELOW: GRANITE DELLS, NEAR PRESCOTT, C. 1920S (ALBERTYPE POSTCARD). The Granite Dells are beautiful geological formations of granite that have eroded over the last billion years into what is seen today. Rocks that defy gravity and spheres of granite rising high into the sky are just a few phenomena of the Dells. Two reservoirs, Willow and Watson, were built within the Dells to supply water for the Chino Valley Irrigation District. (Above, published by Corbin and Bork; below, published by B.B. Shimonowsky & Bro., Post Exchange.)

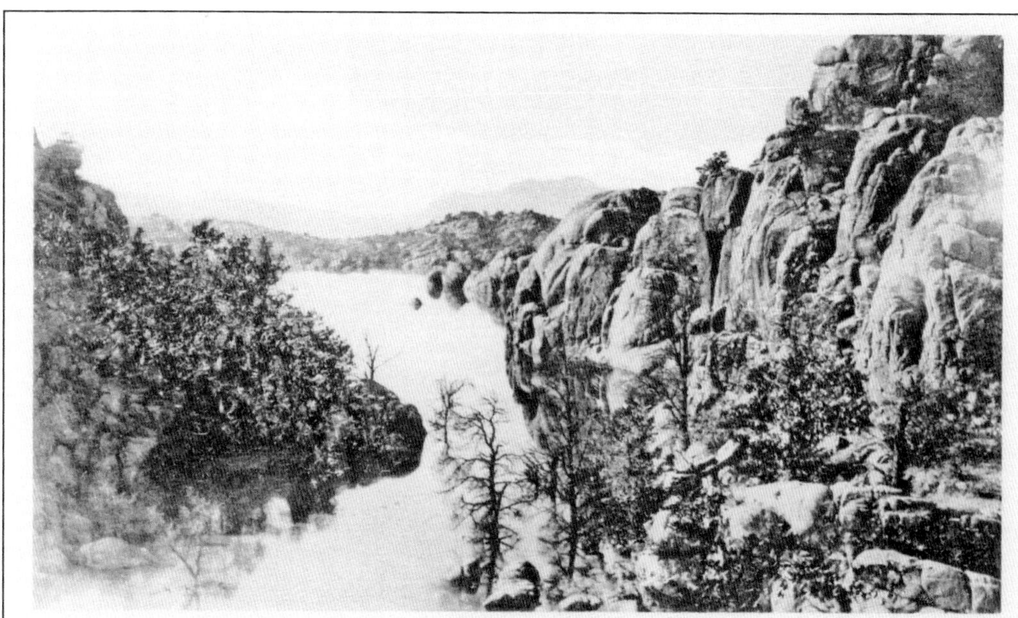

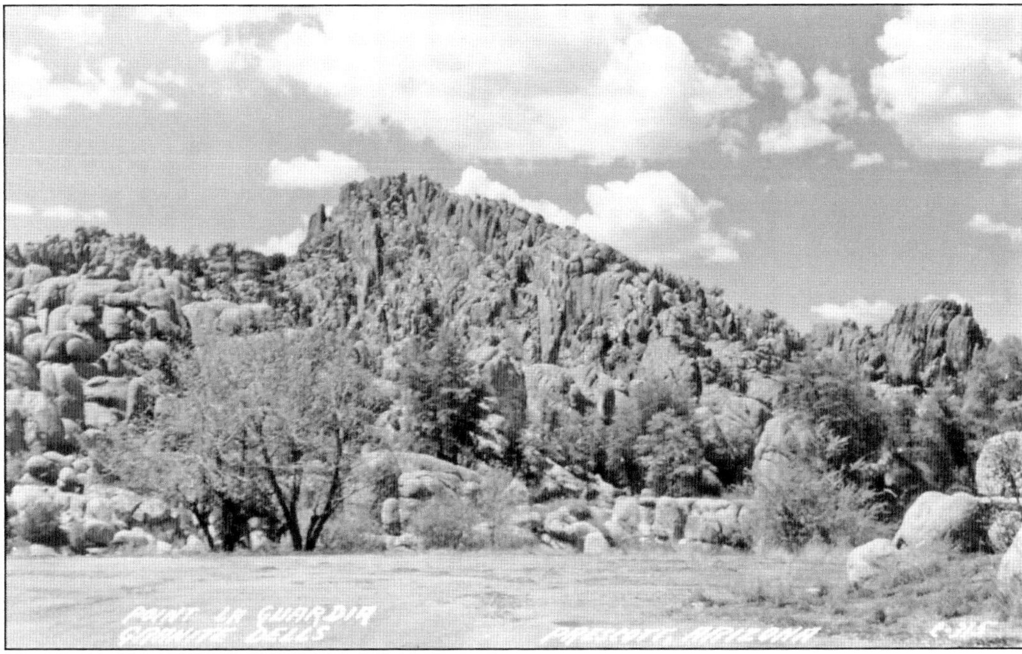

ABOVE: GRANITE DELLS, POINT LA GUARDIA, POSTMARKED JULY 1, 1942 (REAL PHOTO POSTCARD); BELOW: GRANITE DELLS, C. 1905 (UNDIVIDED BACK POSTCARD). La Guardia Point was named after Achilles LaGuardia, the father of New York mayor Fiorello H. LaGuardia. The elder LaGuardia was the bandmaster at Fort Whipple for many years. (Above, published by L.L. Cook Co.; below, published by W.H. Timerhoff, Druggist.)

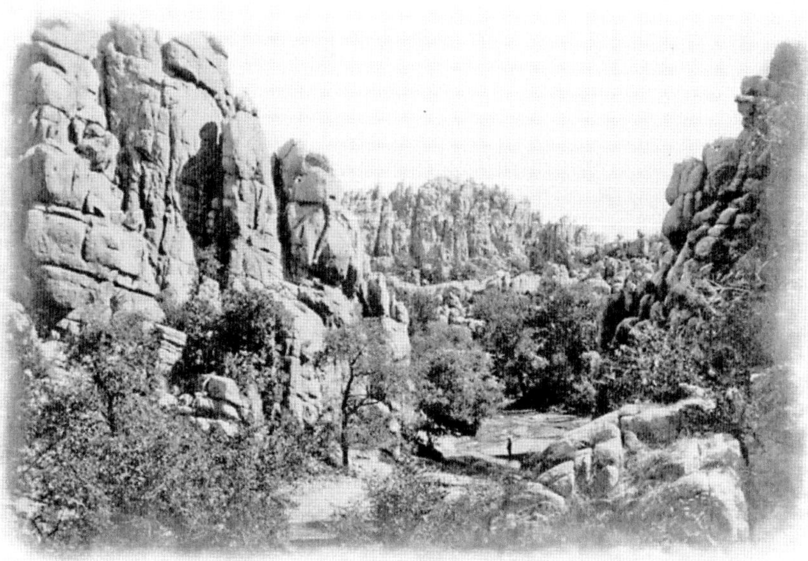

W. H. TIMERHOFF, DRUGGIST. **Point of Rocks Near Prescott, Arizona.**

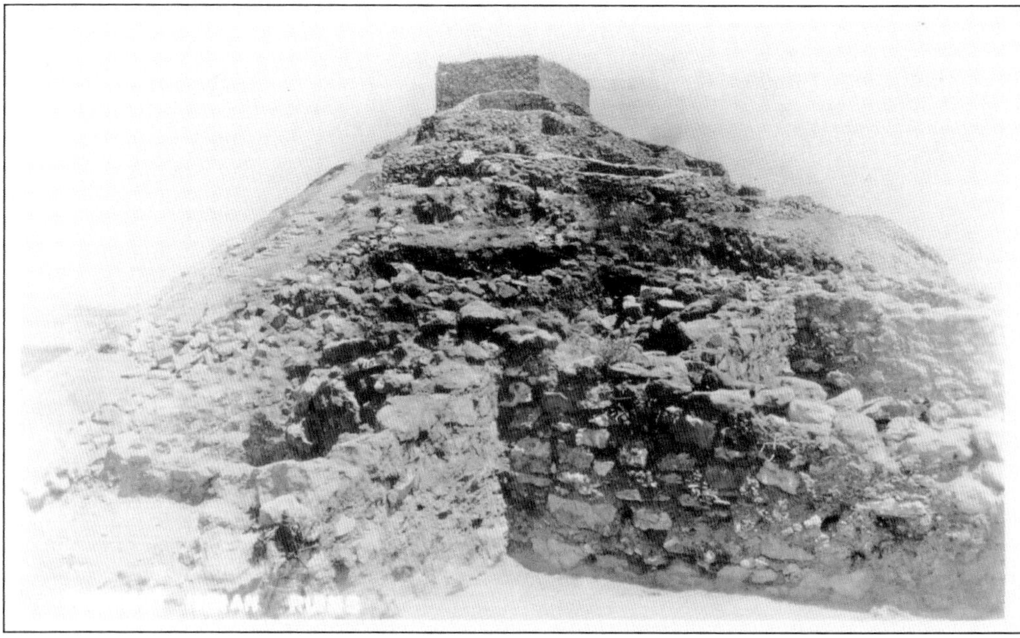

TUZIGOOT, INDIAN RUINS, HANDWRITTEN DATE APRIL 6, 1942 (REAL PHOTO POSTCARD). Located near Clarkdale, Tuzigoot was excavated from 1933 to 1936 and declared a National Monument by Franklin D. Roosevelt on July 25, 1939. Built on a small hill above the floodplain of the Verde River, the site consists of stone masonry walls that reached two and three stories high.

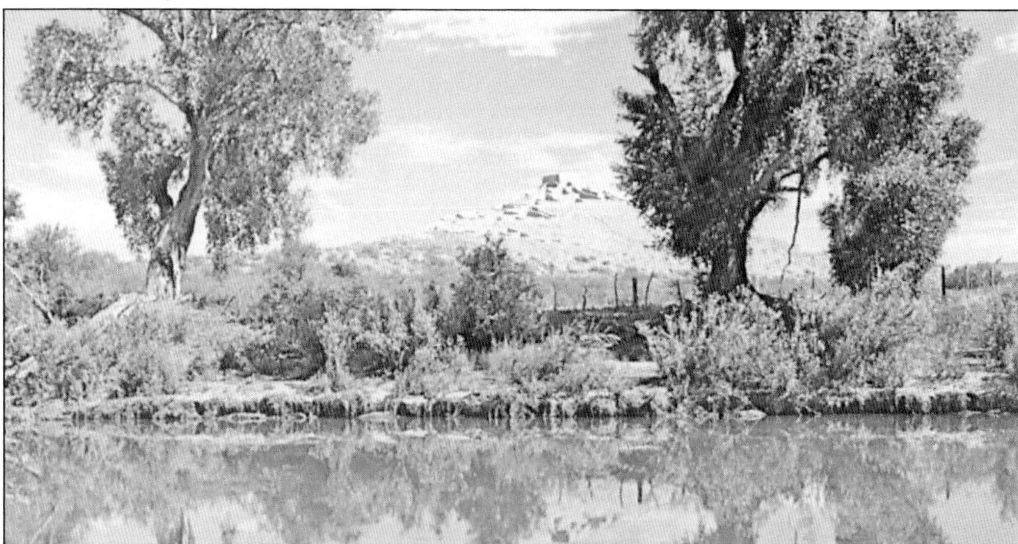

TUZIGOOT, TUZIGOOT NATIONAL MONUMENT, C. 1960S (REAL PHOTO POSTCARD). Atop a small hill along the Verde River, the Tuzigoot pueblo was built by ancient Sinagua people between 1125 and 1400 AD. Tuzigoot, which in Apache means "crooked water," consisted of 110 rooms and was two and, in some places, three stories high. The monument was sold to Yavapai County for $1 in the 1930s by the United Verde/Philip Dodge Mining Company. (Published by Bradshaw Photos, photograph by Bob Bradshaw.)

RIGHT: MONTEZUMA CASTLE, C. 1930S (CURT TEICH HAND-COLORED POSTCARD); BELOW: MONTEZUMA CASTLE, C. 1950S (REAL PHOTO POSTCARD). The ancient Sinagua people built this extremely well-preserved prehistoric building high up a limestone cliff along Beaver Creek. Constructed between 1100 and 1425 AD, this five-story, 25- to 30-room building may have been home to as many as 50 people at one time. It was named after the Aztec emperor Montezuma, as the early explorers to the area mistakenly believed the ruin was an extension of the Aztec construction. (Right, published by Herz Post Card.)

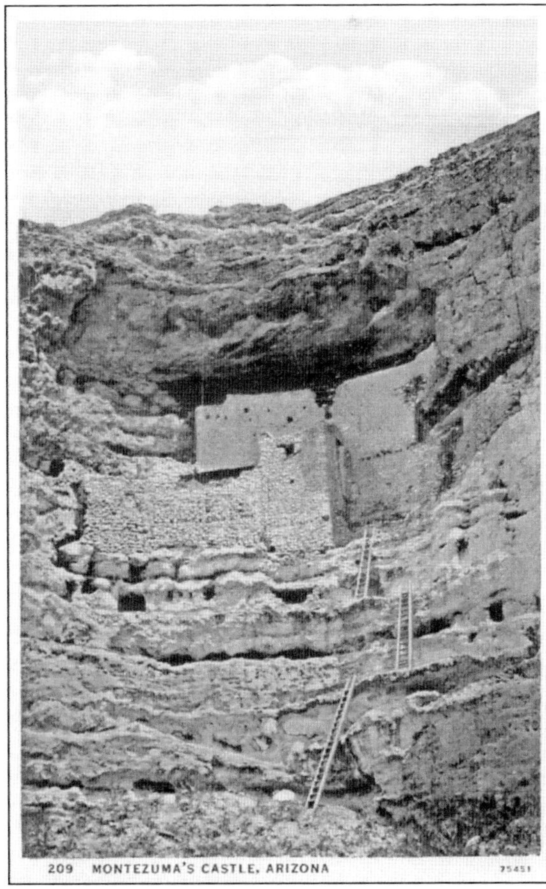

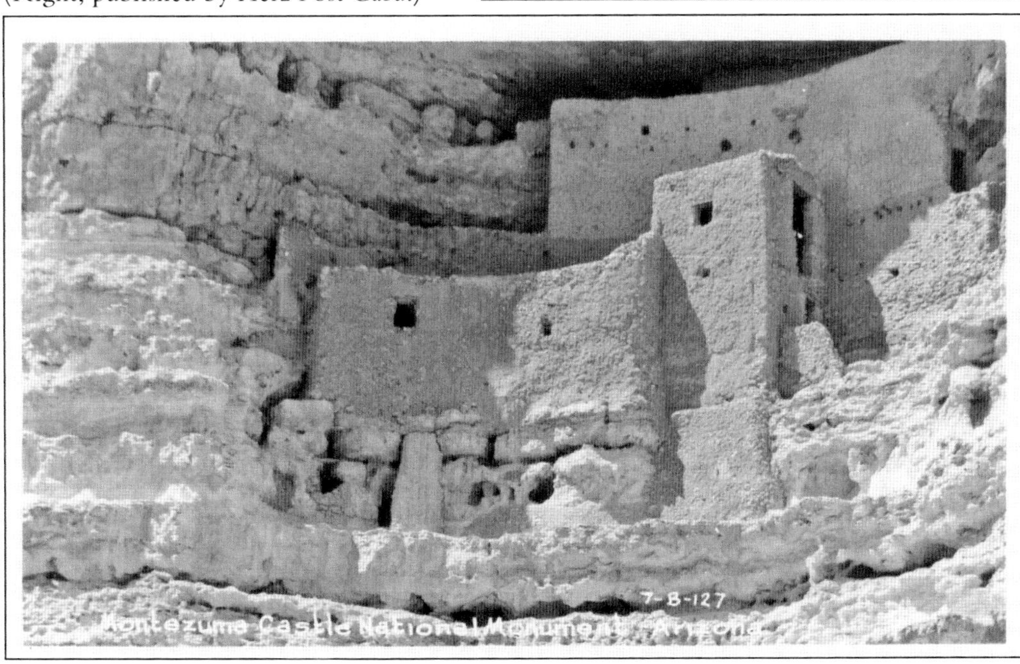

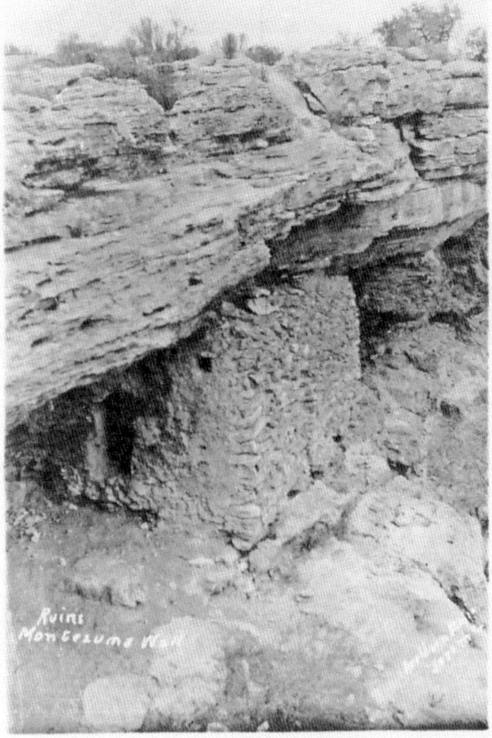

LEFT: MONTEZUMA WELL, RUINS, C. 1920S (REAL PHOTO POSTCARD); BELOW: MONTEZUMA WELL, LAKE BASIN, C. 1917 (CURT TEICH HAND-COLORED POSTCARD). An ancient sinkhole, more than a million gallons of water flow every day through Montezuma Well. Due to its natural lack of oxygen, the well is unable to support aquatic life but worked well for Native Americans, who first moved to the region about 2,000 years ago. Homes were built around the rim of the well and irrigation canals were dug so that water from the well could be used on crops. (Left, published by Aveldson Studios, Jerome; below, published by C.T. American Art Colors.)

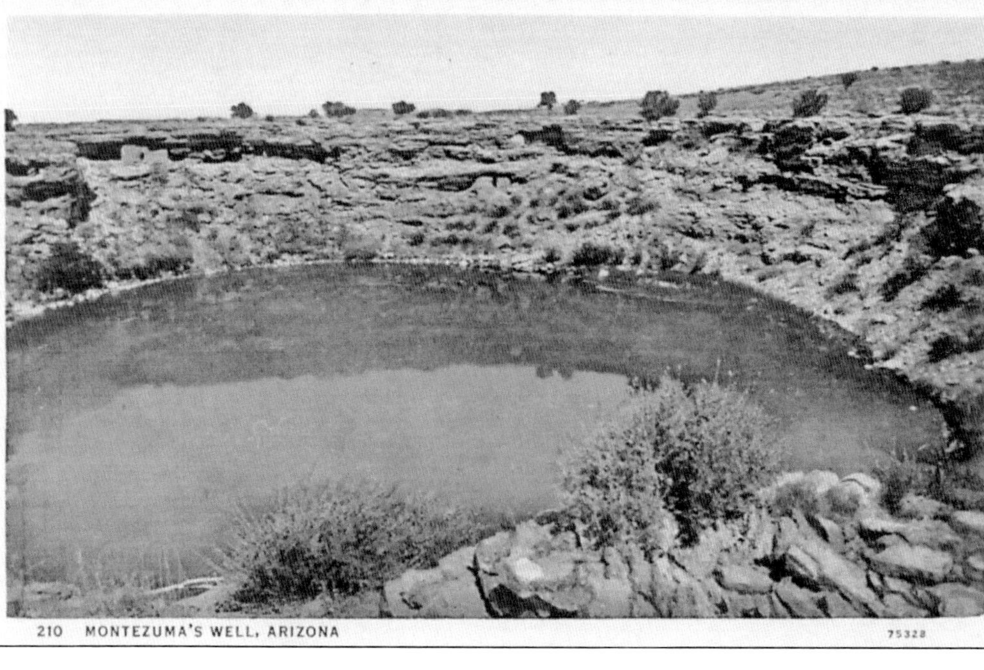

Three

Lakes, Rivers, and Streams

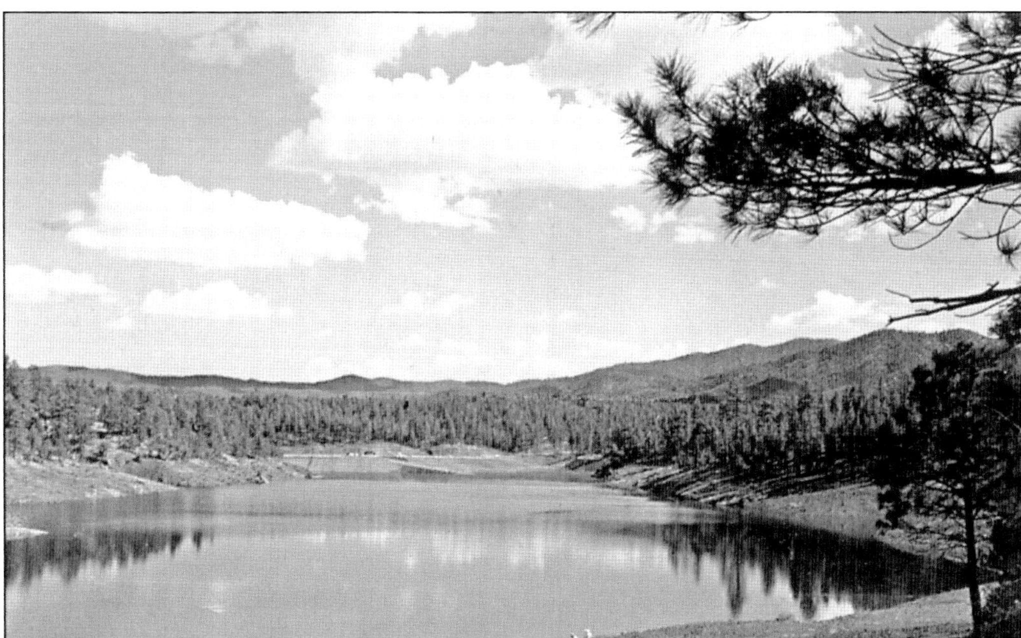

Lynx Lake, Postmarked August 10, 1968 (Real Photo Postcard). Lynx Creek was dammed in 1952, creating 55-acre Lynx Lake. Just off Walker Road a few miles from Highway 69, Lynx Lake is surrounded by hiking trails and ponderosa forests. There are a number of archaeological sites near Lynx Lake that provide a glimpse into the region's past. (Published by Bradshaw Photos, photograph by Bob Bradshaw.)

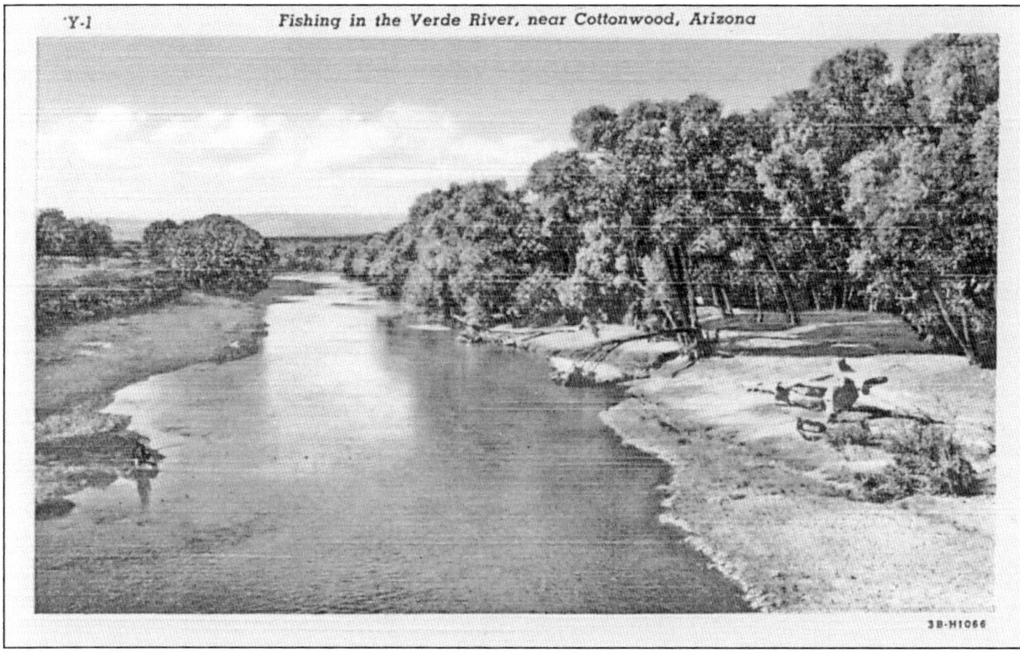

ABOVE: THE VERDE RIVER NEAR COTTONWOOD, C. 1943 (CURT TEICH LINEN POSTCARD); BELOW: THE VERDE RIVER NEAR CLARKDALE, 1907–1929 (DIVIDED BACK POSTCARD). With its headwaters fed by the Big Chino Wash near Paulden, the Verde River flows 170 miles until it reaches the Salt River near Fountain Hills, Arizona. In 1986, a section of the Verde River became part of the Arizona park system. For six miles, the river from Clarkdale to the Bridgeport Highway 89A bridge is known as the Verde River Greenway State Natural Area. (Above, published by C.T. Art-Colortone.)

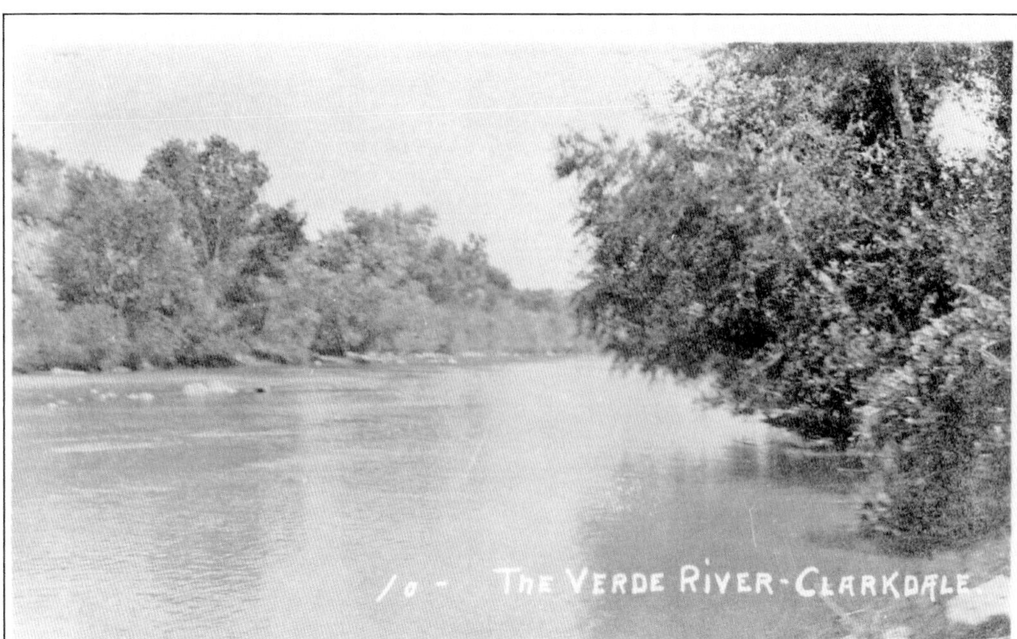

WATSON LAKE

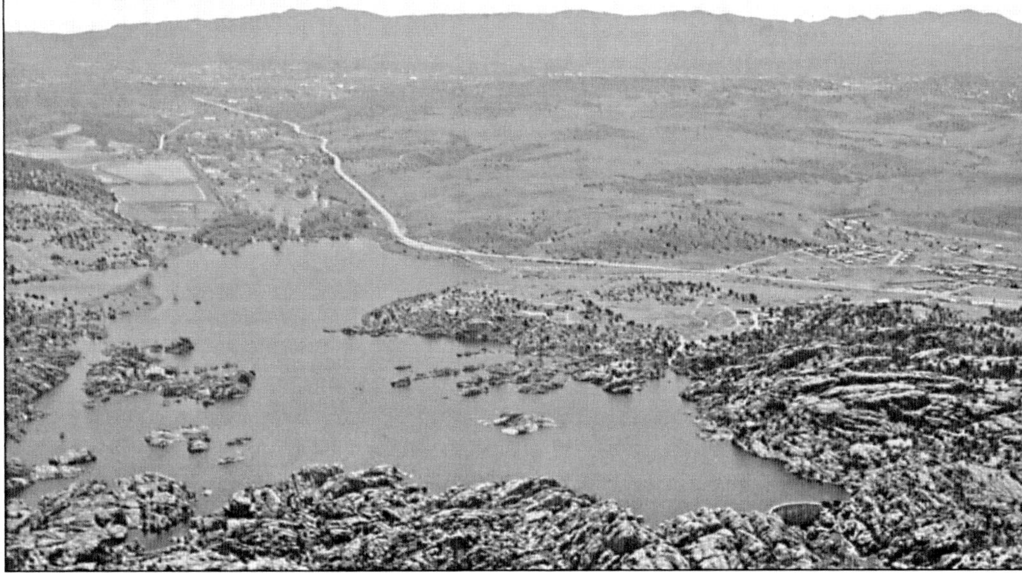

Watson Lake, c. 1960s (Real Photo Postcard). An aerial photograph shows Watson Lake long before housing and development expanded over the hills visible in the postcard. Built in the early 1900s, Watson Lake is now part of the Prescott park system. The lake is surrounded by miles of hiking trails and supports other recreational uses, such as kayaking and fishing. (Published by Petley Studios, photograph by Bob Petley.)

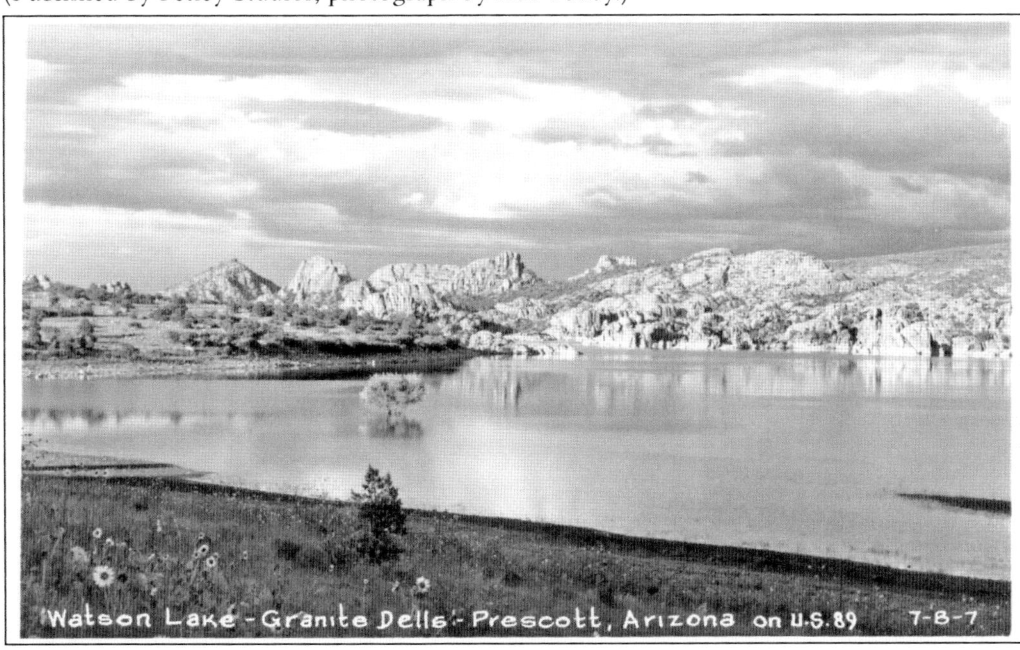

Watson Lake, Watson Lake and Granite Dells, c. 1940 (Real Photo Postcard). This view is from a position near where the present-day launch ramp, docks, and kayak rental trailers are located. Bird lovers flock to the lake to observe thousands of migrating birds that make Watson Lake their home during certain times of the year or as a rest-over as they fly south.

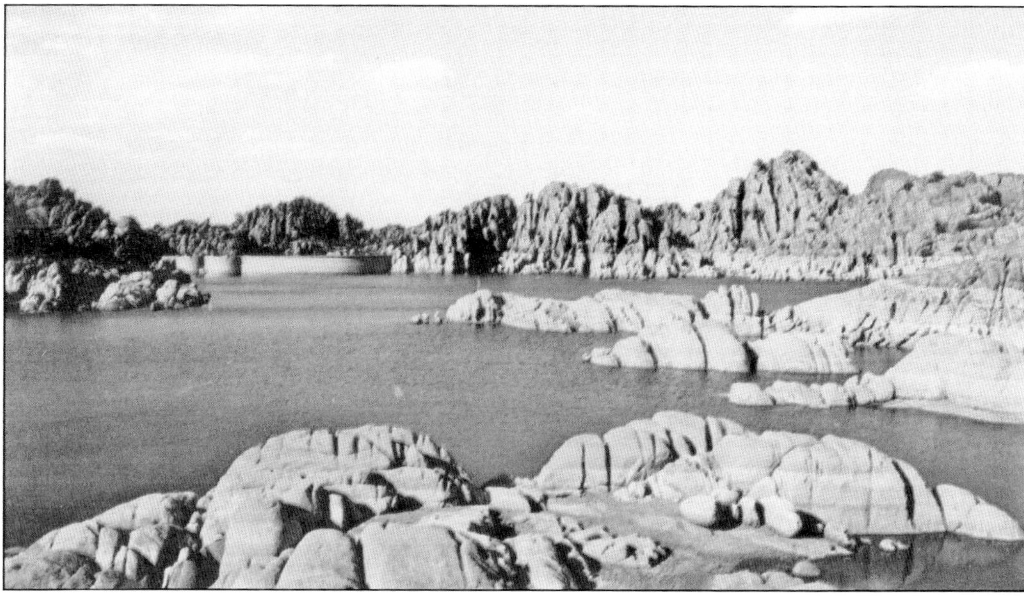

ABOVE: WATSON LAKE, C. 1960S (REAL PHOTO POSTCARD); BELOW: WATSON LAKE, C. 1970S. (REAL PHOTO POSTCARD). Since 2004, the US Environmental Protection Agency has listed Watson Lake as "impaired waters" due to high levels of nitrogen, dissolved oxygen, and phosphorus. The pollutants from fertilizers and animal waste have been washing into the lake from Granite Creek for years and have settled on the bottom of the reservoir. A number of ideas are now being considered on how to best clean up the lake. (Above, published by Bradshaw's Photos, photograph by Bob Bradshaw; below, published by Bob Bradshaw, courtesy John Bradshaw.)

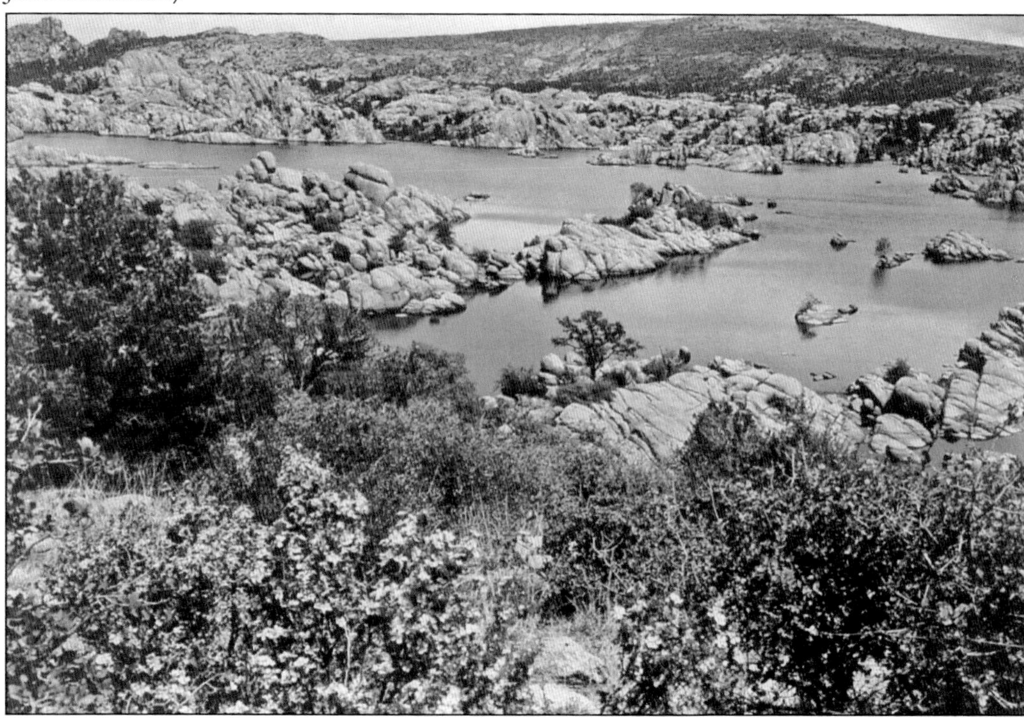

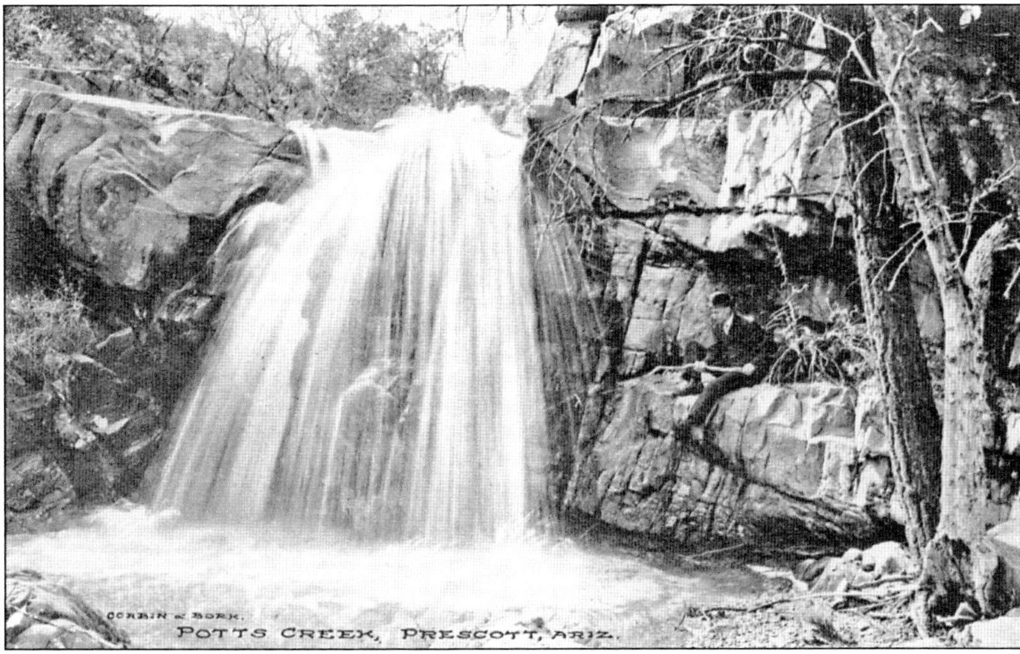

Potts Creek, Waterfall, c. 1910 (Albertype Postcard). Potts Creek, formally known as Butte Creek, is located near Thumb Butte and is part of Prescott's 50-mile Circle Trail. In the late 1800s, the City of Prescott, in searching for new sources of drinking water, called for plans to dam Potts Creek, creating Potts Creek Reservoir. The reservoir plans were never acted upon. (Produced by Corbin and Bork, courtesy Skull Valley Historical Society.)

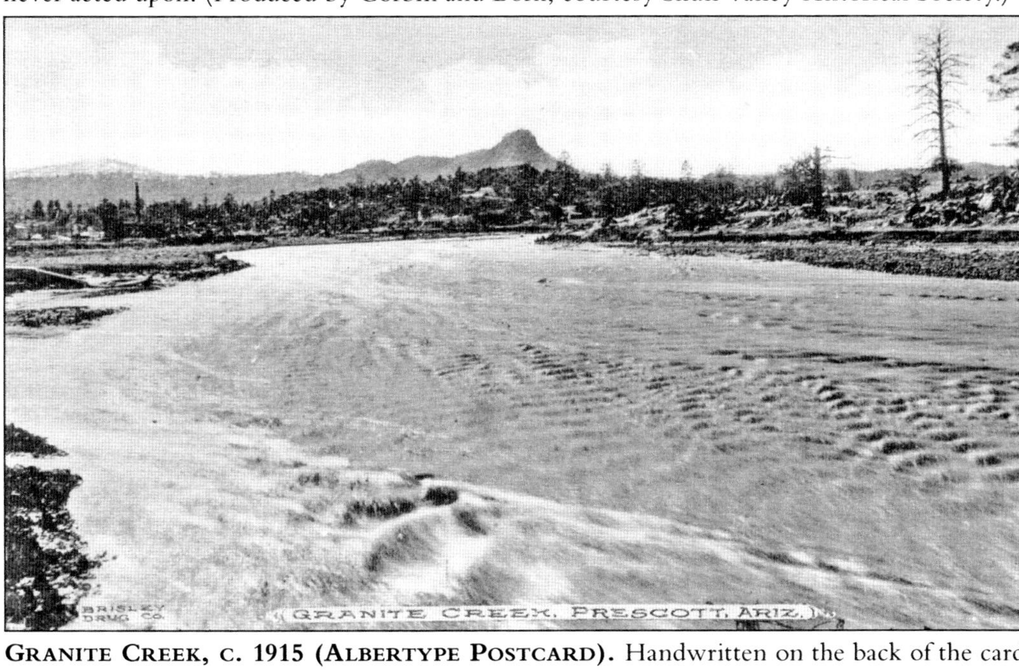

Granite Creek, c. 1915 (Albertype Postcard). Handwritten on the back of the card, someone a long time ago wrote, probably from Fort Whipple, "This creek is only a little ways from the barracks there was not a drop of water in it all the time I have been here until a couple of days ago." (Published by Albertype.)

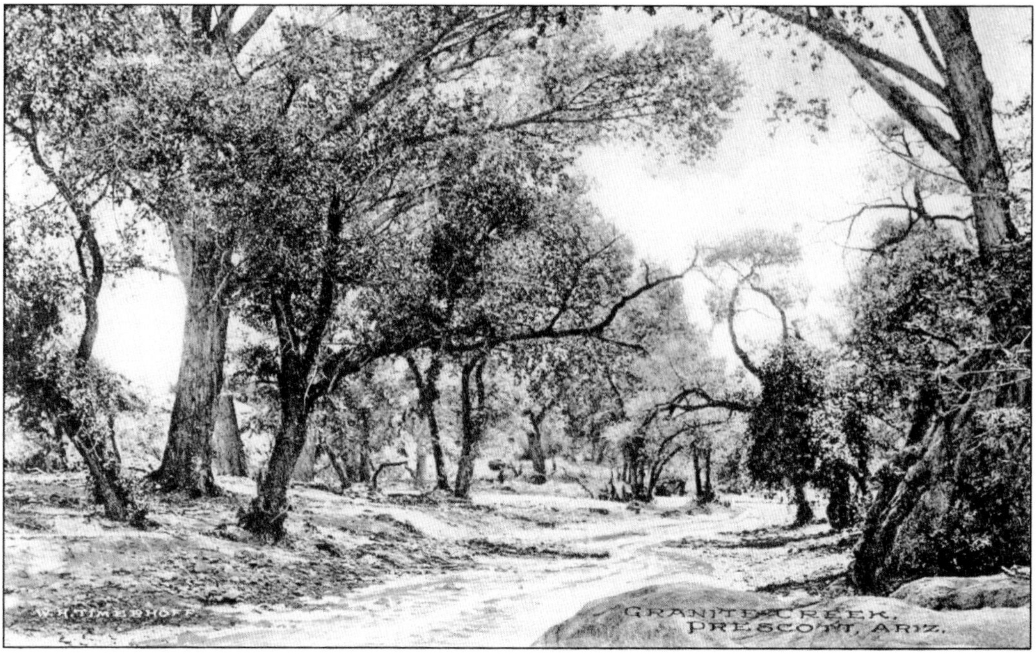

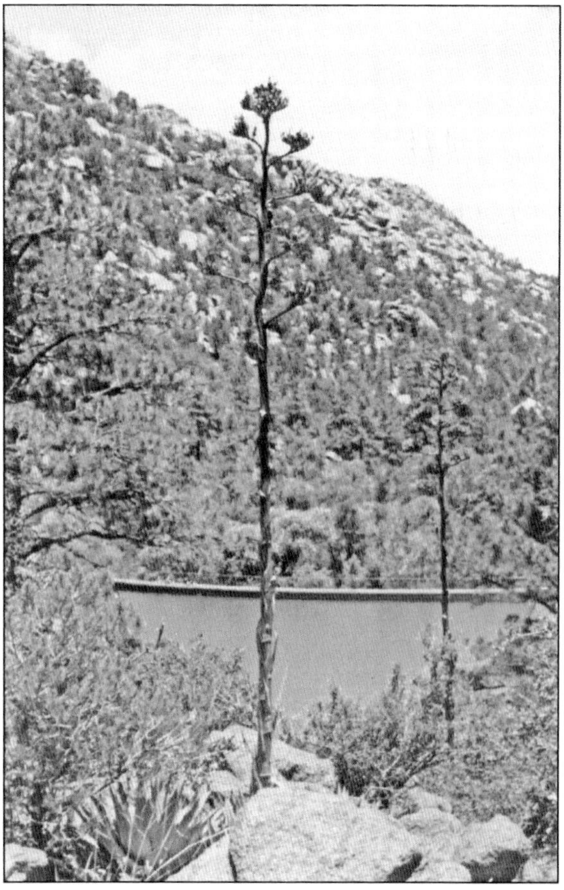

Granite Creek, c. 1915 (Albertype Postcard). Starting high in the Bradshaw Mountains and Prescott National Forest, Granite Creek flows for 38 miles as it winds down the mountain through Prescott and past Fort Whipple. It continues into Watson Lake, through the Granite Dells, and meanders past the airport into Chino Valley, eventually emptying into the Verde River. (Published by W.H. Timerhoff, Druggist.)

Granite Basin Lake, Postmarked July 7, 1973 (Real Photo Postcard). Located in the Granite Basin Recreation Area at the base of Granite Mountain, Granite Basin Lake opened to the public in 1934. The dam was a Depression-era employment project by the Work Projects Administration and was constructed purely for recreational purposes. Although there is no swimming in the lake, people can fish or use small boats such as kayaks or canoes to paddle around. (Published and photograph by Charles Kendall.)

Four

Roads and Highways

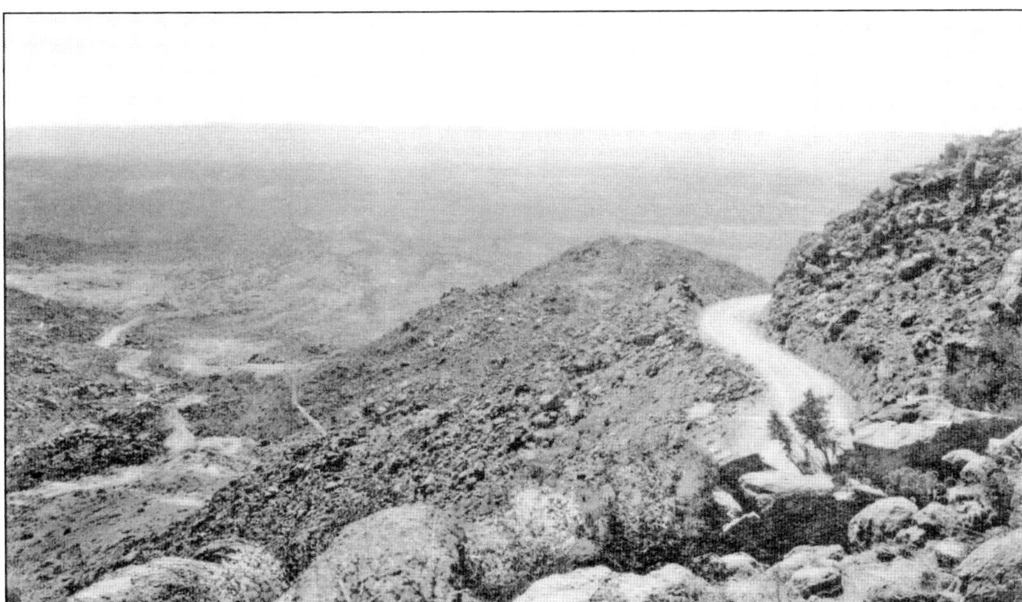

Highway 89, Yarnell Hill, c. 1930s (Albertype Hand-Colored Postcard). Descending 2,500 feet in only four miles, the Wickenburg Road was once the main highway for travel from Phoenix to Prescott. The highway was built as a narrow dirt road in 1923 and was paved in 1933. As early as 1955, the state was looking into improving the old highway. With increased traffic usage and easier access for trucks, the state added two northbound lanes in the late 1960s. (Published by Albertype.)

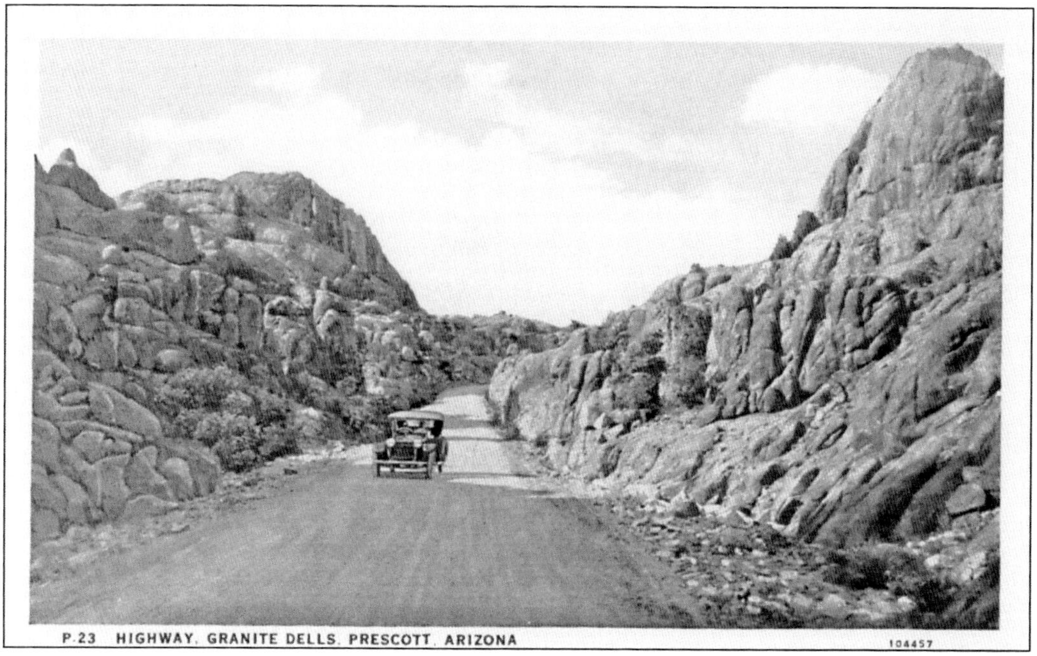

ABOVE: HIGHWAY 89, C. 1922 (CURT TEICH HAND-COLORED POSTCARD); BELOW: HIGHWAY 89 THROUGH THE DELLS, HANDWRITTEN DATE JUNE 1928. (ALBERTYPE POSTCARD). The Bianconis, who owned a ranch and farm just north of the Granite Dells, are credited with helping improve the first road through them in the early 1920s. Originally called the Prescott–Ash Fork Road and later named US Highway 89, it has had a few minor alterations since the 1920s, such as paving in the 1930s and later widening to accommodate larger vehicles. (Above, published by C.T. American Art; below, published by Owl Drug and Candy Company.)

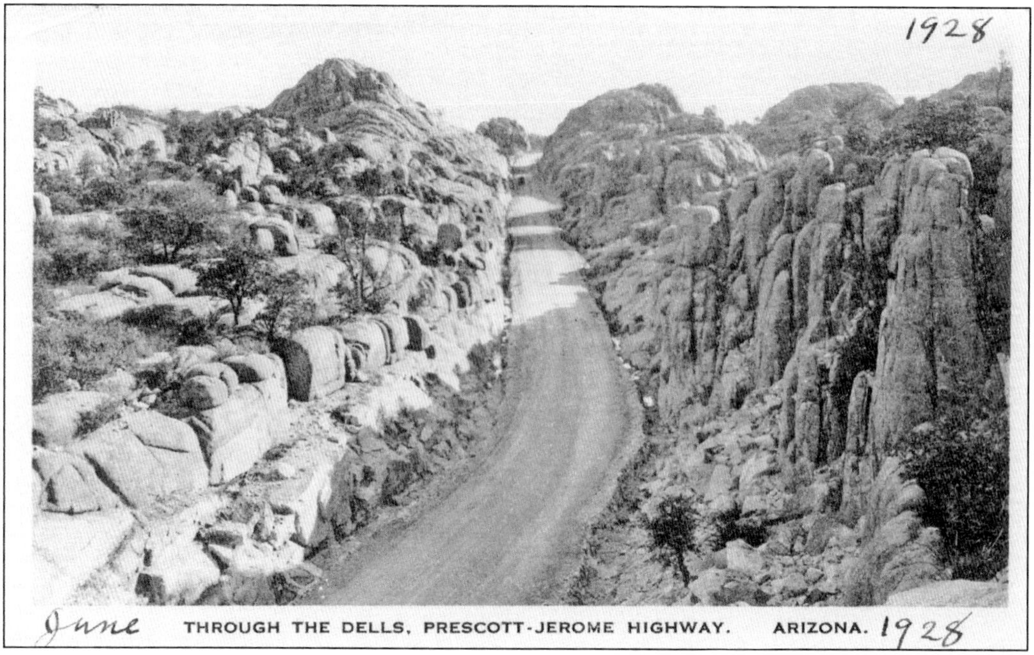

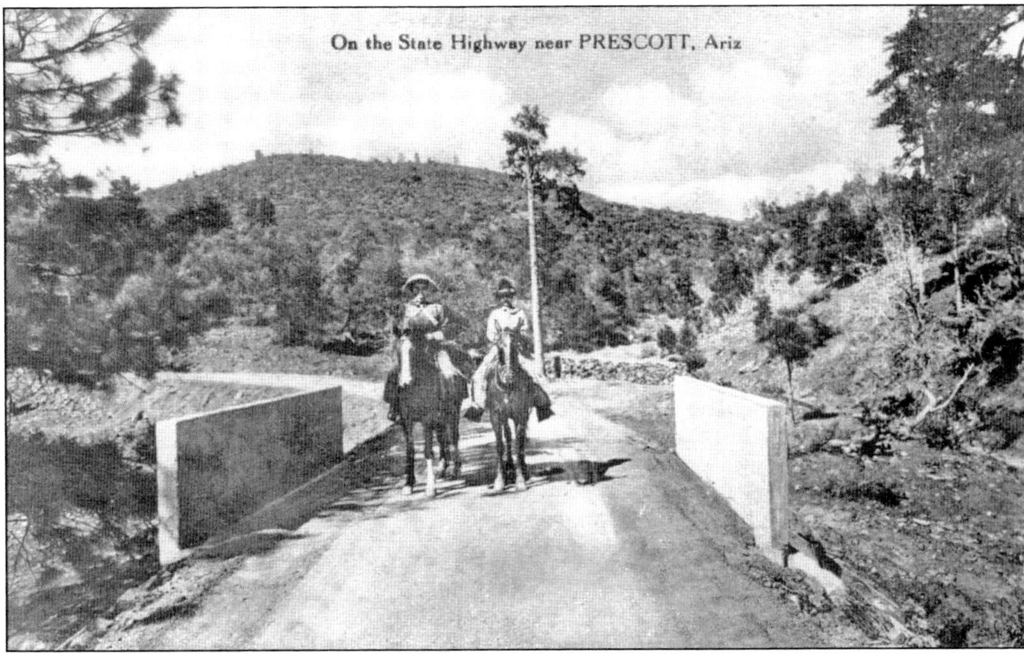

SENATOR HIGHWAY, HORSEBACK, C. 1920S (ALBERTYPE POSTCARD). This bridge is on County Road Number 1, better known as the Senator Highway. When it achieved statehood in 1912, Arizona had 1,500 miles of highways, and none of them were paved. It was not until 1937 that all primary state highways were either paved or oiled. (Published by Brisley Drug Co.)

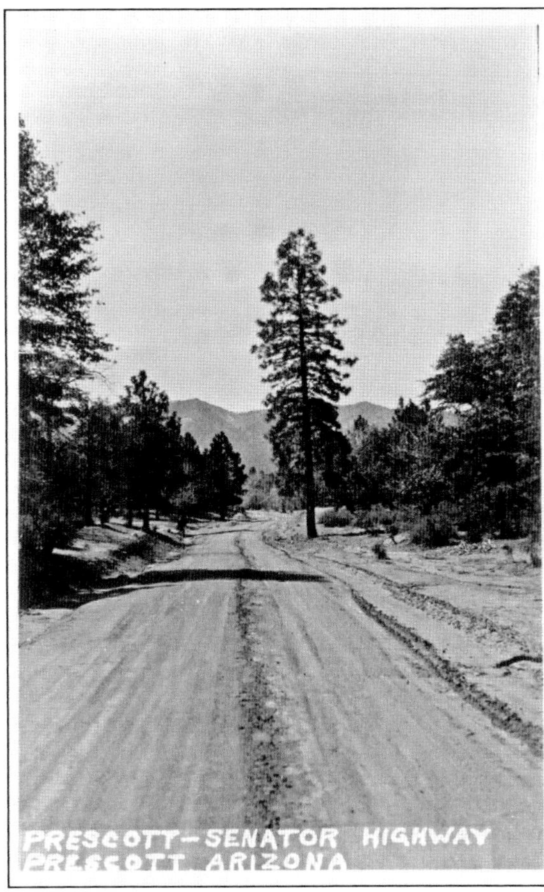

SENATOR HIGHWAY, C. 1930S (REAL PHOTO POSTCARD). The Senator Highway, named after the Senator Mine, was an early Arizona toll road. Construction started in 1866 with private finding and eventually reached Crown King in the 1880s. It became a state highway in 1912 with the intention of creating a highway between Prescott and Phoenix.

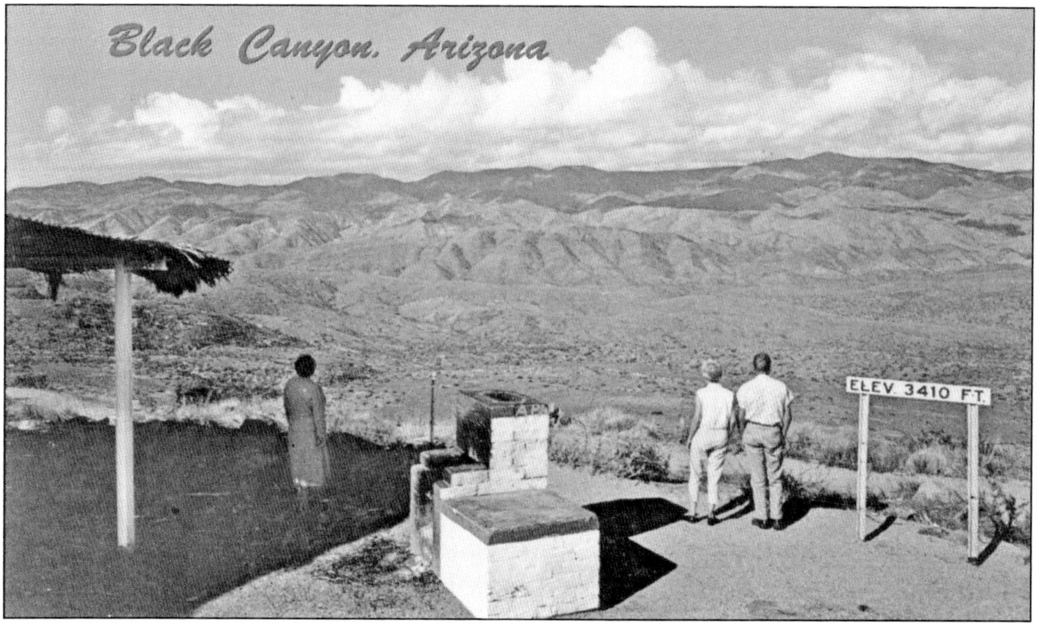

HIGHWAY 17, BLACK CANYON HIGHWAY, POSTMARKED OCTOBER 14, 1965 (REAL PHOTO POSTCARD). Prior to the completion of Highway 17 from Phoenix to Flagstaff in 1971, the Black Canyon Highway (then called Highway 69) was still a two-lane road. This busy rest stop with views of Bumble Bee below was a popular roadside spot to have a picnic before completing the journey. (Published by Petley Studios, photograph by Bob Petley.)

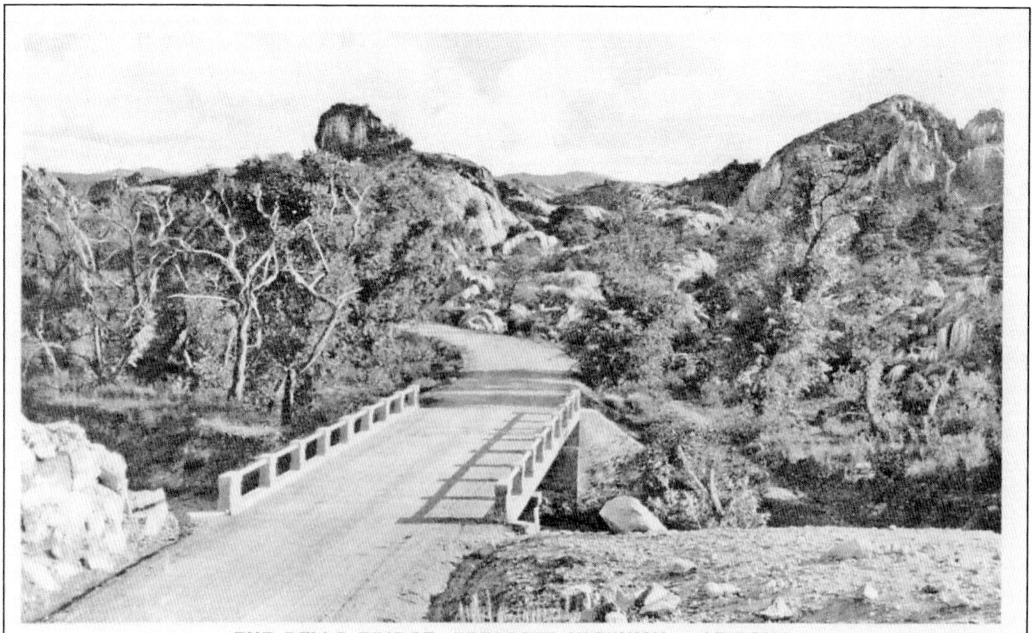

THE DELLS BRIDGE, PRESCOTT HIGHWAY. ARIZONA.

HIGHWAY 89, THE DELLS BRIDGE, C. 1920S (ALBERTYPE POSTCARD). Although the bridge is still standing and looks pretty much as it did back then, it is no longer in use and is blocked off to vehicle and foot traffic. The highway was later realigned more to the west and bypassed this section of the Dells altogether. (Published by Brisley Drug Co.)

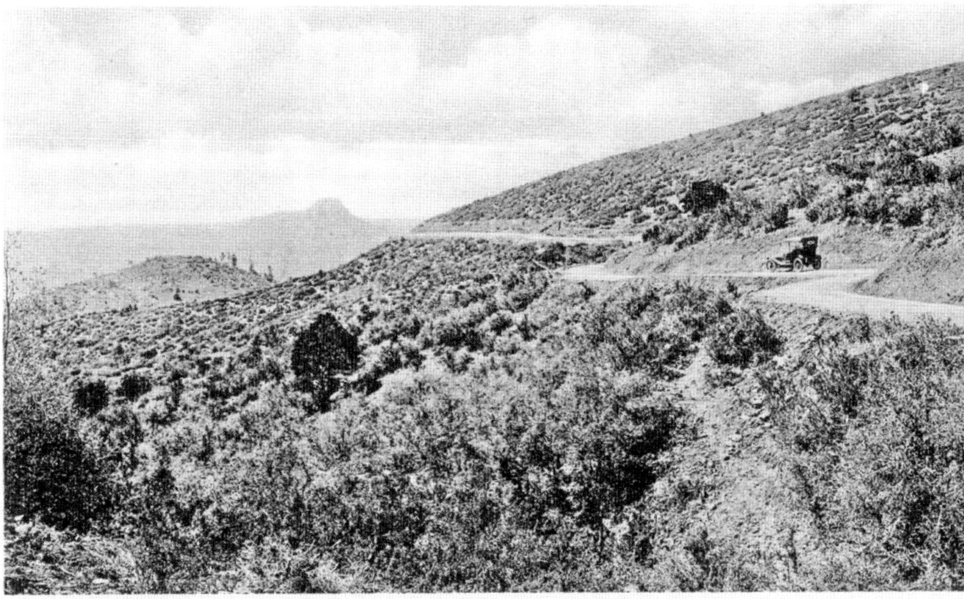

ABOVE: STATE HIGHWAY, POSTMARKED AUGUST 11, 1924 (ALBERTYPE POSTCARD); BELOW: STATE HIGHWAY NEAR PRESCOTT, C. 1910 (ALBERTYPE POSTCARD). After concluding that the Senator Highway was not the best route to Phoenix, a group from Prescott lobbied to have a road constructed from Prescott to the White Spar Mine and down to Yarnell Hill, Wickenburg, and finally Phoenix. The White Spar Highway opened in 1923 and was later given the designation of US 89. (Both, published by Owl Drug and Candy Company.)

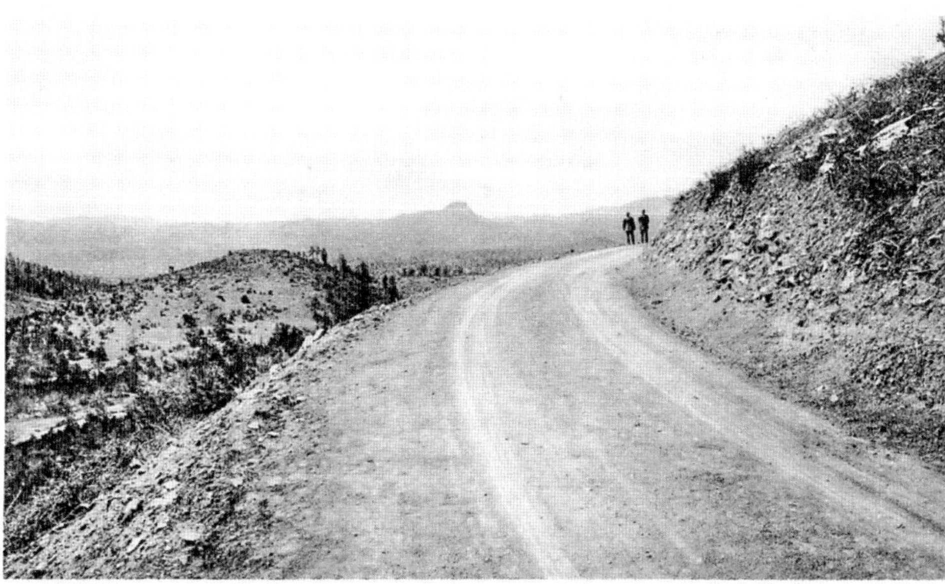

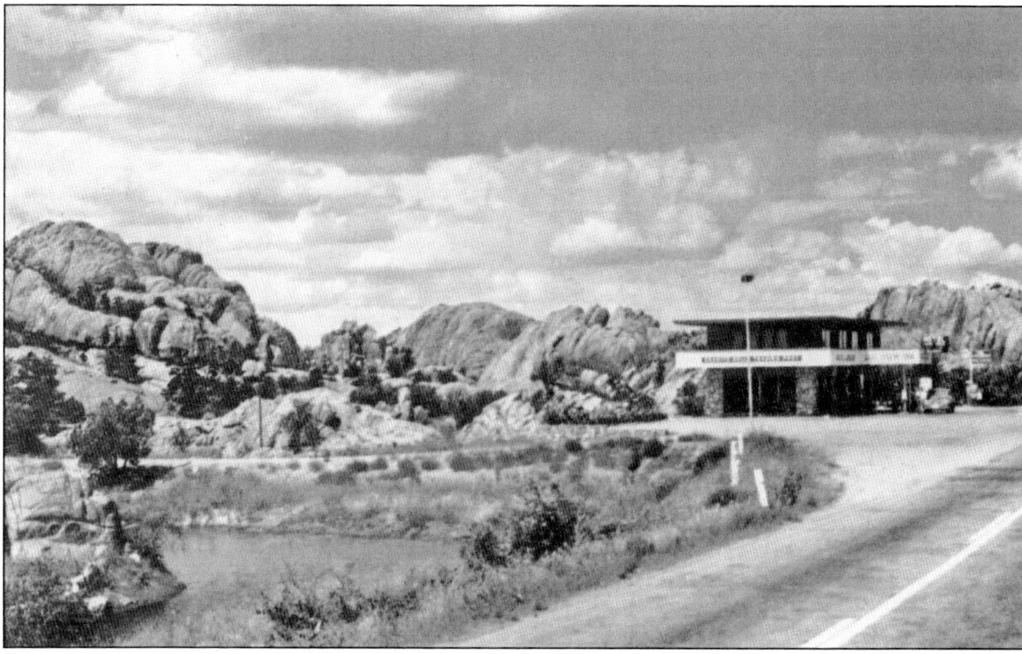

HIGHWAY 89, C. 1960S (EKTACHROME POSTCARD). Still in use today, the old Granite Dells Trading Post and gas station has seen many uses over the years. Built sometime prior to 1946, the building has had at least three commercial remodelings, in 1976, 1986, and lastly in 1989. In addition to the trading post, it has been a dress shop and souvenir store, and it is currently a plumbing business. (Published by Gods Gardens, Inc.)

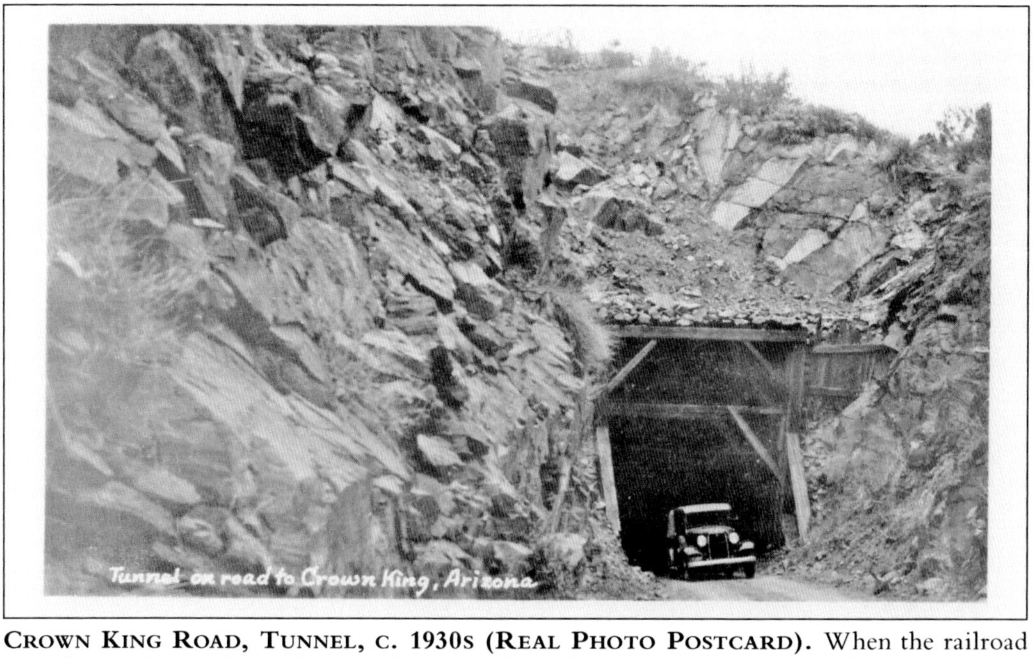

CROWN KING ROAD, TUNNEL, C. 1930S (REAL PHOTO POSTCARD). When the railroad ceased operating to Crown King in the 1920s, the railroad tracks were removed, and a road was created along the old railroad bed. The old tunnels have since been removed, but the same road is still in use today. (Courtesy Tony Meager.)

Five

Railroading throughout the County

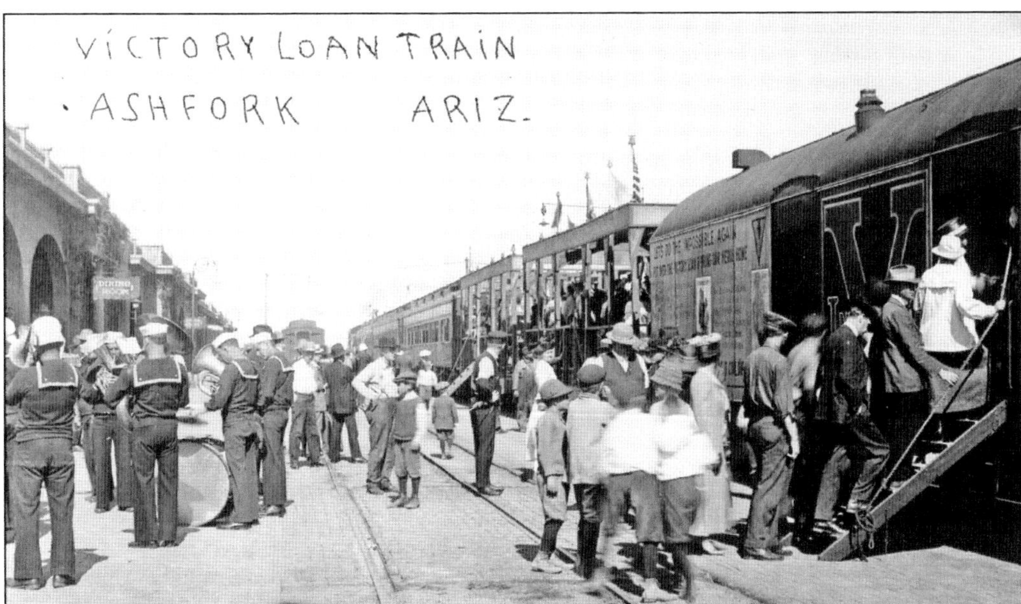

Ash Fork, Victory Loan Train, c. 1919 (Real Picture Postcard). With the conclusion of World War I in 1918, the War Trophy Train, also known as the Victory Loan Train, toured the country to encourage people to buy Victory Loan Bonds. The train carried soldiers from the Army, Navy, and Marines, along with exhibits of military hardware from the allied armies as well as items captured from the enemy. One item of interest was a French "Mosquito tank." (Courtesy Nancy Burgess.)

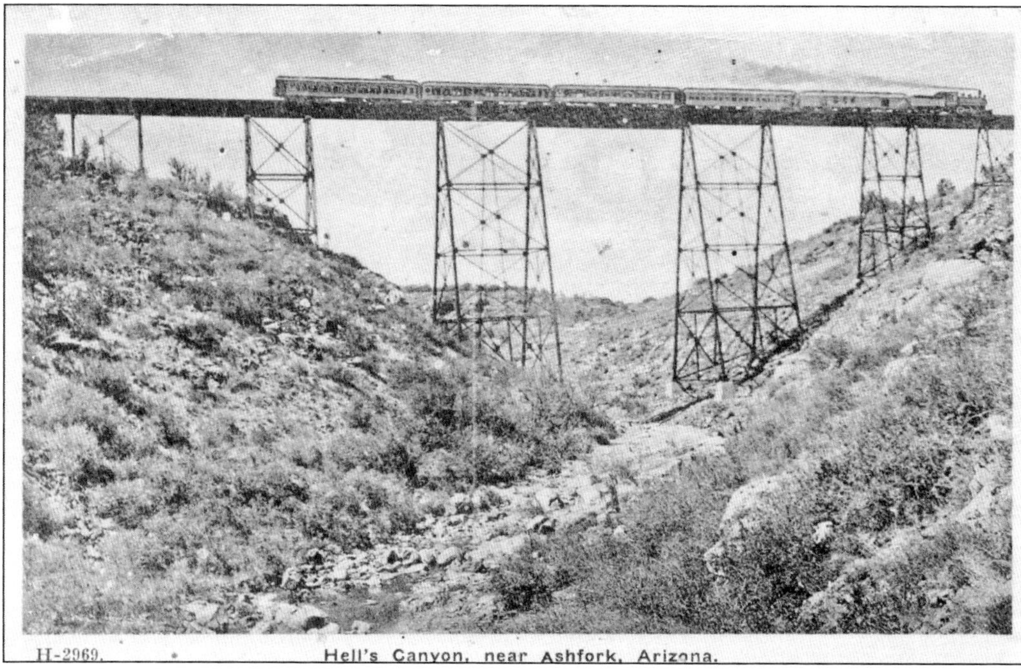

ABOVE: HELLS CANYON, POSTMARKED APRIL 11, 1925 (DIVIDED BACK POSTCARD); BELOW: RAILROAD AND HIGHWAY 89, HELLS CANYON, POSTMARKED MAY 11, 1943 (ALBERTYPE POSTCARD). A Santa Fe Railroad locomotive crosses the old steel bridge over Hells Canyon near present-day Drake, between Ash Fork and Prescott. The Burlington Northern Santa Fe (BNSF) still travels along the same line as it did almost 100 years ago. If one were to look down from the side of the road today on Highway 89, this scene would look nearly identical to this postcard in 1943. (Above, published by Fred Harvey; below, courtesy Tony Meager.)

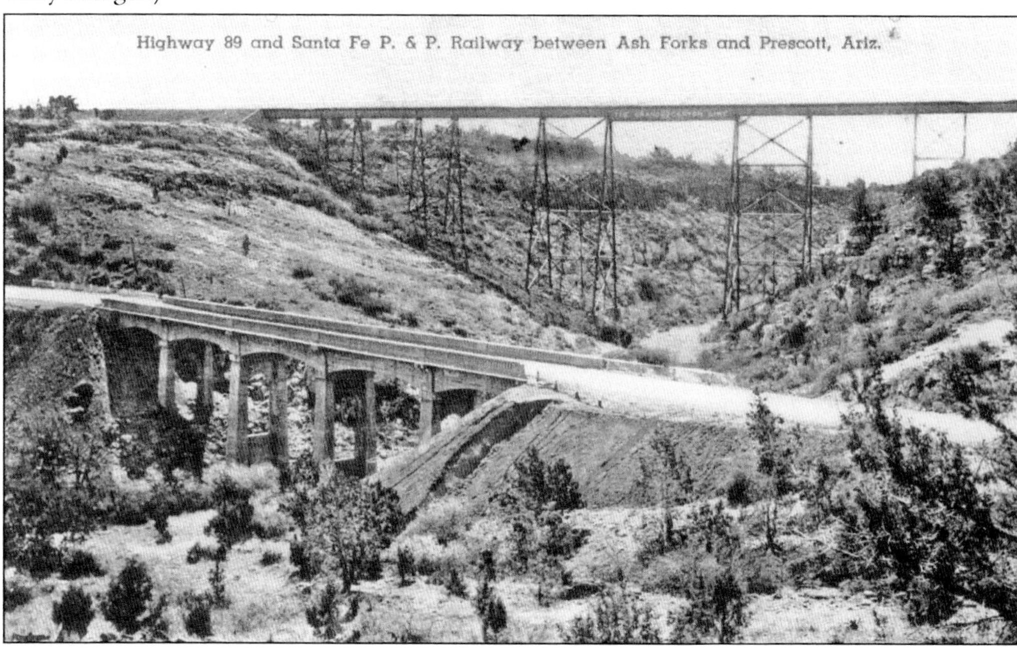

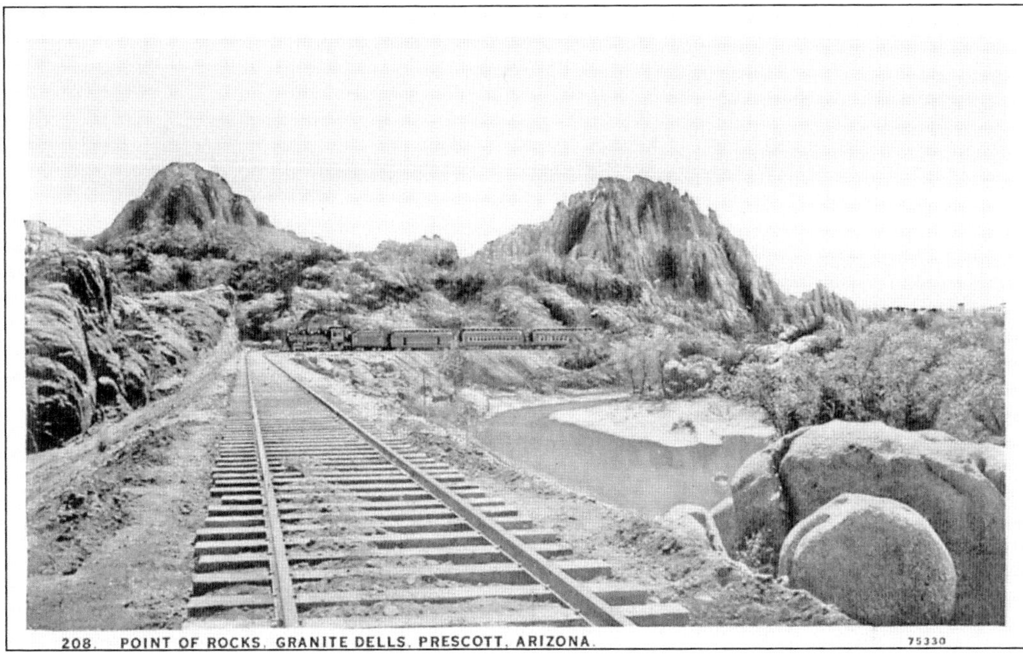

ABOVE: GRANITE DELLS, C. 1917 (CURT TEICH HAND-COLORED POSTCARD); BELOW: TRAIN THROUGH THE GRANITE DELLS, POSTMARKED DECEMBER 11, 1908 (HAND-COLORED POSTCARD). After the last train rambled through the Dells in 1984, the City of Prescott began planning a walking trail along the old rail right-of-way. In June 1999, on National Trails Day, the Peavine Trail opened to hikers and bikers alike. There are currently 5.2 miles of hiking along the Peavine Trail and another 4 miles on the Iron King Trail, which intersects the Peavine and winds to Prescott Valley. The photograph features a portion of the Santa Fe, Prescott & Phoenix Railway. (Above, published by Central News and Novelty Co.; below, published by Brisley Drug Co., courtesy Tony Meager.)

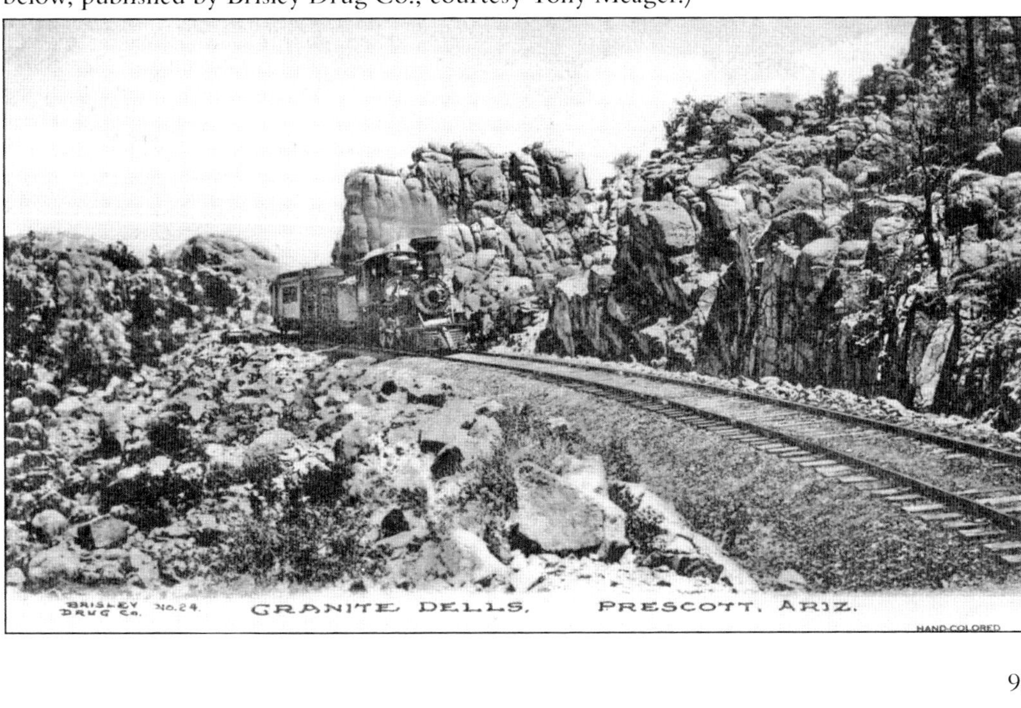

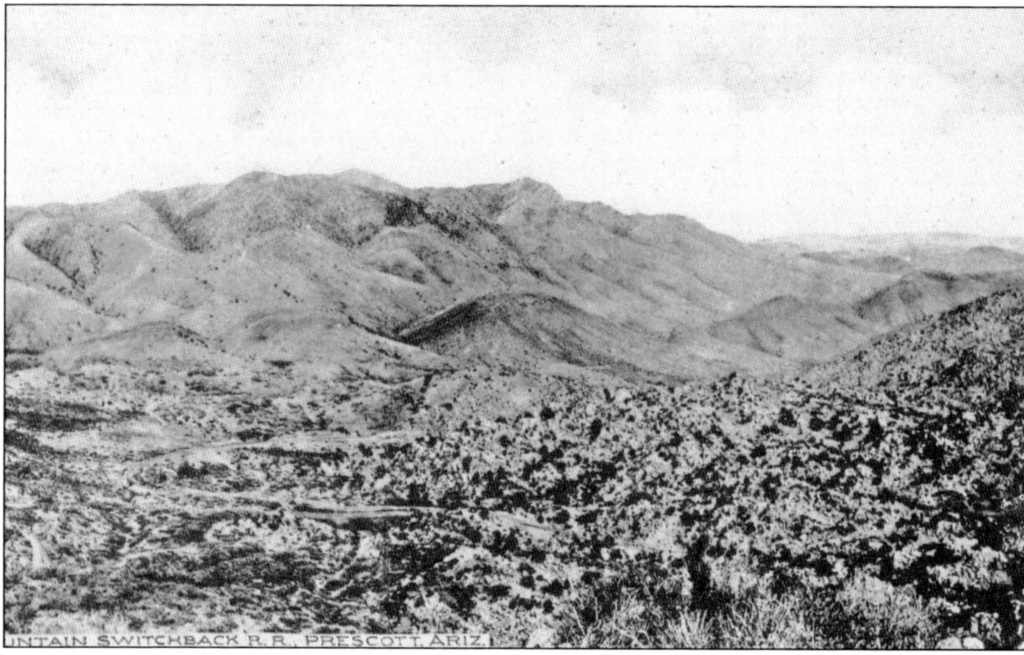

SWITCHBACK, C. 1910 (BLANK BACK POSTCARD). Bradshaw Mt. Railroad was known as Murphy's Impossible Railroad due to the engineering of five switchbacks, a tunnel, and a number of extremely high trestles up the steep mountain. Completed in 1904, the railroad connected Crown King and the Prescott & Eastern Railroad in Mayer. Because the mines began to close within the next few years, the railroad ceased operations, and the tracks were torn up in 1927.

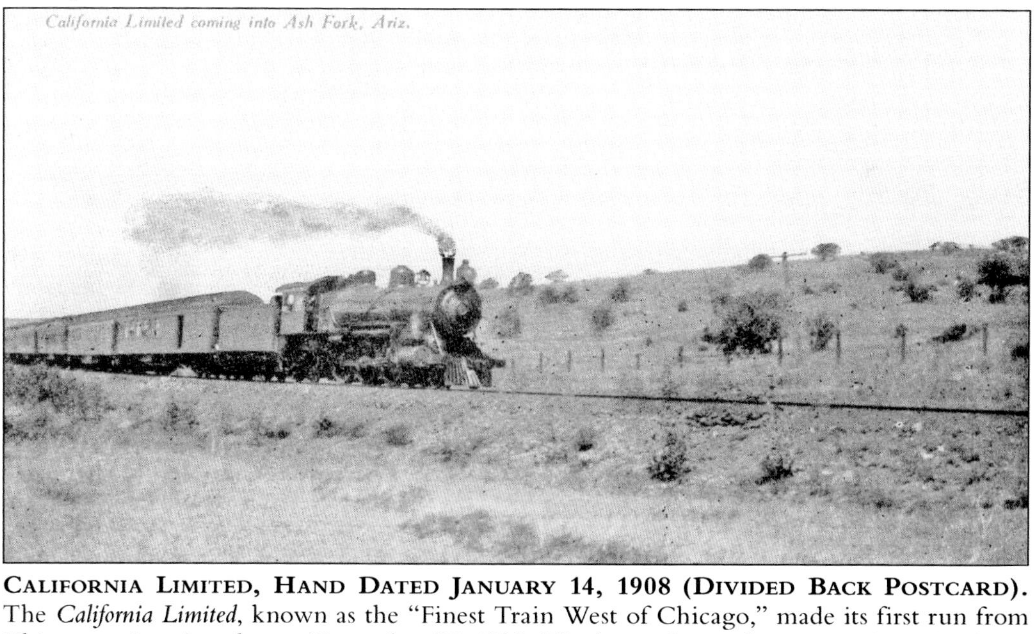

CALIFORNIA LIMITED, HAND DATED JANUARY 14, 1908 (DIVIDED BACK POSTCARD). The *California Limited*, known as the "Finest Train West of Chicago," made its first run from Chicago to Los Angeles on November 27, 1892. The last train service was on June 15, 1954. The *California Limited* was also the first of the Santa Fe line to have Fred Harvey food service. (Published by Fred Harvey, courtesy Nancy Burgess.)

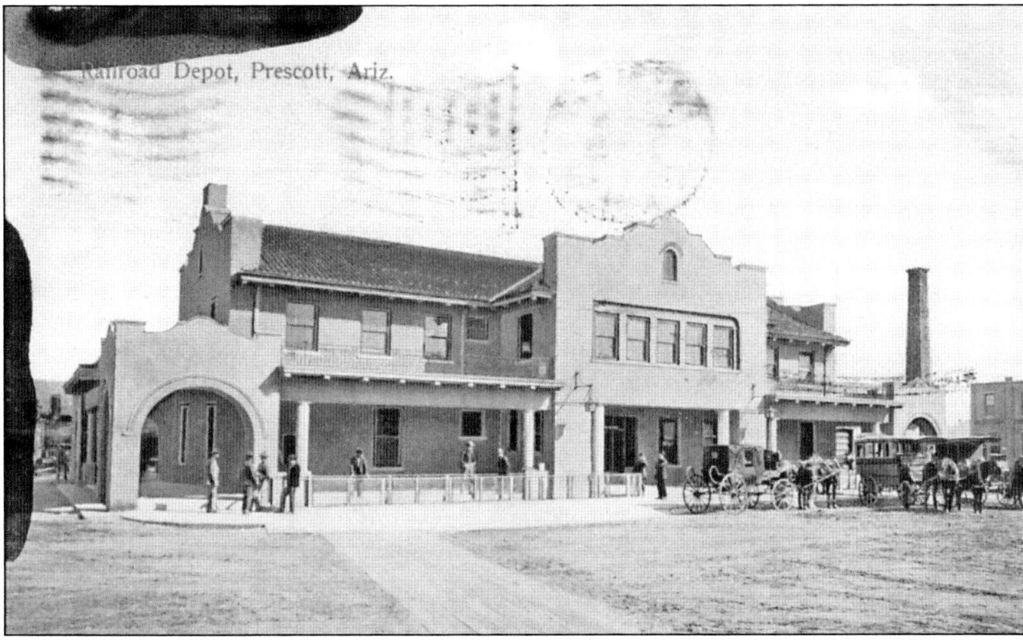

ABOVE: PRESCOTT DEPOT, POSTMARKED MARCH 3, 1909 (DIVIDED BACK POSTCARD); BELOW: PRESCOTT DEPOT, C. 1910 (ALBERTYPE HAND-COLORED POSTCARD). The first train through Prescott arrived on December 31, 1886. The depot, built in 1907 in a Mission Revival style, still stands on Sheldon and Cortez Streets and currently is leased as offices. (Above, published by M. Reider Publ., courtesy Skull Valley Historical Society; bottom, published by Brisley Drug Co.)

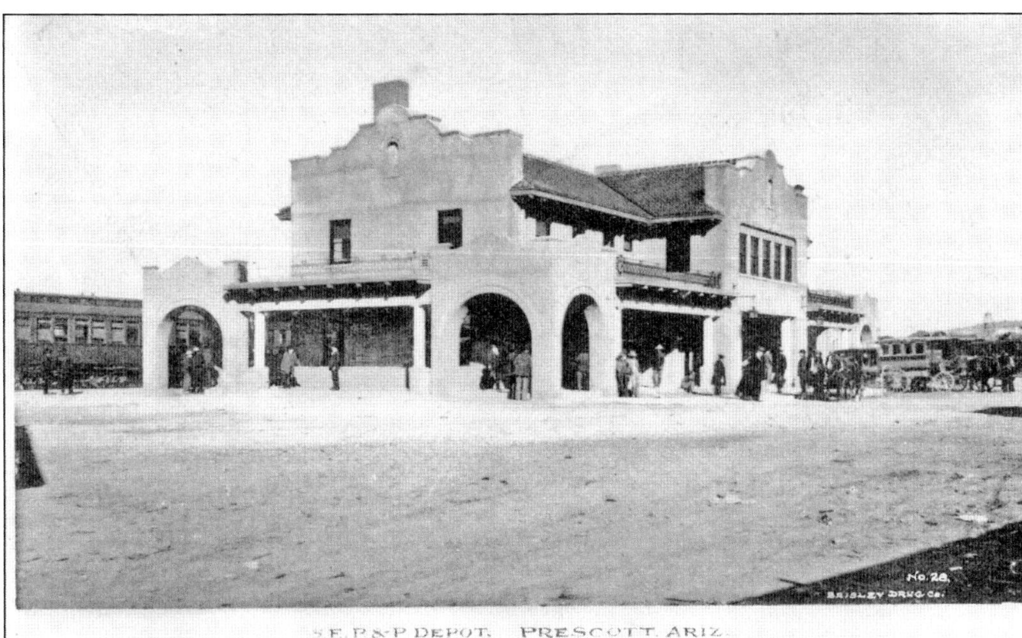

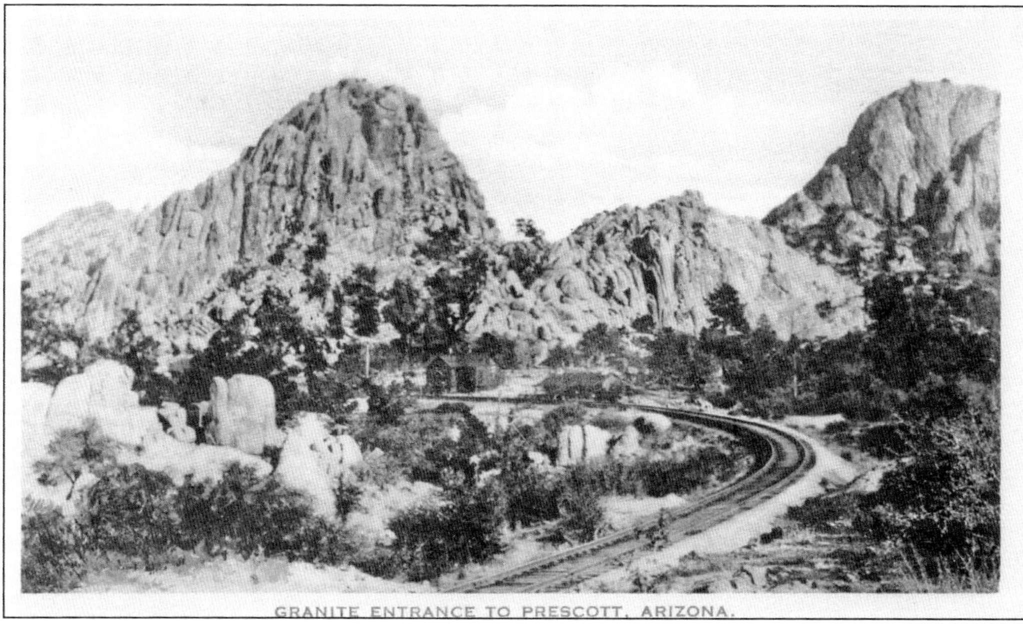

GRANITE DELLS STATION, C. 1910 (ALBERTYPE POSTCARD). Originally constructed in 1893 for the Santa Fe, Prescott & Phoenix Railway, the old station at Entro was still on site into at least the 1950s. It is unknown what happened to the depot, but one story has it being turned into a private residence and later burning down. (Published by Brisley Drug Co., courtesy Tony Meager.)

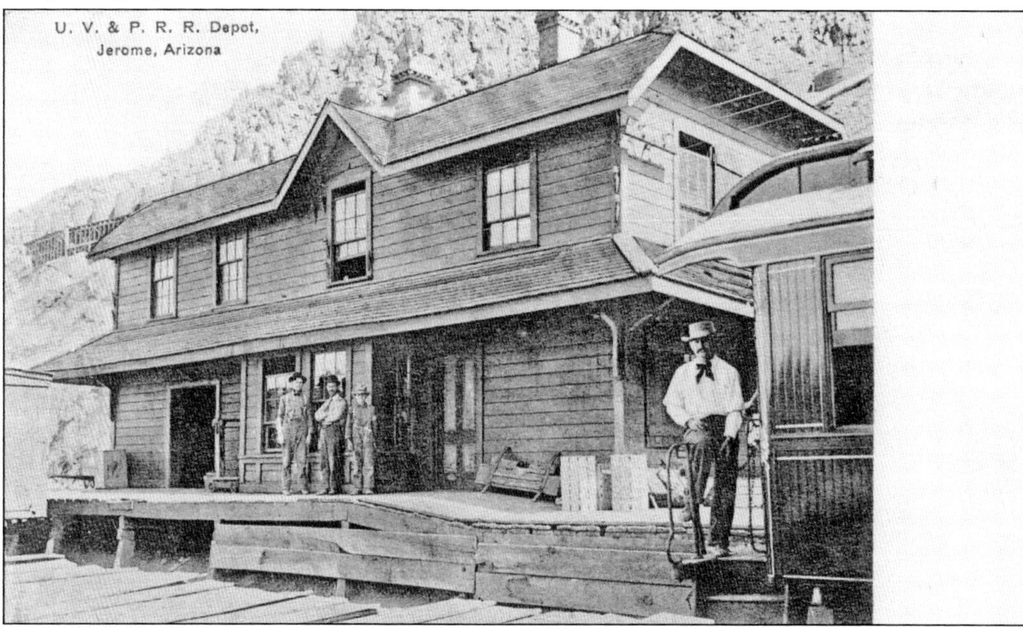

UNITED VERDE & PACIFIC RAILROAD DEPOT, C. 1910 (DIVIDED BACK POSTCARD). The United Verde & Pacific Railway was a 26-mile narrow-gauge railroad from the smelter in Jerome to an existing Santa Fe line near Drake. The line started service in 1895, and the last train left the Jerome station in May 1920. (Published by the Mitchell Drug Co., courtesy Tony Meager.)

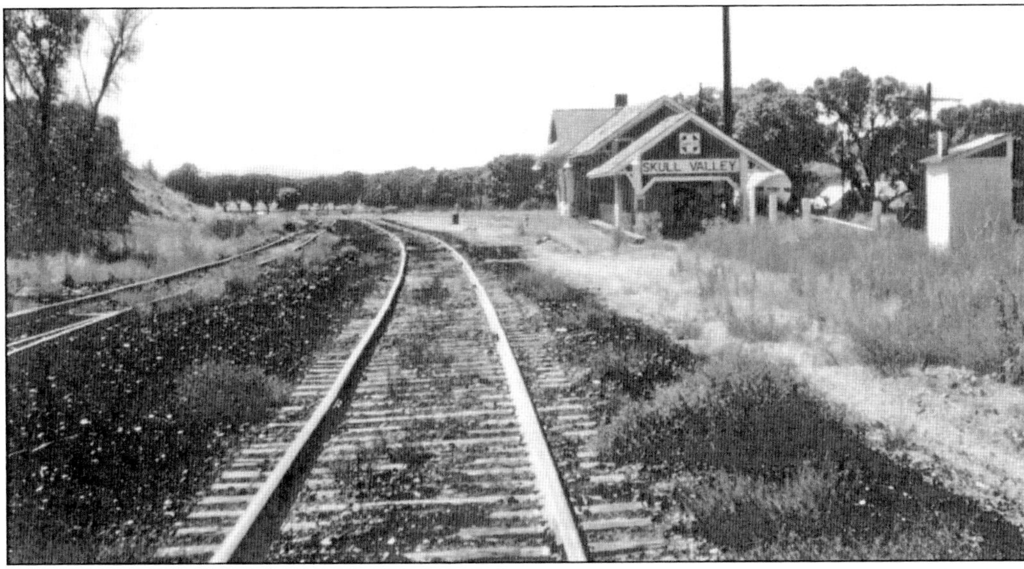

SKULL VALLEY, RAILROAD STATION, C. 1969 (REAL PHOTO POSTCARD). The Skull Valley railroad depot was originally named Cherry Creek Depot, in Dewey. The depot was constructed by the Prescott & Eastern Railroad in 1898. Beginning on October 15, 1898, the Prescott & Eastern started in the Point of Rocks in the Granite Dells and ran for 26 miles to Mayer. The closing of the mines in the Bradshaws and the World War I Armistice seemed to be the death knell of the railroad. The depot was relocated to Skull Valley in 1926. By 1949, all the tracks between Prescott and Mayer were entirely removed. (Photograph by Ken Jackway, courtesy Skull Valley Historical Association.)

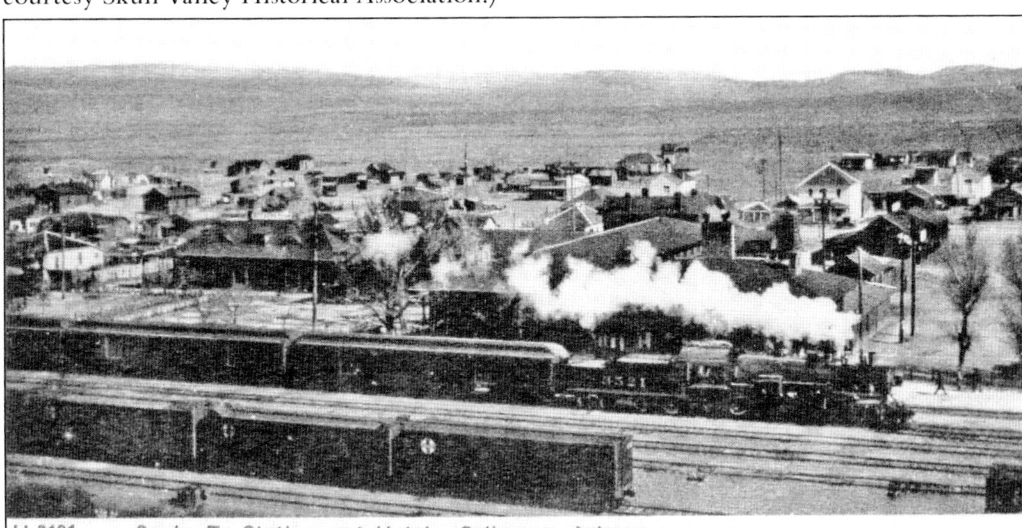

SELIGMAN, SANTA FE, RAILROAD, C. 1920. (REAL PHOTO POSTCARD.) The townsite was once a stage stop on the Mojave Road and was later named Prescott Junction, as it was the location of the junction of the Santa Fe main line and the Prescott & Arizona Central Railroad spur line to Prescott. The P&AC line to Prescott was discontinued in 1891, and a new line, the Santa Fe, Prescott & Phoenix Railroad, began at Ash Fork instead of Seligman. The town was renamed in 1886 after Jesse Seligman, one of two brothers who helped finance the local railroads. (Published by Fred Harvey.)

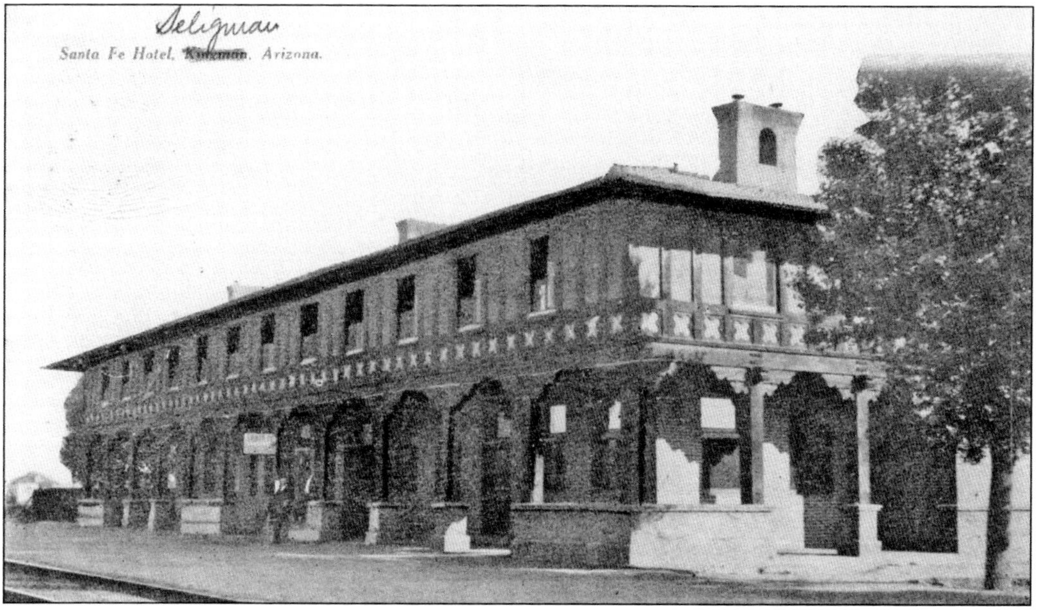

Seligman, Santa Fe Hotel, c. 1915. (Advertising Postcard.) In 1905, Fred Harvey decided to add one of his restaurants and hotels to the Seligman station, so the "Havasu" Harvey House opened for business. The hotel became a popular stop for the trains, so passengers could stay at the hotel or have a meal in the dining room. In 1971 Amtrak took over rail passenger service and then discontinued the stop in Seligman in 1984. It was demolished in 2008. (Published by Fred Harvey.)

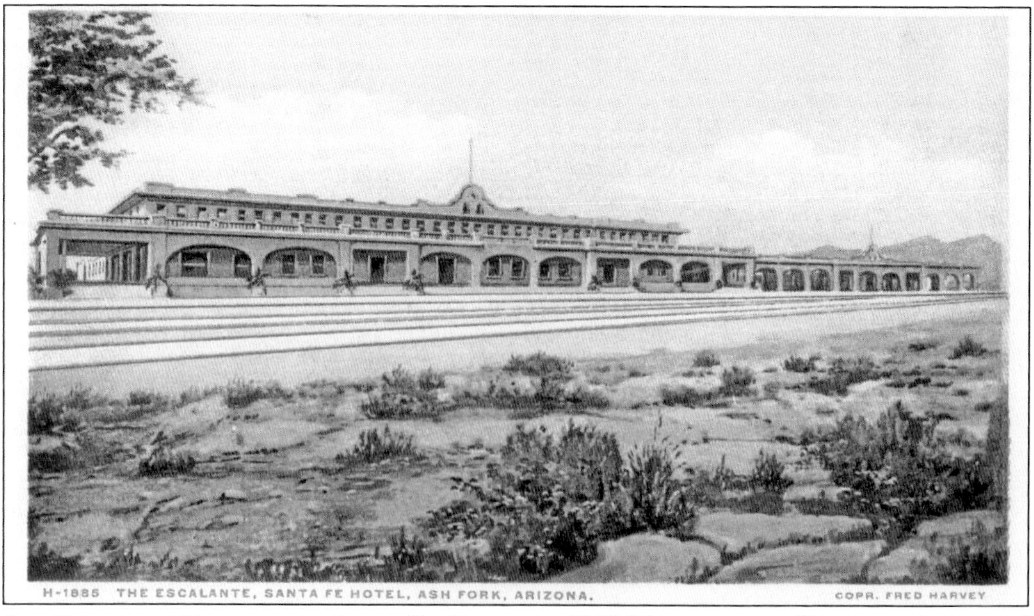

Ash Fork, the Escalante, Santa Fe Hotel, c. 1908 (Advertising Postcard). Located in Ash Fork at the Santa Fe junction with the Prescott-Phoenix line, the Escalante was built in 1907 after the original station, built in 1893, burned down in 1905. The Escalante, one of the famed Harvey Houses built by the Fred Harvey Company, was a meal stop for trains heading in all directions. The hotel closed in 1948 and was torn down in 1968. (Published by Fred Harvey.)

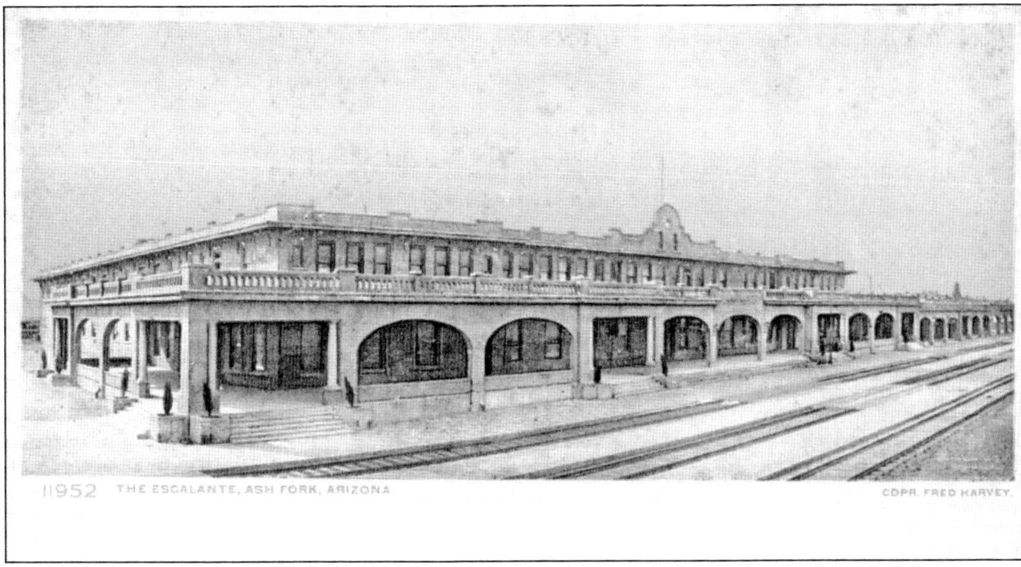

ASH FORK, THE ESCALANTE, C. 1915 (ADVERTISING POSTCARD). On the back of the card, someone wrote, "This is sure a small station we stopped there about 25 minutes." Built at a cost of $150,000, the Escalante consisted of a dining room, a lunch counter, barbershop, newsstand, and an Indian gift shop. (Published by Fred Harvey.)

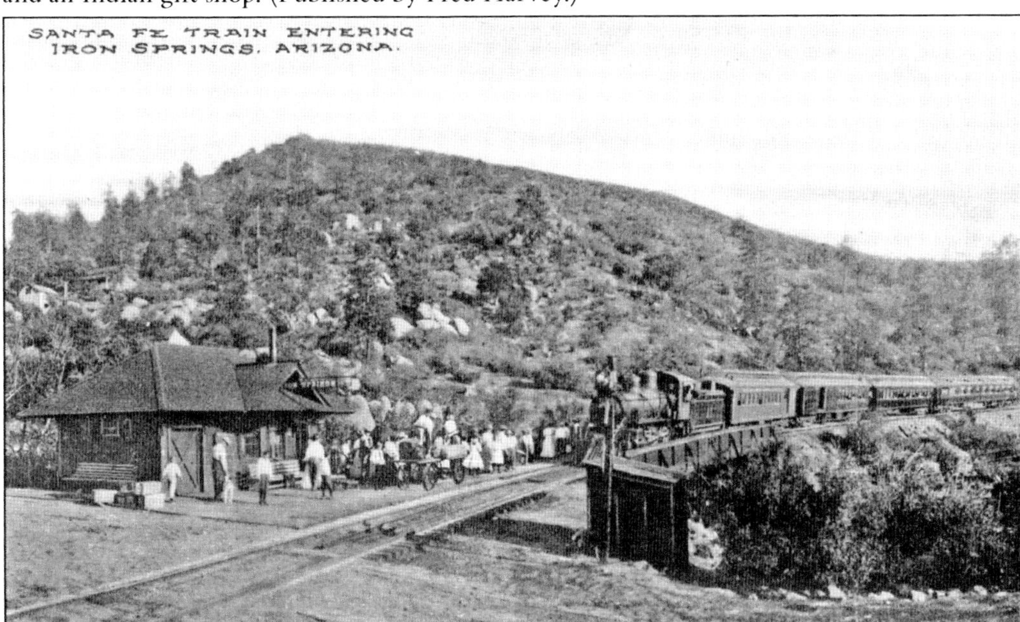

IRON SPRINGS DEPOT, C. 1910 (DIVIDED BACK POSTCARD). The station was constructed in 1909 to accommodate a summer camp for Phoenix's business elite and their families. The name "Iron Springs" comes from an early settler, Bob Atkinson. After setting up a stage station at his home between Prescott and Skull Valley in 1874, Atkinson planted an orchard below the spring and used an iron pipe to irrigate his trees. From that pipe, the name Iron Springs stuck. The station was used until 1934. (Published by Fred Harvey, courtesy Tony Meager.)

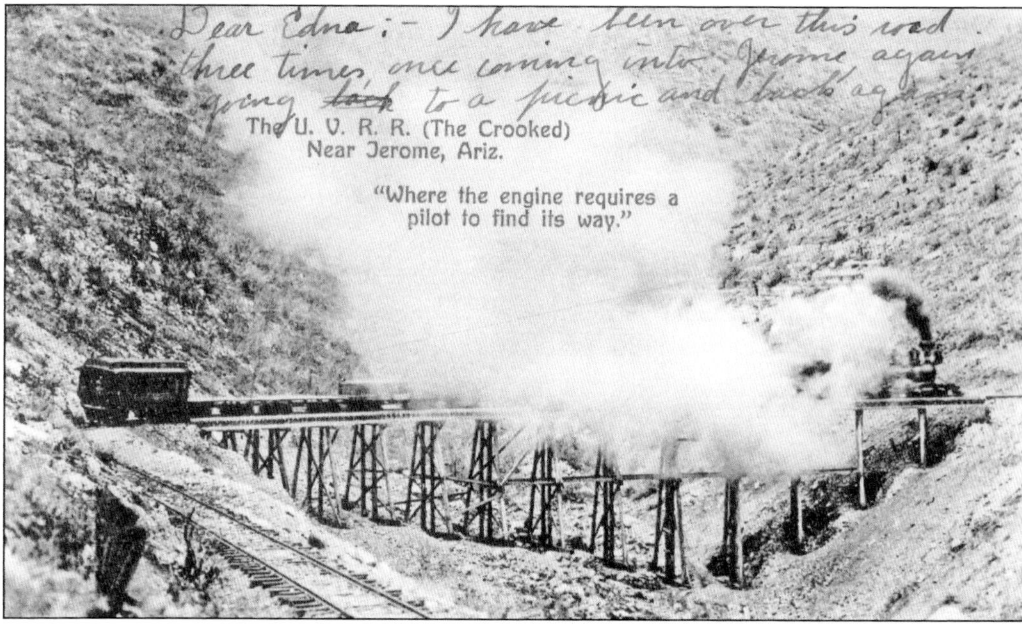

United Verde & Pacific Railroad, Postmarked August 27, 1907 (Real Photo-Postcard). Funded entirely by William Clark, owner of the United Verde Mine, the narrow-gauge railroad cost $600,000 to construct; with inflation, that would be more than $16 million today. Clark was able to keep the cost down because narrow-gauge railways used less steel for track and timber for crossties. The rolling stock was also considerably smaller than the full-size engines and rail cars. (Published by Lynn Boyd Drug, courtesy Nancy Burgess.)

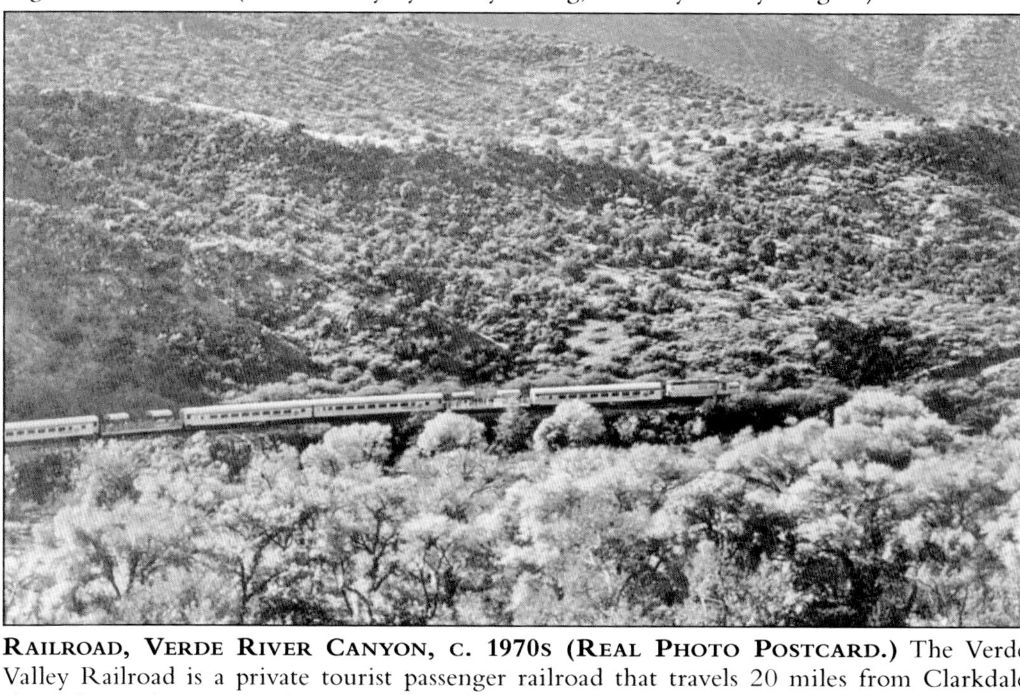

Railroad, Verde River Canyon, c. 1970s (Real Photo Postcard.) The Verde Valley Railroad is a private tourist passenger railroad that travels 20 miles from Clarkdale along the Verde River to the ghost town of Perkensville and back. (Published by the Bradshaw Studios, courtesy of John Bradshaw and Bradshaw Color Studios.)

Six

Mining in Yavapai County

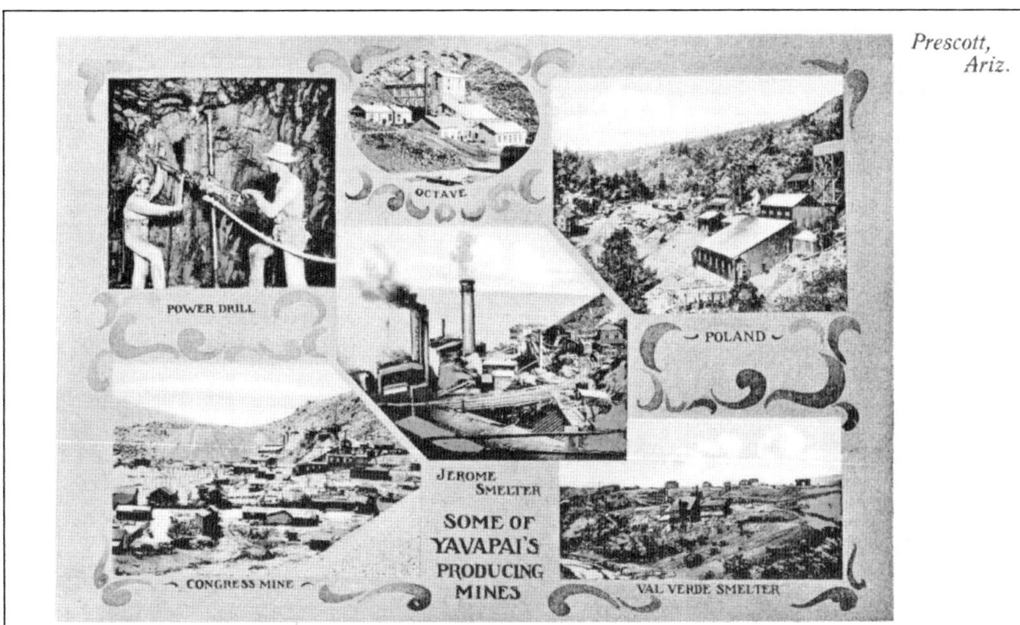

Yavapai Mines, c. 1910 (Multi-View Postcard). There are over 1,500 known mines in Yavapai County and probably hundreds of smaller mines and claims that are unaccounted for. The names range from A&A Mine near Jerome to the Zonia Mine in Peeples Valley. Then there are names such as Doodlebug Mine, Copperopolis, Mark Twain Mine, Midnite Test Mine, and the Silver Christmas Mine. Although copper, gold, and silver were the mainstays for prospectors, numerous other ores and minerals were found in Yavapai County, including lead, opals, garnets, zinc, and cinnabar. (Published by Souvenir P.C., courtesy John Taylor.)

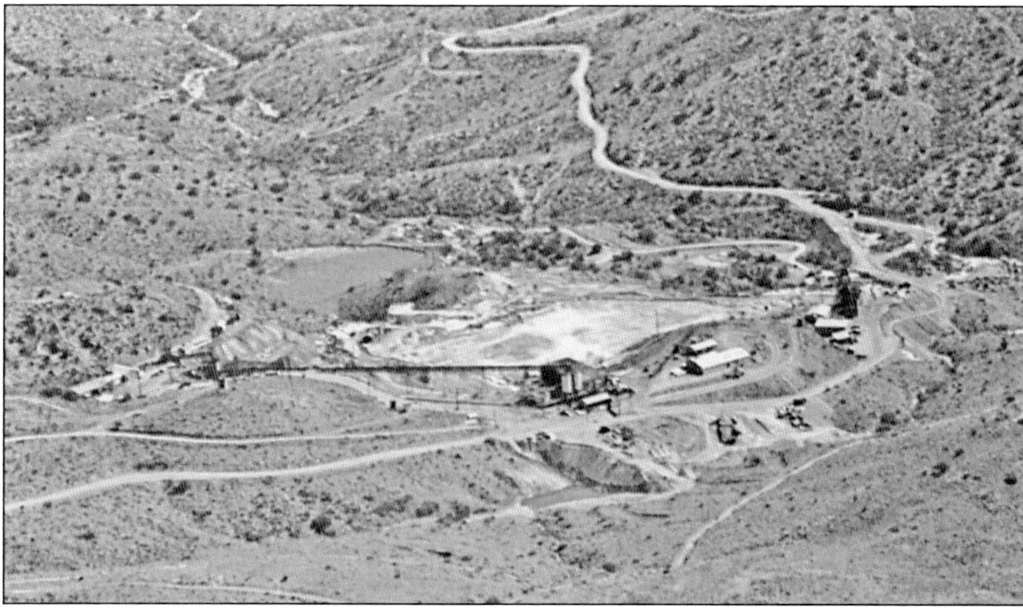

BAGDAD, CYPRUS MINE, C. 1960 (REAL PHOTO POSTCARD). This aerial view shows the Cyprus Mine's Old Bruce Division. Originally discovered in 1882, the Old Dick Mine changed owners and names many times over the years, finally shutting down in 1977. The Cyprus Mine is no longer in existence, having been swallowed by the larger open-pit mine. (Published by Kingman Photo Services, photograph by David C. Lincoln.)

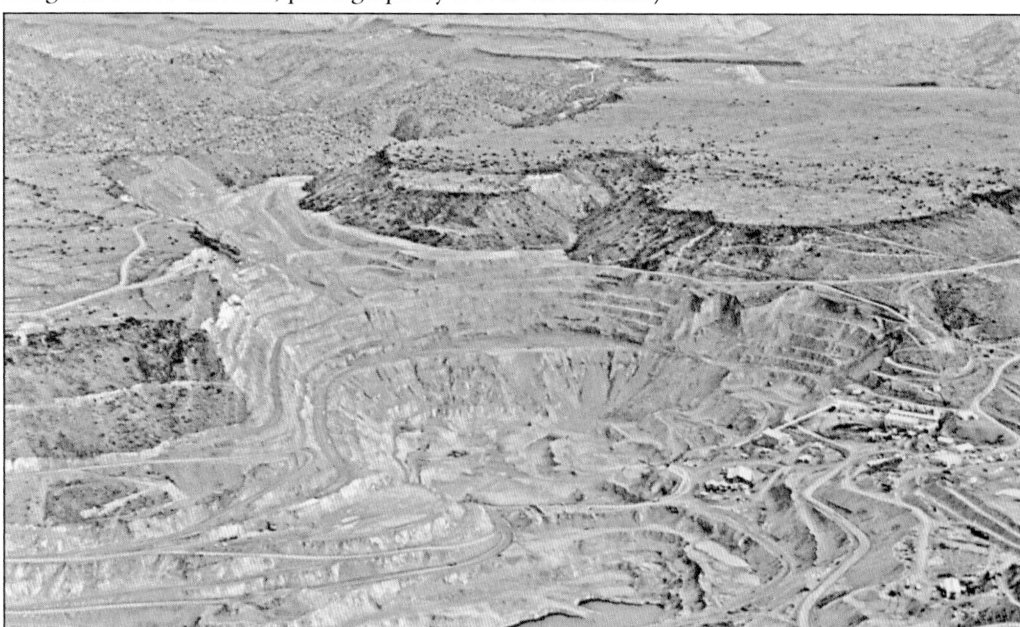

BAGDAD, OPEN PIT MINE, C. 1960S (REAL PHOTO POSTCARD). This aerial view shows the open-pit mine and mill areas. Open-pit mining began in Bagdad in 1945 and now operates 24 hours a day, producing up to 75,000 metric tons per day of copper and molybdenum. (Published by Kingman Photo Services, photograph by David C. Lincoln, courtesy Bagdad Historical Society.)

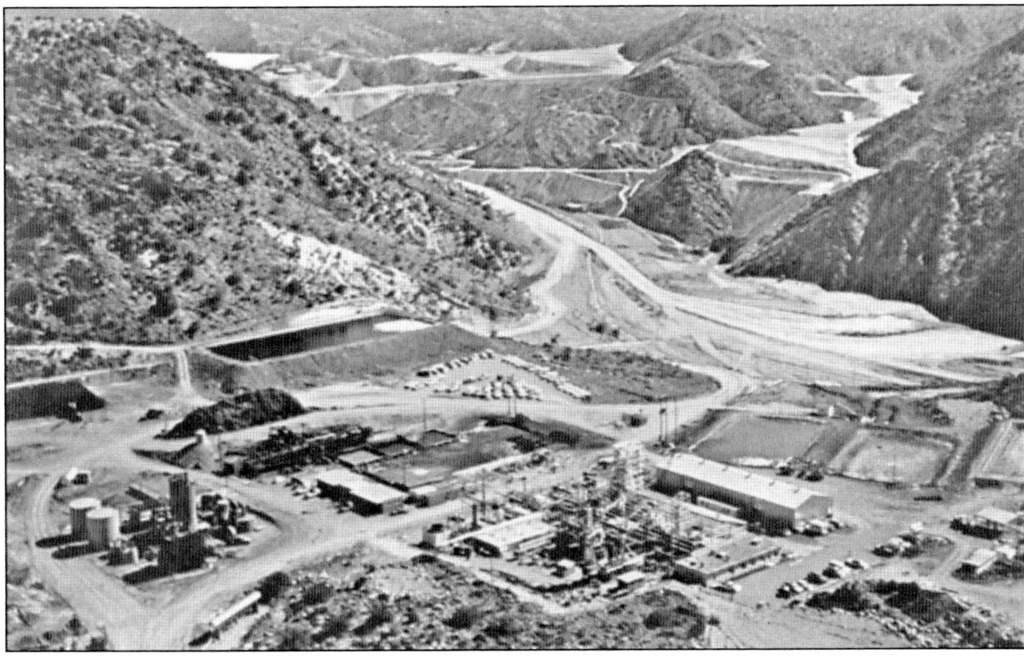

BAGDAD, ACID PLANT, C. 1960S (REAL PHOTO POSTCARD). Pictured are the acid plant, refinery, and leach plant area for the Bagdad Copper Corporation Mine. Bagdad is a company town. The town, houses, and commercial buildings, along with the open-pit copper mine, are owned and operated by Freeport-McMoRan. The original Bagdad claim was recognized in 1882 but remained undeveloped until the late 1920s. Bagdad saw a boom after World War II, when lead and copper became in demand. (Published by Kingman Photo Services, photograph by David C. Lincoln, courtesy Bagdad Historical Society.)

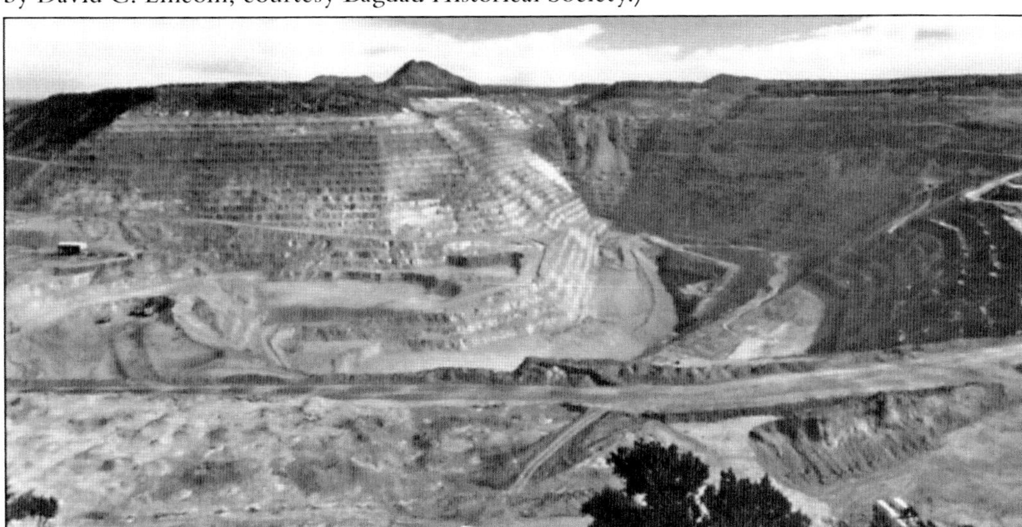

BAGDAD, OPEN-PIT MINE, C. 1960S (REAL PHOTO POSTCARD). Mining in the early years consisted of tunnels dug by miners with picks, shovels, and dynamite. Then, in 1945, the open-pit mining method became popular. Through the years, the pit has grown to about 2,200 feet deep and almost a mile and a half wide. (Published by Kingman Photo Services, photograph by David C. Lincoln, courtesy Bagdad Historical Society.)

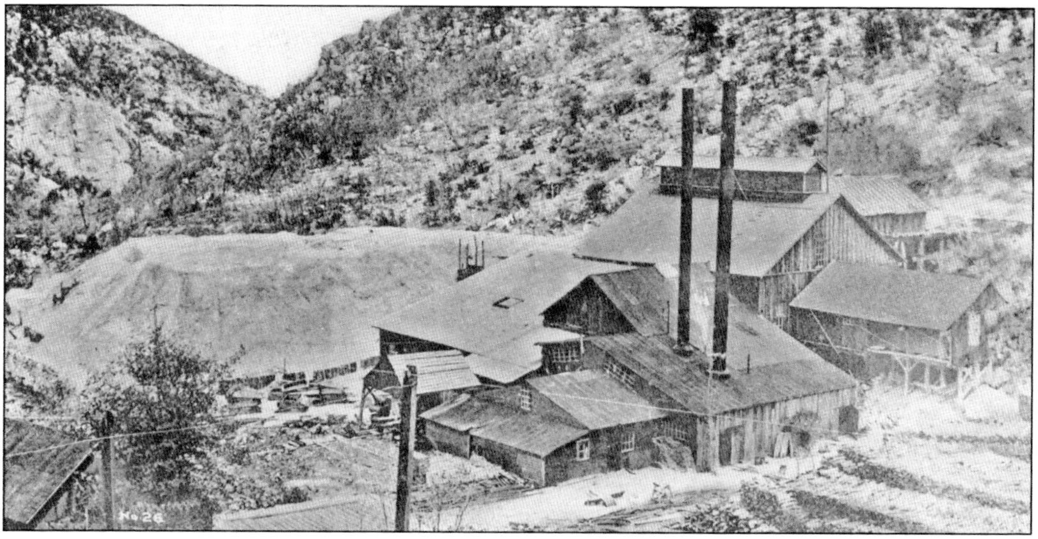

CROWN KING, QUARTZ MILL, POSTMARKED MARCH 18, 1911 (DIVIDED BACK HAND-COLORED POSTCARD). The Crown King Mine was the largest mine in the Bradshaw Mountains. Originally named Crowned King, the name was shortened, which led to naming the small mining community Crown King. A shaft once reached 500 feet below the ground, allowing miners to exhume over $40,000 a month of ore. The mine closed in 1899. (Published by Brisley Drug Co.)

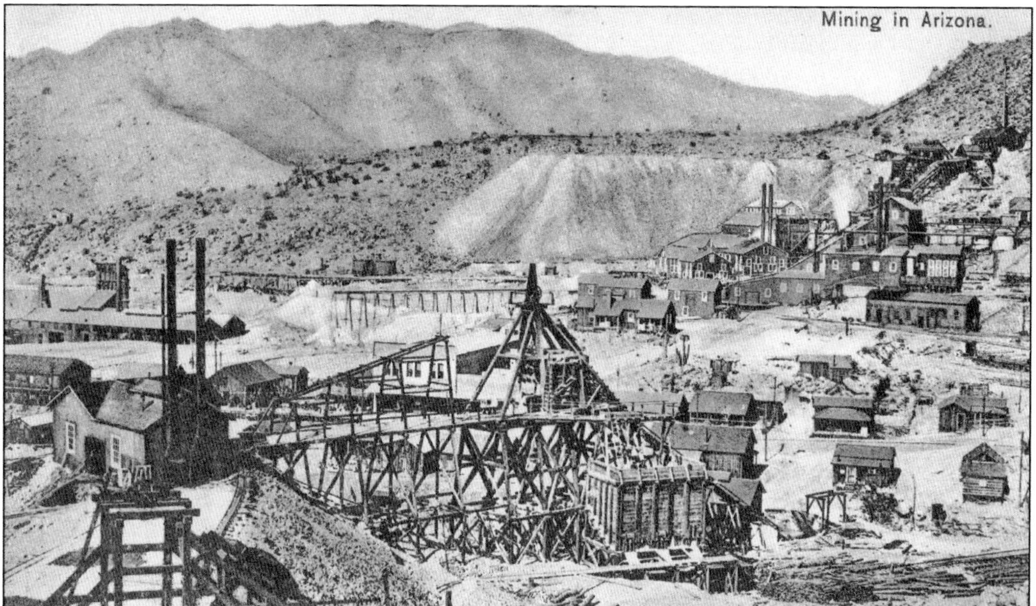

CONGRESS, POSTMARKED 1912 (HAND-COLORED POSTCARD). Dennis May, an early prospector in Yavapai County, first discovered gold along Date Creek, about eight miles northwest of Congress, in 1870. Around 1880, May, along with two other prospectors, began working what would become the Congress Mine. The claim for the Congress Mine was filed on March 25, 1884. The mine shut down for three years in 1891 so that a railroad from Ash Fork to Phoenix could be built with a spur in Congress. By 1900, the mine became Arizona's biggest producer of gold and had the territory's deepest shaft at 2,700 feet. (Courtesy John Taylor.)

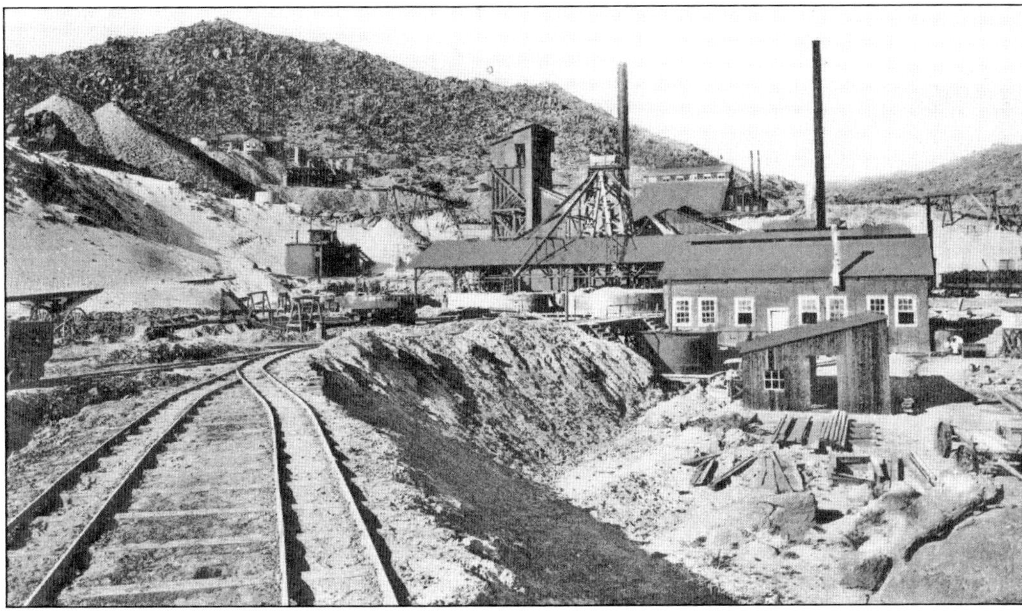

CONGRESS, POSTMARKED 1907 (HAND-COLORED POSTCARD). In May 1901, Pres. William McKinley visited the Congress Mine. By 1902, the main shaft reached a depth of 3,200 feet as ore became scarcer. Over the next three years, ore got harder and harder to locate. In 1905 and 1906, a boom in gold production was seen as the shaft reached 4,000 feet. The mine closed down for good in 1910. There have been a number of speculative groups interested in the mine over the years, but none ever came to be. (Published by M. Reider Publ., courtesy John Taylor.)

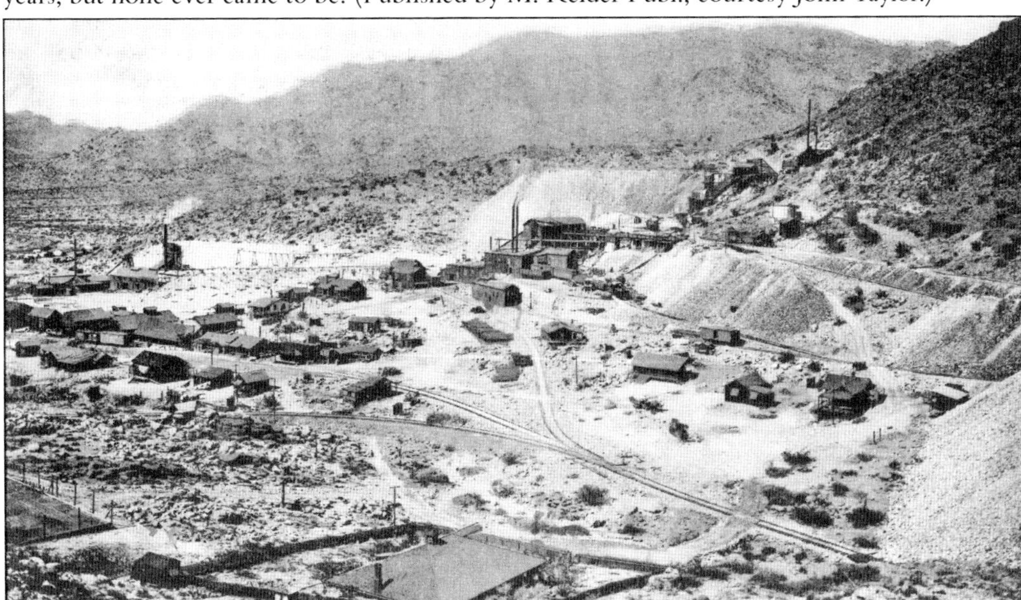

CONGRESS, POSTMARKED 1907 (HAND-COLORED POSTCARD). In the early years of the Congress Mine, from 1889 to 1891, the mine produced over 71 tons of ore. Compare that to the period from 1894 until the mine closed 1910, when it produced 307,000 tons of ore. Over the 21-year lifespan of the mine, it produced over $7.6 million in gold and silver. (Published by M. Reider Publ., courtesy John Taylor.)

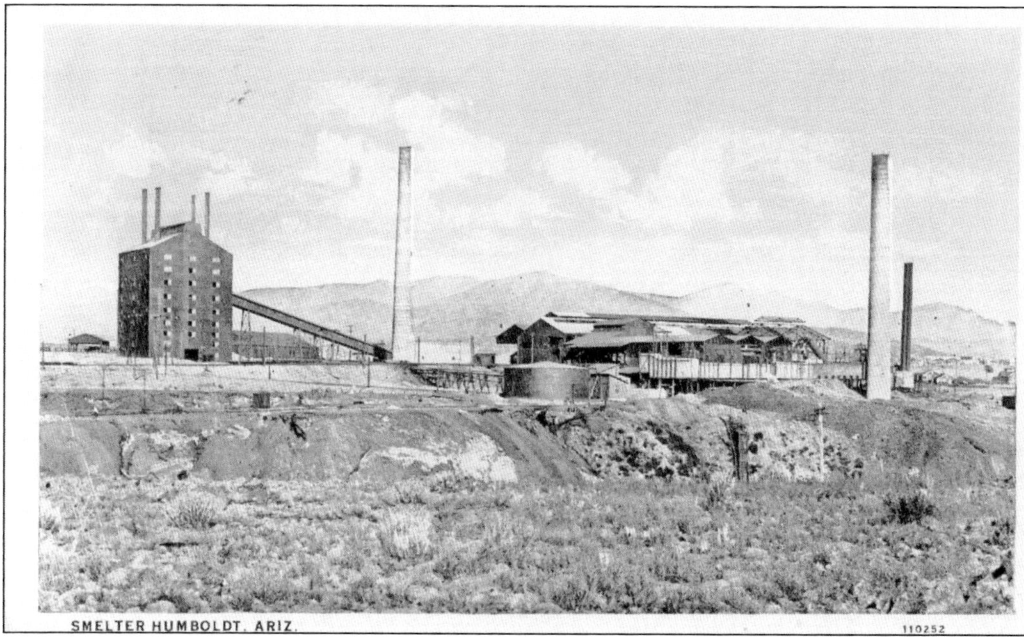

ABOVE: HUMBOLDT, SMELTER, C. 1926 (CURT TEICH HAND-COLORED POSTCARD); BELOW: HUMBOLDT, SMELTER AND SAMPLE MILL, C. 1910 (DIVIDED BACK POSTCARD). The Humboldt Smelter sits on 182 acres near the Iron King Mine in the town of Dewey-Humboldt. The smelter began operations in the late 1800s and operated until the 1960s. The original smelter burned down in 1904 and was rebuilt in 1906. The new smelter ran until 1918 and then intermittently for five years starting in 1922. The smelter reopened in 1930 and ran until the 1960s, when it was closed permanently. Due to high levels of arsenic, lead, and sulfate, in 2008, the smelter site was named to the EPA's Superfund list for site cleanup. (Above, produced by C.T. American Art Blue Sky; below, courtesy John Taylor.)

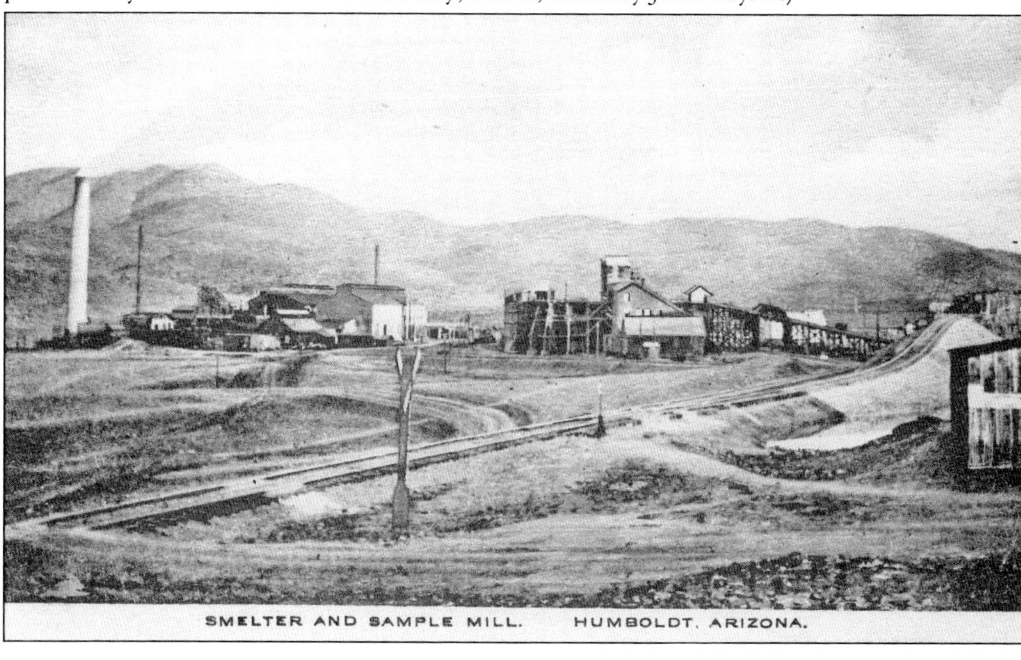

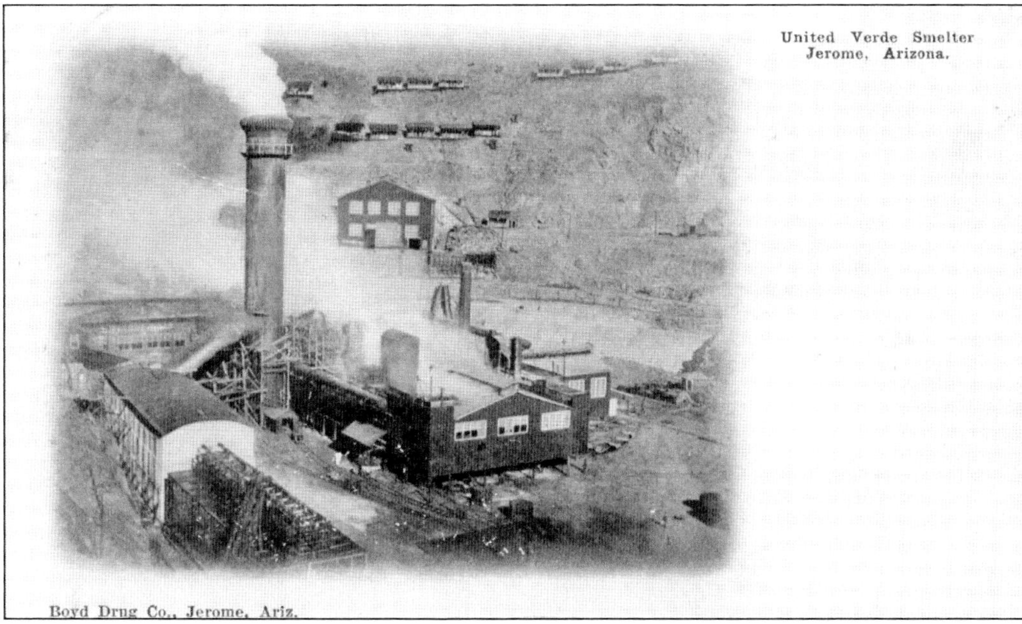

ABOVE: JEROME, UNITED VERDE SMELTER, C. 1904 (UNDIVIDED BACK POSTCARD); BELOW: JEROME, JEROME SMELTERS, C. 1910 (UNDIVIDED BACK POSTCARD). The first smelter, built on unstable ground at the United Verde Mine in the 1880s, was replaced about 1915 by the new smelter in Clemenceau, near Cottonwood. Because of Jerome's remoteness, coke, which was being used to fuel the smelter, was shipped from Wales around Cape Horn to San Francisco, then placed on a train to Ash Fork to be delivered to Jerome. By 1900, the fumes from the smelter killed off almost all of the vegetation on the hills surrounding Jerome. (Above, produced by Lynn Boyd Drug; below, published by Souvenir P.C.)

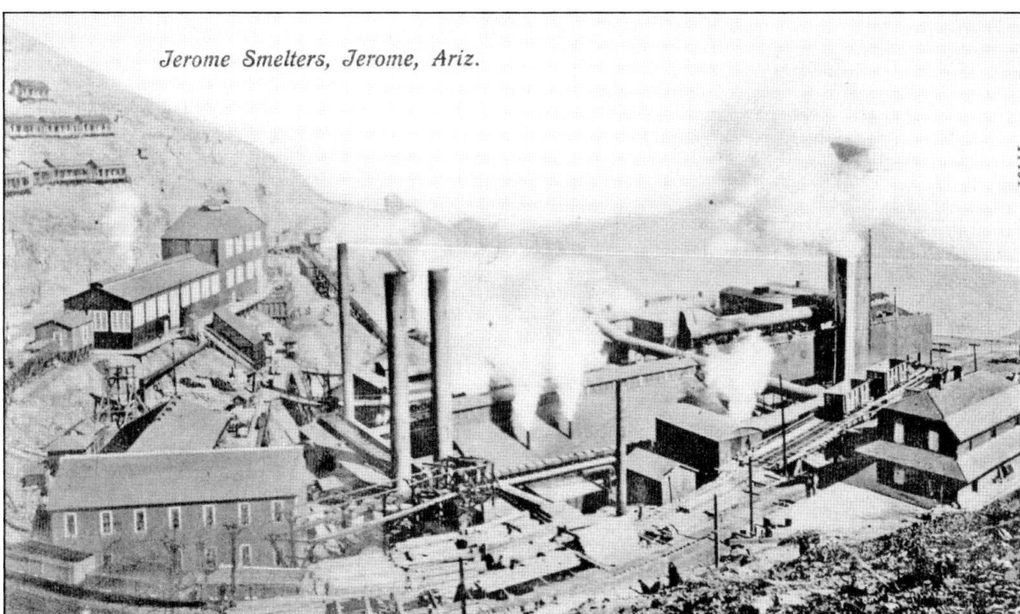

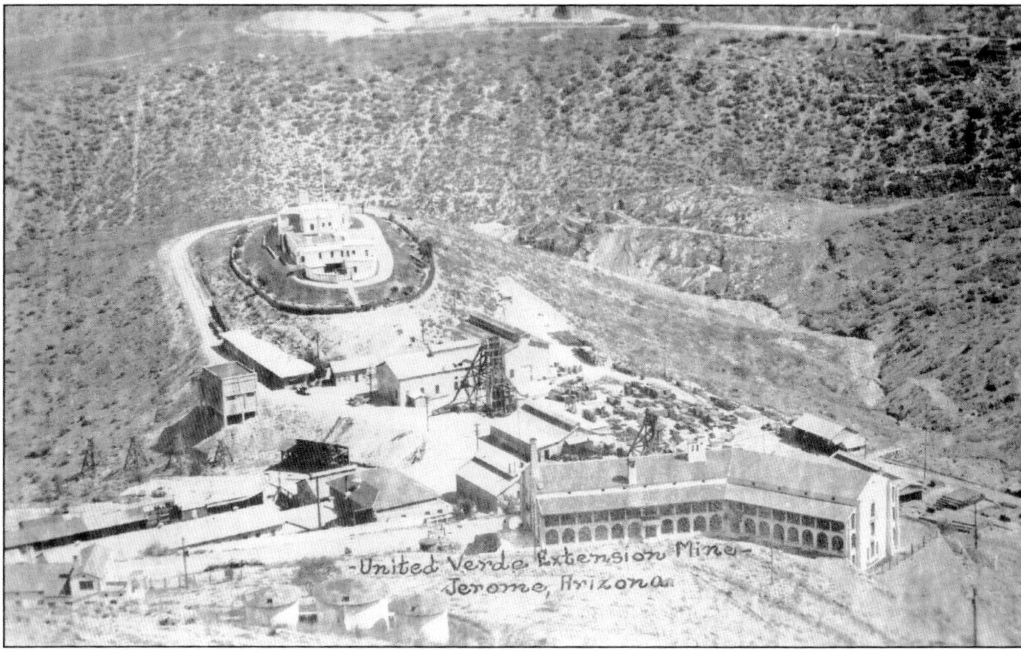

ABOVE: JEROME, UNITED VERDE EXTENSION MINE, C. 1910 (DIVIDED BACK POSTCARD); BELOW: JEROME, LITTLE DAISY MINE, C. 1930 (HAND-COLORED POSTCARD). The United Verde Extension Mine was also known as the Little Daisy Mine. During 1916, the mine produced over $10 million in copper, gold, and silver. Over its lifetime, the mine produced over $125 million in ore. (Above, courtesy John Taylor; below, published by Yavapai Drug, courtesy John Taylor.)

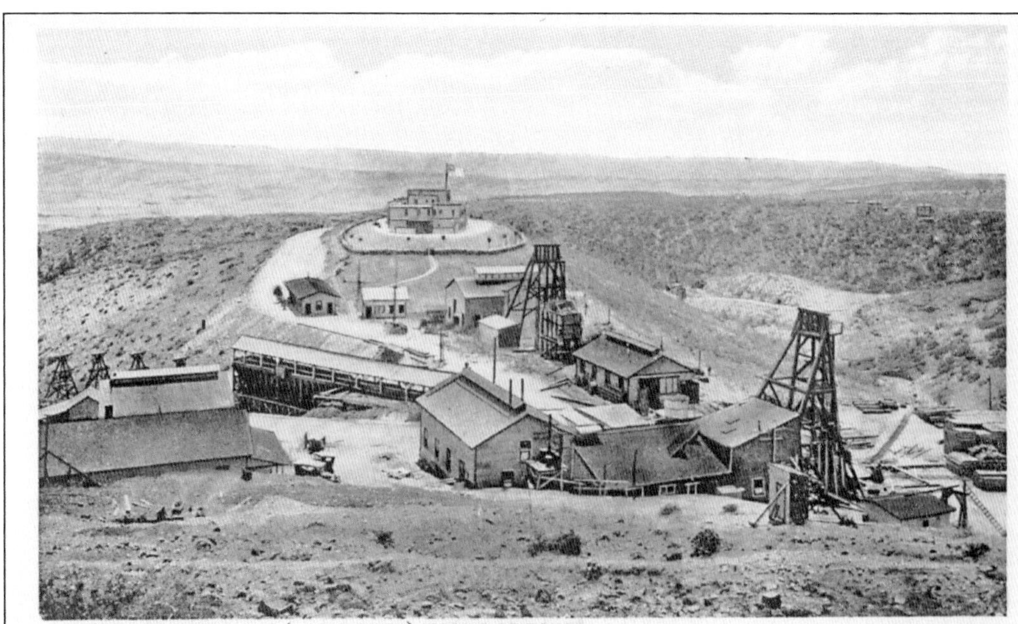

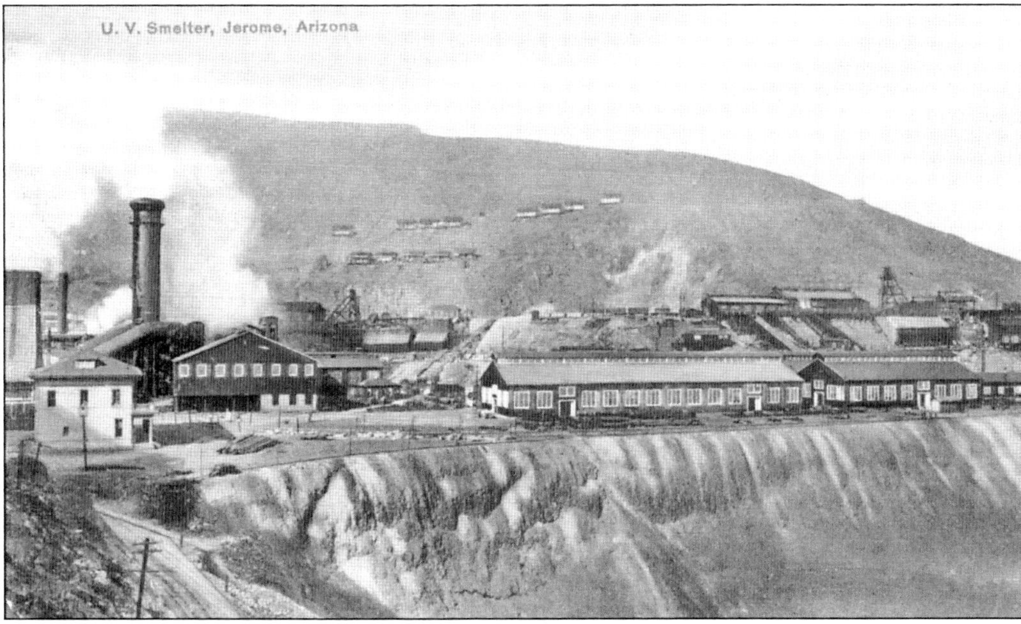

ABOVE: JEROME, UNITED VERDE SMELTER, C. 1910 (HAND-COLORED POSTCARD); BELOW: JEROME, POURING COOPER, C. 1910 (DIVIDED BACK POSTCARD). Smelting plants for metals such as copper, gold, and the like involve extremely high heating processes in which the ore and a reducing agent, such as coke or charcoal, causes a chemical reaction that separates the metal from rock. Once the metal has been separated, it can be poured into molds. Once cooled, it is ready to be transported to other facilities for manufacturing products. (Above, published by R.A. Smith–Jerome, courtesy John Taylor; below, published by Lynn Boyd Drug, courtesy John Taylor.)

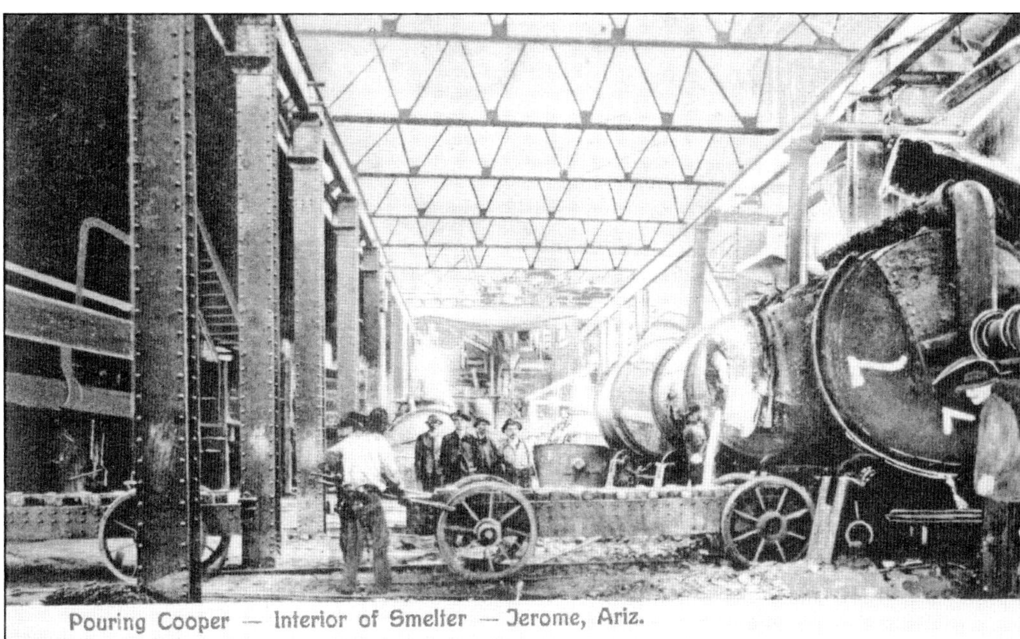

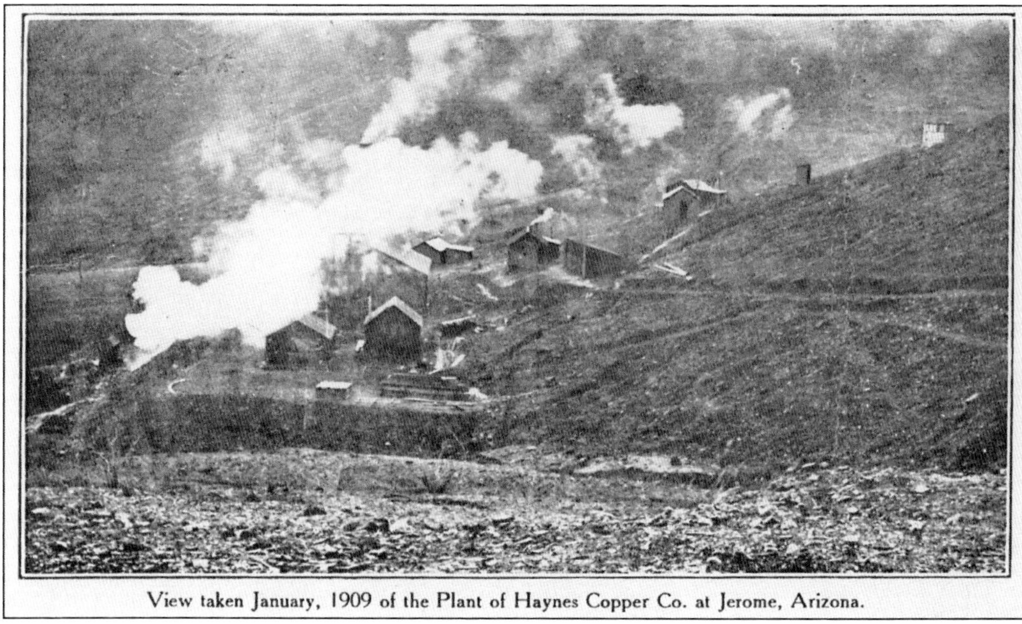

JEROME, HAYNES COPPER CO., POSTMARKED 1914 (DIVIDED BACK POSTCARD). The mines and town of Haynes are long gone, only to be resurrected as a tourist attraction known as the Gold King Mine and Ghost Town. A small mine compared to others in the Jerome area, it boasted a population of 301 people in 1901 and only 14 people by 1914. Although it called itself a copper company, it never really did discover much copper and mostly ended up mining gold. In the 1960s, Don Robertson bought the property with only a few of the original buildings still standing. The rest of the tourist attraction was constructed from old lumber or buildings brought in from other locations. (Courtesy John Taylor.)

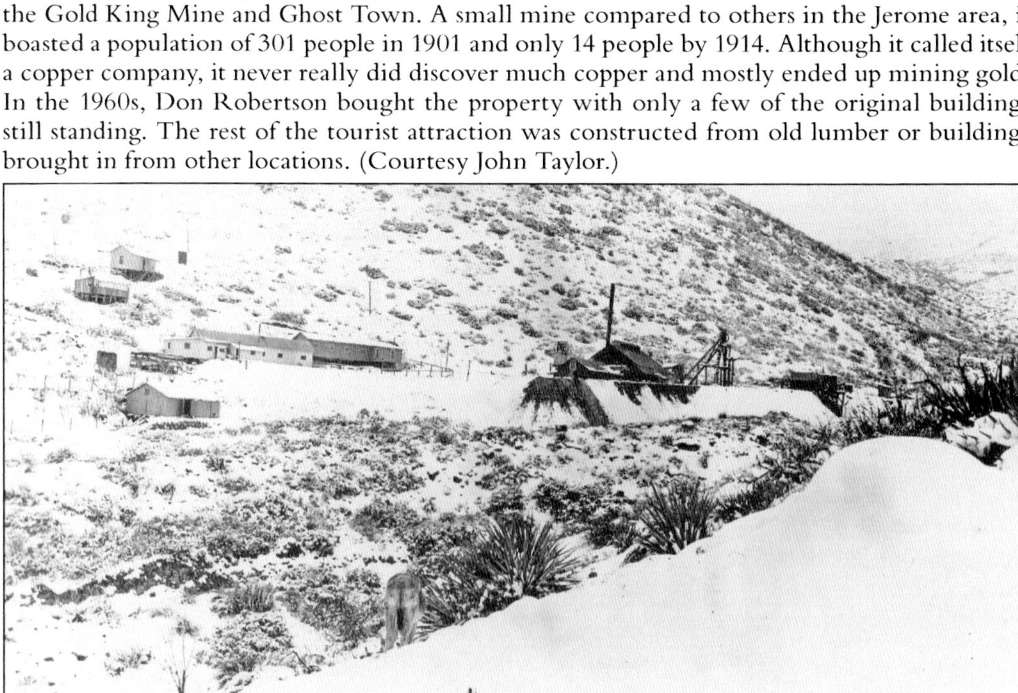

JEROME, SNOW AT THE A&A MINE, C. 1910 (DIVIDED BACK POSTCARD). In 1909, the Arkansas & Arizona Mine received a new diamond drill with expectations of reaching greater depths and new veins of copper. But as the drill reached near the 1,200-foot level, it struck a cave, causing extensive damage to the drill. The mine was forced to cease operations until the drill could be repaired and returned from the East Coast. The mine closed in 1917. (Courtesy John Taylor.)

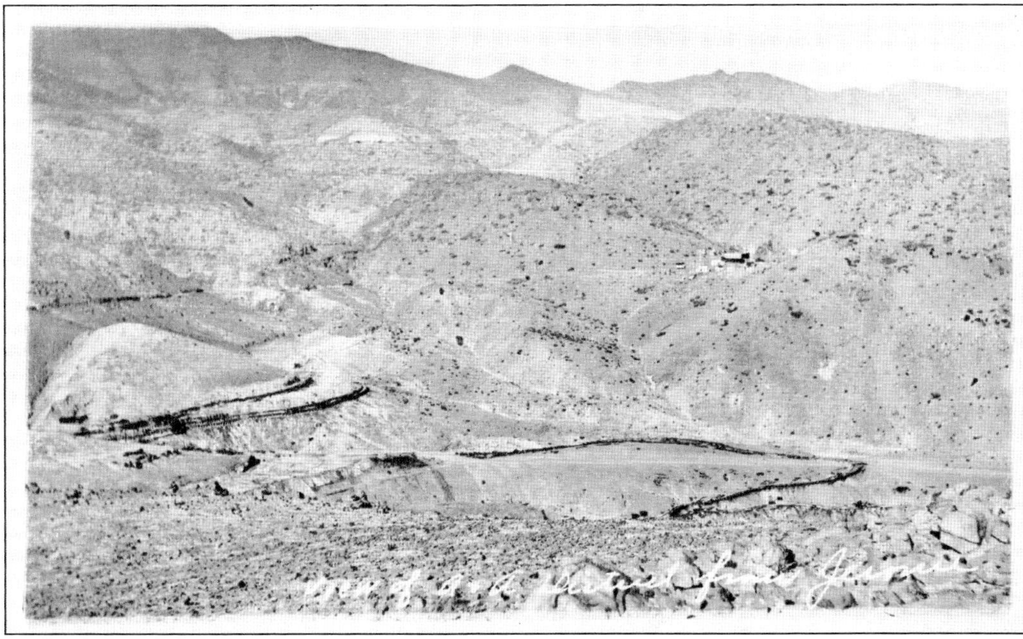

ABOVE: JEROME, VIEW OF THE A&A MINE FROM JEROME, C. 1910 (DIVIDED BACK POSTCARD); BELOW: JEROME, MINE AND TOWN, A&A MINE, POSTMARKED 1916 (DIVIDED BACK POSTCARD). Located just north of the United Verde Copper Mine and down the hill from the Haynes Mine, the Arkansas & Arizona Copper Mine was led by a group of investors from Arkansas. A vein rich in copper was discovered over the hill from the Little Daisy Mine with an extremely large cross-section shared with the A&A Mine. The mine closed for a time in 1914 but reopened in 1915 with the news of the copper vein. (Both, courtesy John Taylor.)

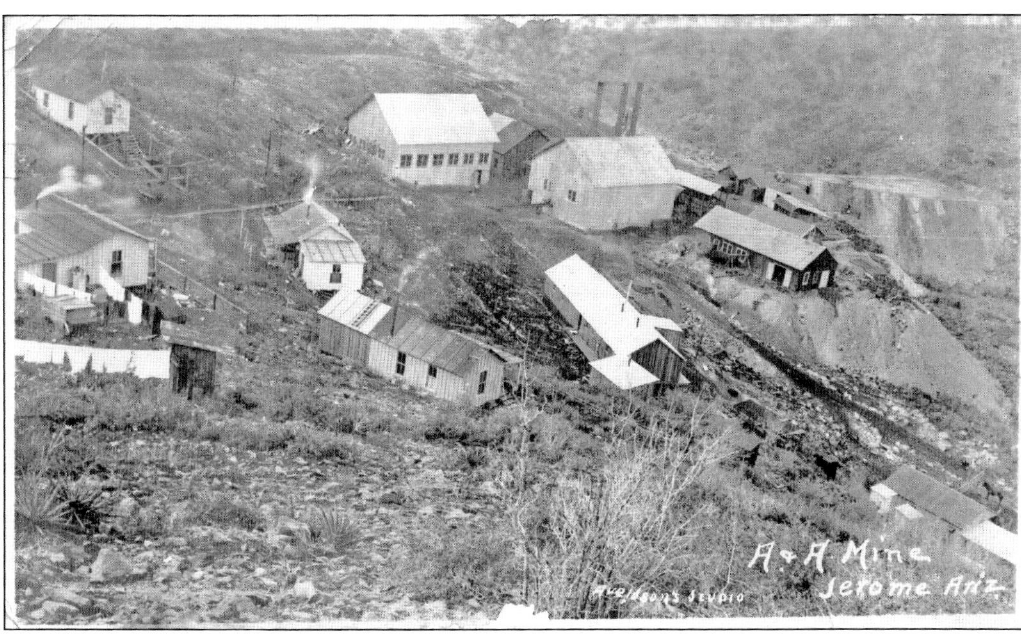

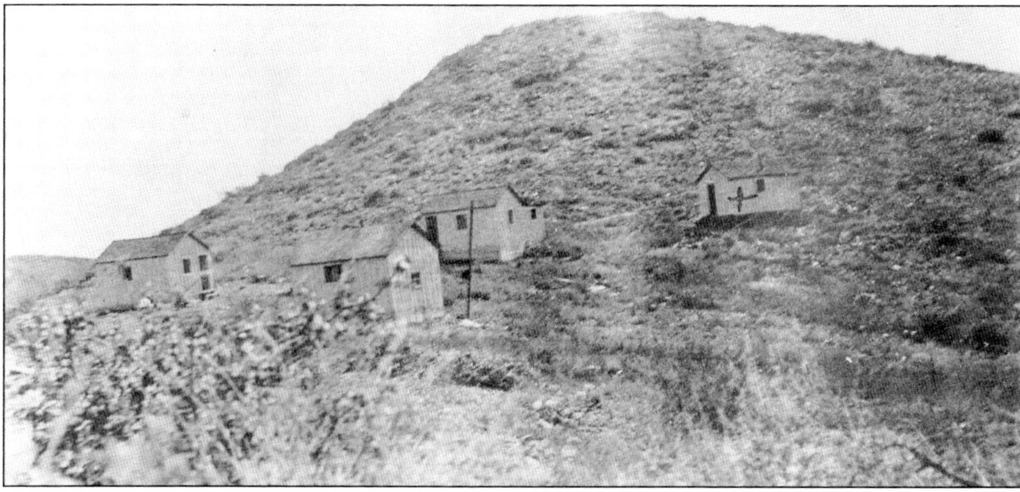

JEROME, BUNKHOUSES FOR THE A&A MINE, POSTMARKED AUGUST 12, 1912 (DIVIDED BACK POSTCARD). Handwritten on the back is "The one with the X is ours and is the best one. Ernest." Housing was at a minimum at the turn of the century, and miners usually shared quarters with other miners on other shifts so everyone had a place to sleep. Notice the lack of trees on the hillsides. Just about every tree within miles of the town of Jerome was cut down to use in the mines or as building material. (Courtesy John Taylor.)

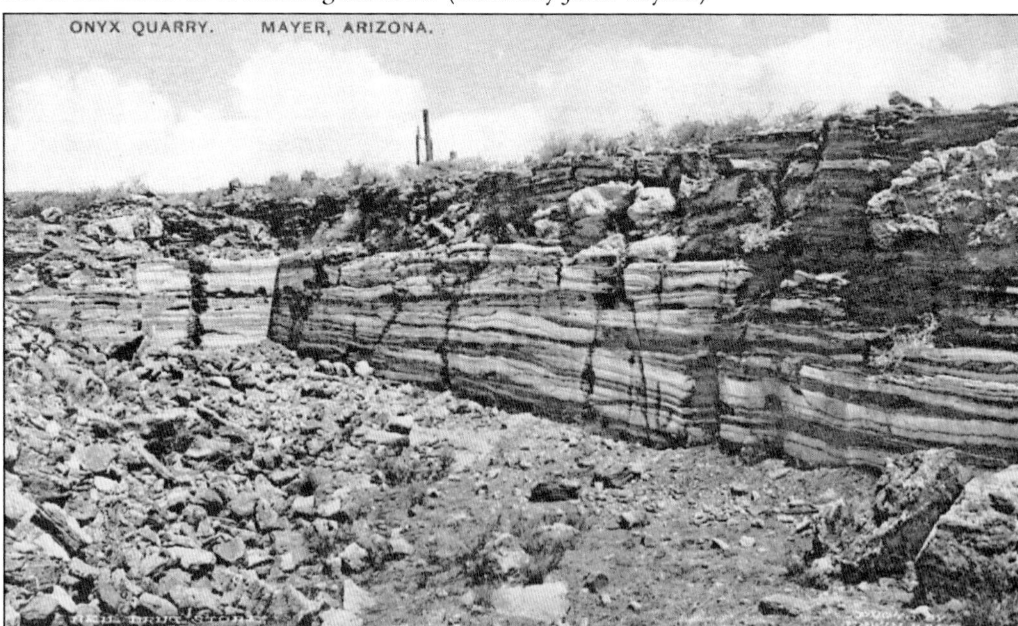

MAYER, ONYX QUARRY, C. 1910 (ALBERTYPE POSTCARD). Joe Mayer, the founder of the town, settled in the area and operated a stage stop between Phoenix and Prescott. He and three business partners, including Bucky O'Neil, opened an onyx quarry near Big Bug Creek. The site was sold in 1890 for a reported $250,000 to a group from Los Angeles. Onyx from Mayer was in high demand in the early part of the 20th century. It was widely used in lamp stands, jewelry boxes, tabletops, and even in automobiles. The quarry shut down in 1929 as the Depression hit the country. Since then, the quarry has opened and closed a number of times, with the site currently in operation today. (Courtesy John Taylor.)

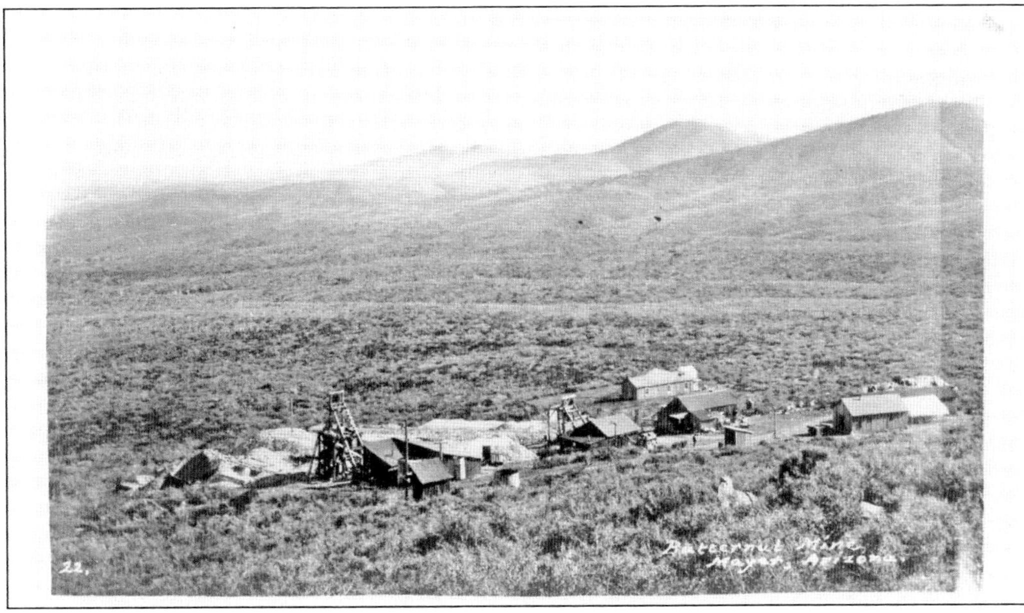

MAYER, BUTTERNUT MINE, 1904–1918 (REAL PHOTO POSTCARD). The Butternut was in the Big Bug district, about three miles northwest of Mayer. The Butternut was not as productive as the nearby Henrietta Mine, only producing about $225,000 in gold during the early part of the 1900s. It finally shut down for good in 1946 after several failed attempts to locate additional ore. (Courtesy Nancy Burgess.)

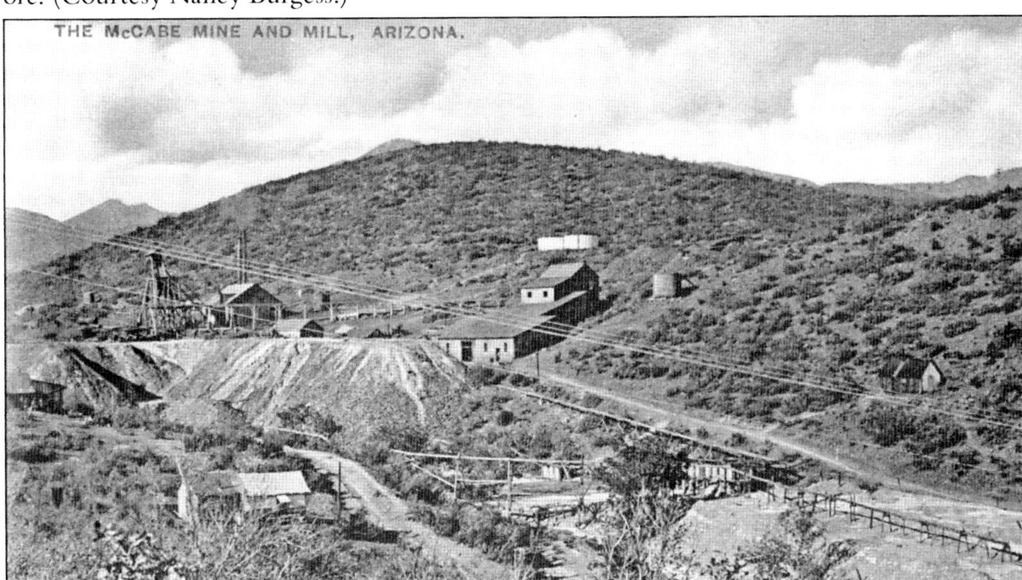

MCCABE MINE, MINE AND MILL, C. 1910 (ALBERTYPE POSTCARD). The only remnant of this small town and mine is the time-ravaged McCabe cemetery. Located about three miles southwest of the Iron King Mine in Humboldt, McCabe's population reached about 600 at its peak. Discovered in the 1860s, the mine closed in 1913. During the next 80 years, attempts were made to reopen the mine, the last being in 1989. The mine and buildings were bulldozed sometime after 1990. (Courtesy John Taylor.)

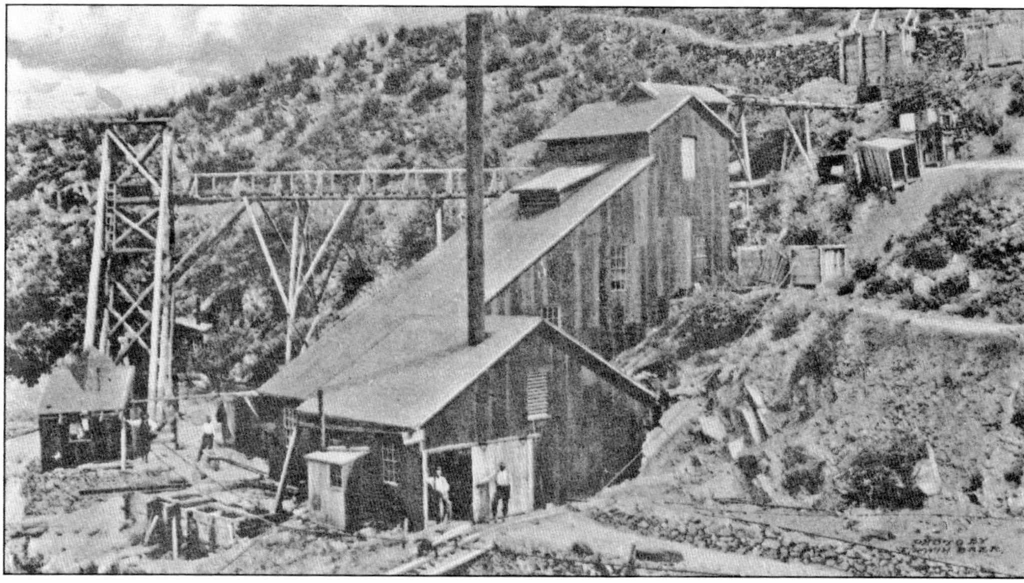

Mount Elliott Mill, c. 1910 (Albertype Postcard). Not much is known about the Mount Elliott Mine, as it was located a few miles from the Poland Mine and incorporated in 1906. In the April 19, 1908, edition of the *Pittsburg Press*, an ad appeared looking for investors. Part of the ad mentioned that the mine had a 10-stamp mill that was capable of crushing 100 tons of rock a day with returns of about $17 a ton in gold and silver. (Published by Neil Drug, courtesy John Taylor.)

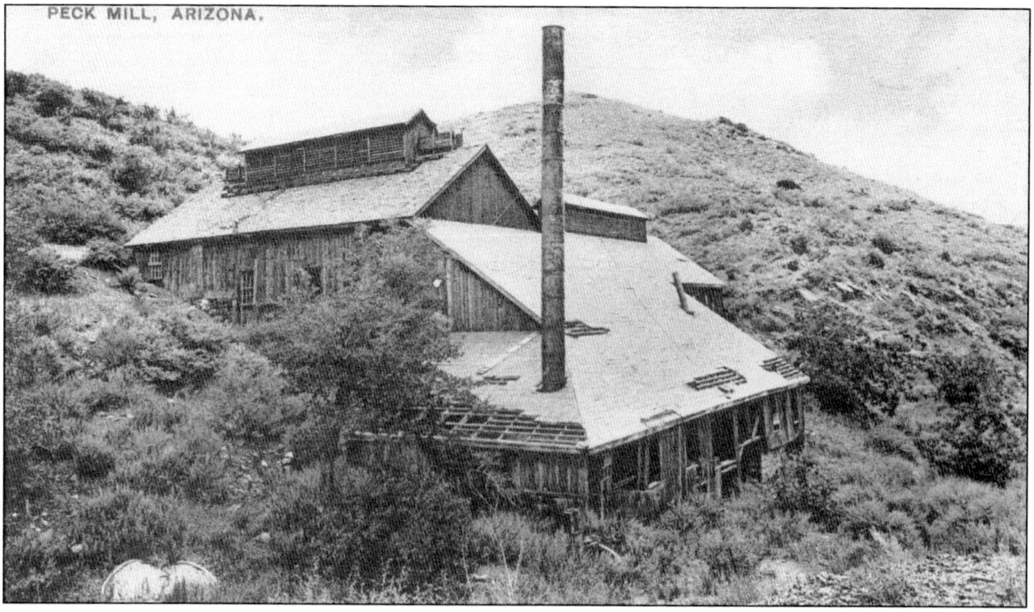

Peck Mine, c. 1910 (Albertype Postcard). In June 1875, E.G. Peck was exploring the Bradshaw Mountains when he noticed a rock sticking out of the ground that turned out to be almost pure silver. With the discovery, the Peck Mine and town of Alexandra were born. From 1875 to 1885, almost $1.5 million worth of ore was dug out of the ground. By 1896, the mine was played out, and the townspeople moved on. In 1903, a new shaft was in operation, but it did not last long, and the town never came back. (Published by Neil Drug, courtesy John Taylor.)

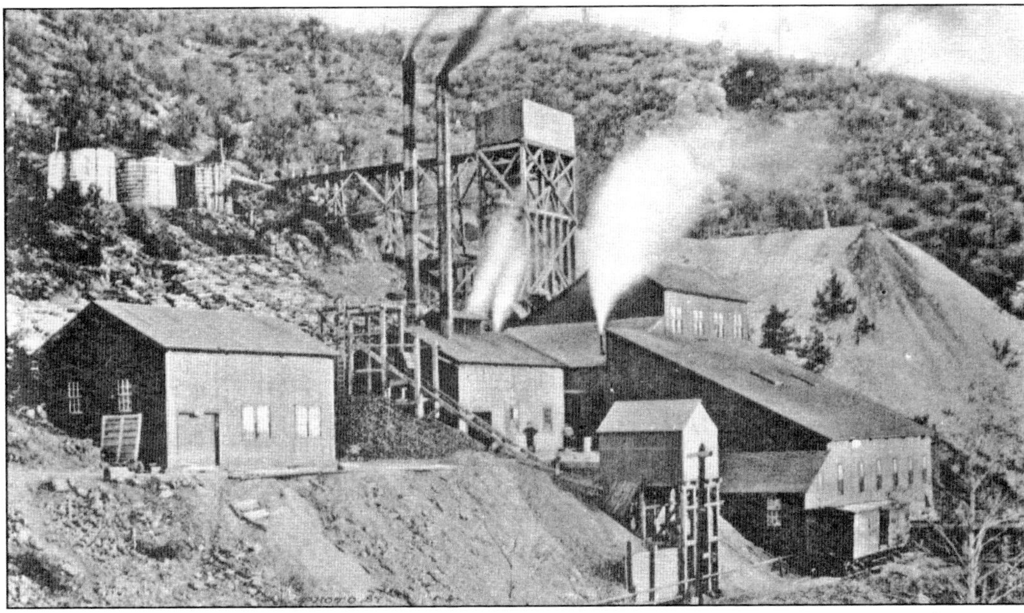

POLAND, C. 1910 (ALBERTYPE POSTCARD). The town of Poland was named after Davis Robert Poland, who in 1872 discovered the mine. The post office opened in 1901, and by 1902, the town had 800 residents. In 1903, a tunnel was completed from Walker to Poland to transport ore to the mill in Poland. The mill ceased operations in Poland by 1911, and the post office closed two years later. By 1939, all production had halted and the mine closed. (Courtesy John Taylor.)

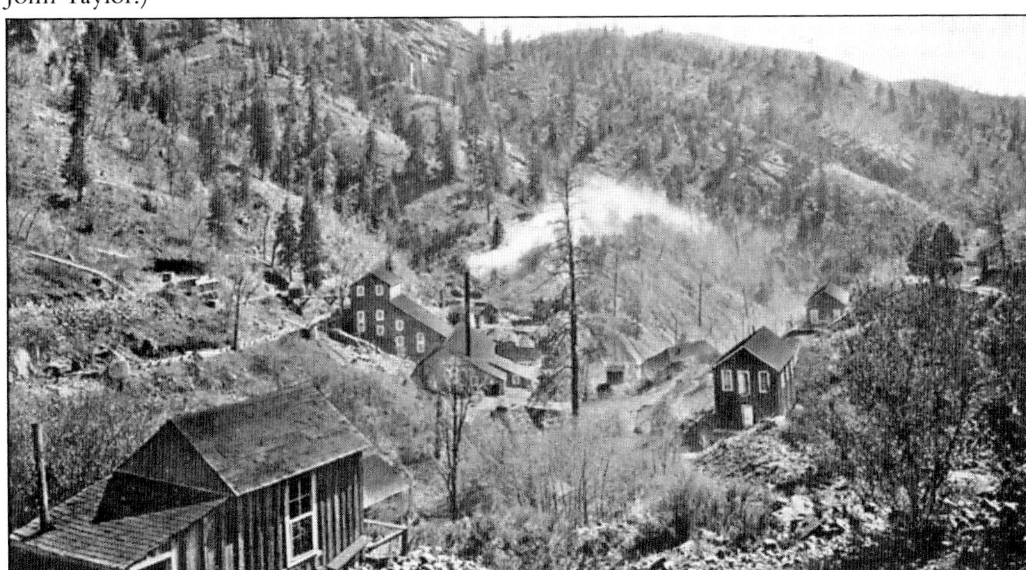

PRESCOTT, SENATOR MINE, POSTMARKED JANUARY 1907 (UNDIVIDED BACK POSTCARD). Discovered along the Hassayampa River in the 1860s, the Senator Mine was one of the longest-active mines in the county. Starting out as a humble mining camp, it grew into a small town with saloons, hotels, restaurants, and even a church and school. The post office arrived in 1901. The mine continued operations, producing copper, gold, zinc, and lead, well into the 1930s. (Courtesy John Taylor.)

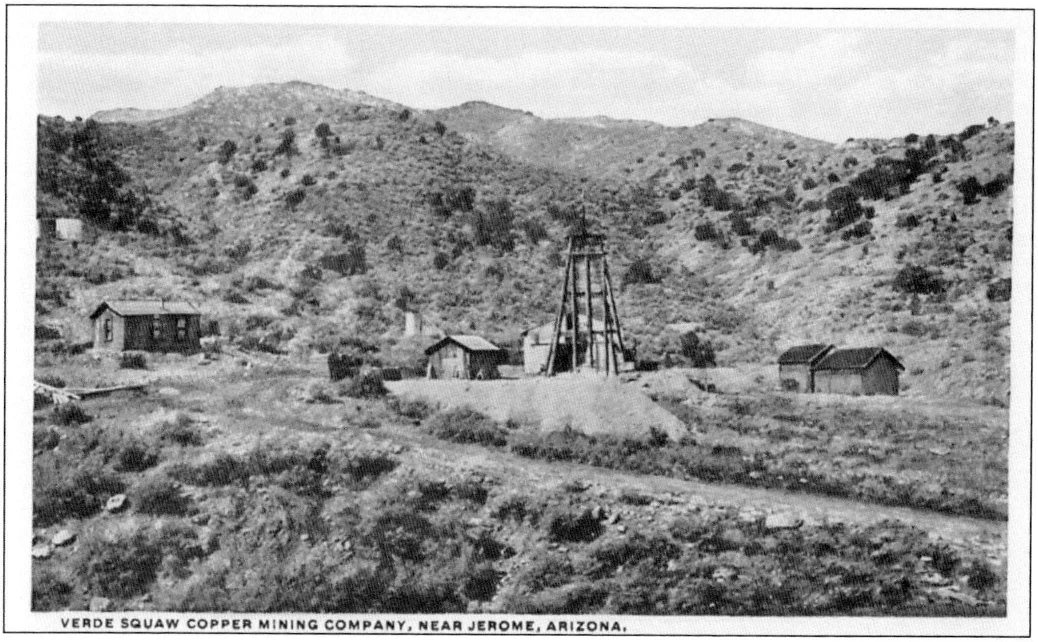

VERDE, VERDE SQUAW COPPER MINE COMPANY, C. 1930S (CURT TEICH HAND-COLORED POSTCARD). Discovered at the base of Great Squaw Peak near the Verde River around 1900 by David W. Barter, it was not until January 8, 1917, that the Verde Squaw Copper Mining Company was incorporated. Operating 15 claims over 275 acres in the Verde Valley about four and a half miles south of Camp Verde, the mine received a promising report in the 1918 *Arizona Mining Journal*: "I have never seen better surface indications that there must be high-grade copper ore in large bodies below the permanent ground water level." (Courtesy John Taylor.)

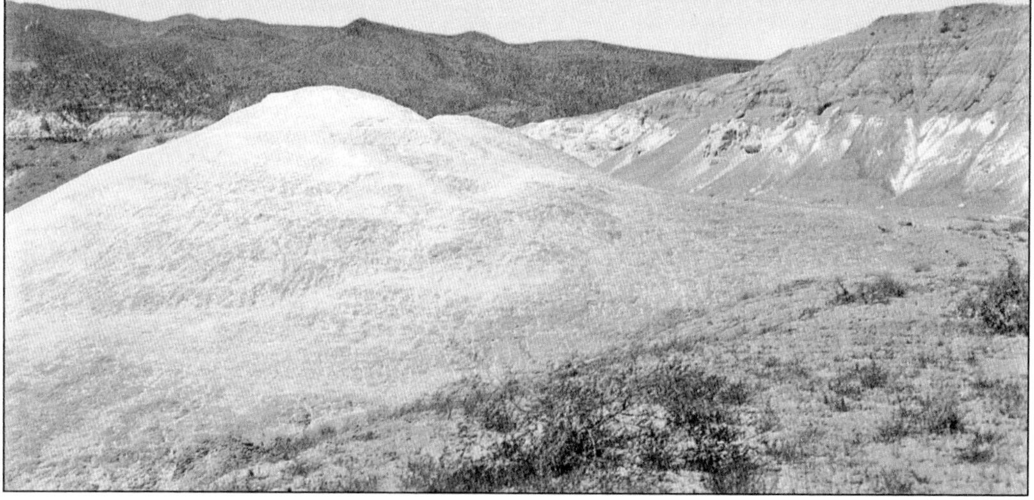

CAMP VERDE, SALT MINE, C. 1960S (REAL PHOTO POSTCARD). Not all mines in Yavapai County were for copper, gold, or silver; at least one was for salt. About two miles south of Camp Verde is the Camp Verde Salt Mine, one of the oldest known mines in the United States. Artifacts and the mummified body of an Indian miner were found in an underground tunnel dating back to the 14th century. In the 1920s and 1930s, the mine produced 100 tons of salt cake daily. (Published and photograph by Bob Bradshaw.)

Seven

Other Cards from Yavapai County

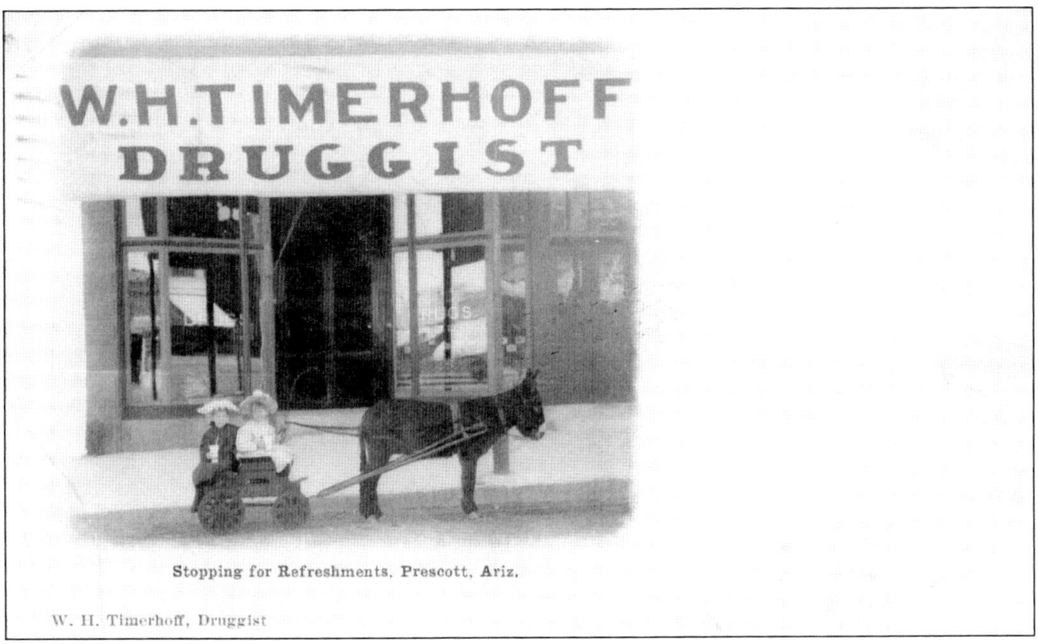

Prescott, W.H. Timerhoff, Druggist, Postmarked January 22, 1908 (Undivided Back Postcard). After relocating to Prescott from Flagstaff, Timerhoff, druggist and future mayor of Prescott, purchased W.P. Corilland's drugstore at 121 North Cortez Street in 1904. The drugstore and soda fountain lasted well into the 1930s. The building was recently used as an antique shop. (Published by W.H. Timerhoff, Druggist.)

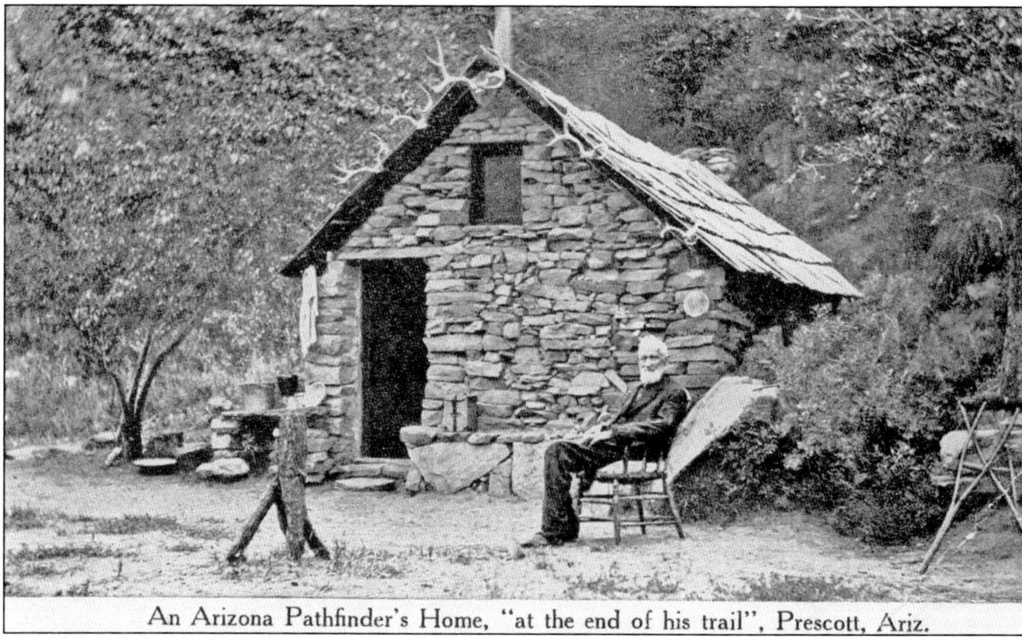

PATHFINDERS HOME, C. 1910 (DIVIDED BACK POSTCARD). Built before the beginning of the 20th century, this small rock cabin with its wood shingle roof and deer antlers was similar to many throughout Yavapai County. Although the man resembles one of Yavapai County's early settlers, Charles Genung, who died in 1916, he has not been positively identified as such.

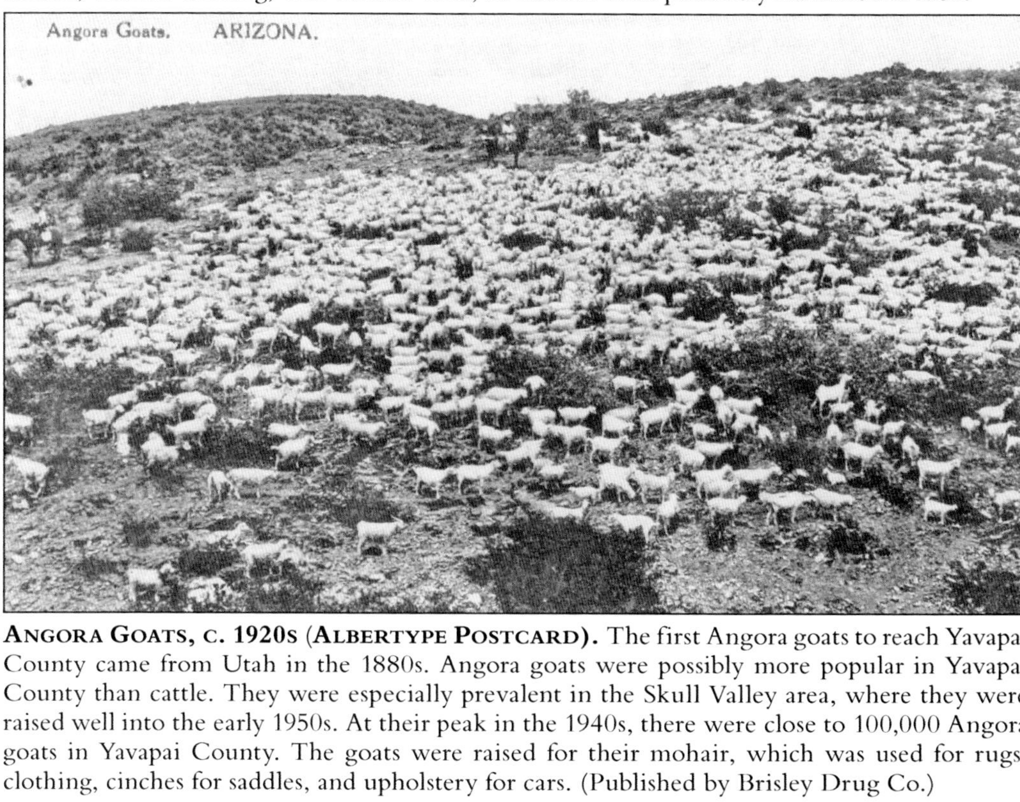

ANGORA GOATS, C. 1920S (ALBERTYPE POSTCARD). The first Angora goats to reach Yavapai County came from Utah in the 1880s. Angora goats were possibly more popular in Yavapai County than cattle. They were especially prevalent in the Skull Valley area, where they were raised well into the early 1950s. At their peak in the 1940s, there were close to 100,000 Angora goats in Yavapai County. The goats were raised for their mohair, which was used for rugs, clothing, cinches for saddles, and upholstery for cars. (Published by Brisley Drug Co.)

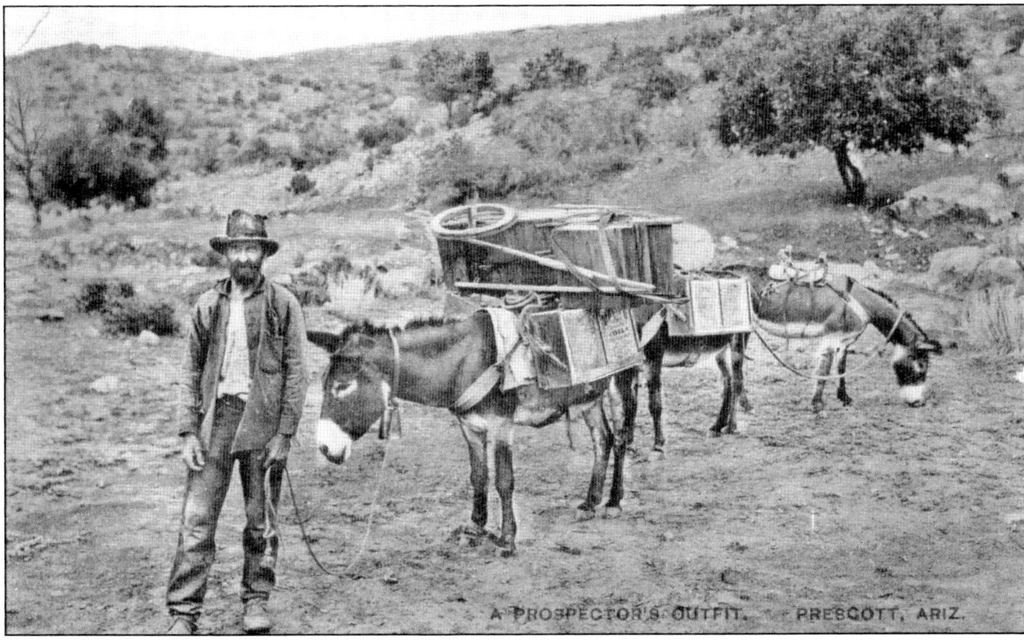

PROSPECTOR, C. 1910S (ALBERTYPE POSTCARD). This prospector and his burros have turned up on a number of postcards throughout the early 1900s. Although a majority, like this old Albertype, say it is from Prescott, some early hand-colored cards just say Arizona. Also, like earlier postcards, some are published by local drugstore companies, while others are printed in bulk and sold throughout Arizona. (Published by Brisley Drug Co.)

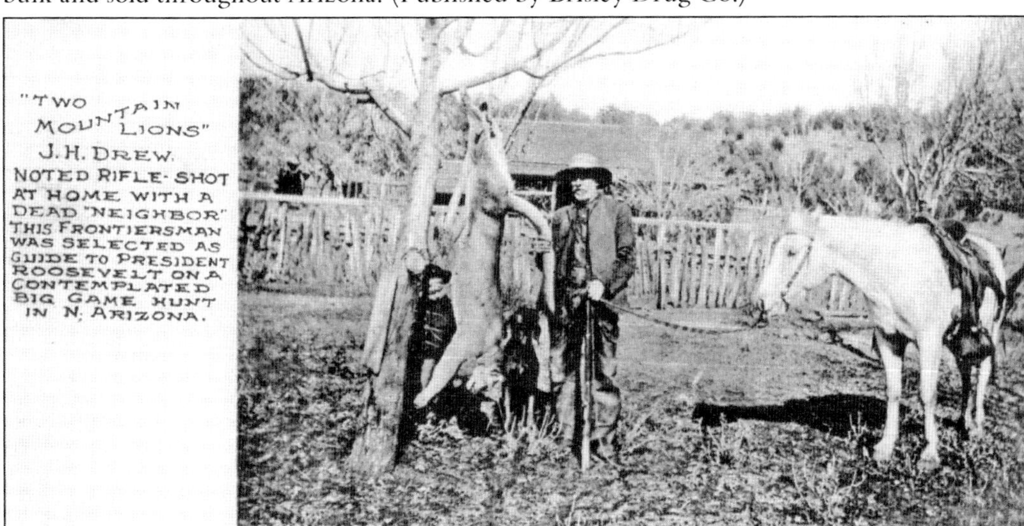

LION HUNTER, C. 1910S (ALBERTYPE POSTCARD). The front of the card reads, "Two Mountain Lions, J.H. Drew noted rifle shot at home with a dead neighbor. This frontiersman was selected as guide to President Roosevelt on a contemplated big game hunt in N. Arizona." From the February 26, 1902, edition of the *Weekly Journal-Miner*: "J.H. Drew killed a 200-pound mountain lion on Walnut Creek last week. The animal is said to have had a head on him as large as an African lion. The lion measured eleven feet and eight inches from the tip of his nose to the tip of his tail." (Published by Brisley Drug Co.)

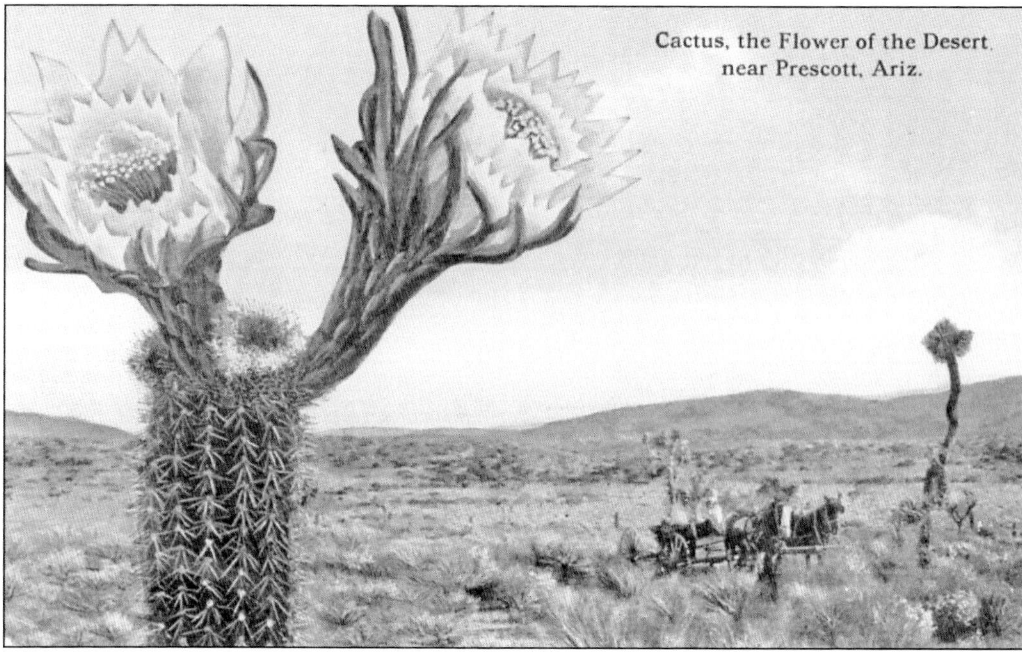

CACTUS FLOWER, C. 1913 (CURT TEICH HAND-COLORED POSTCARD). The state flower of Arizona is the saguaro cactus blossom. Also called a sahuaro, this fragrant flower was adopted as the state flower in 1931. (Published by Owl Drug and Candy Company.)

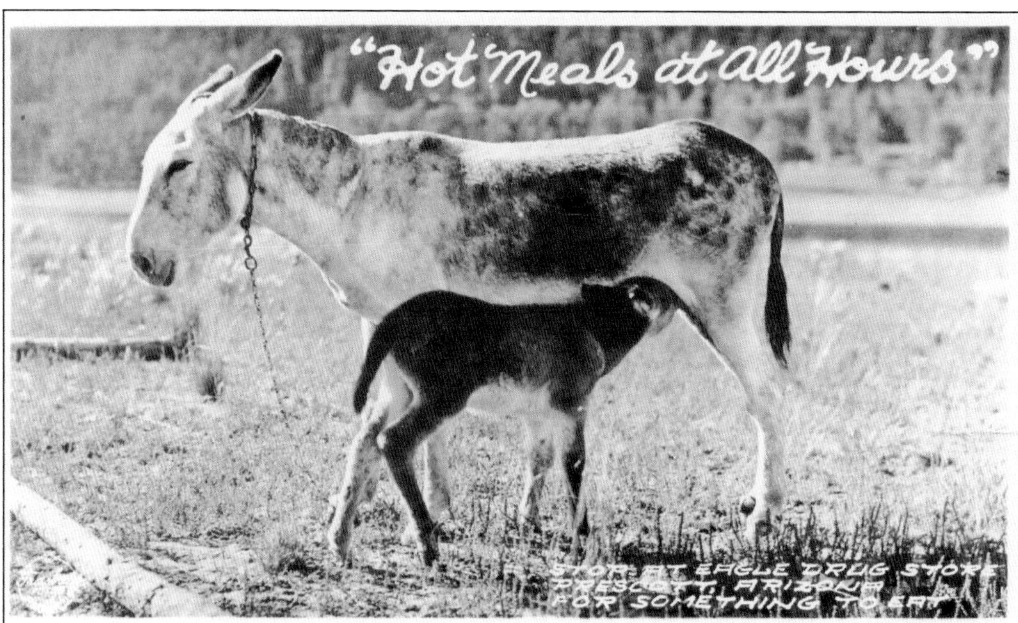

HOT MEALS, EAGLE DRUG, POSTMARKED OCTOBER 10, 1940 (REAL PHOTO POSTCARD). This generic postcard has been used by other businesses as advertising over the years. Eagle Drug started out when Charles Freericks purchased Heil's Drugstore in 1918. Over the next 67 years, Eagle Drug changed hands a number of times, and it was last located at 1000 Willow Creek Road in 1985, when it closed for good. (Published by Frashers, Inc.)

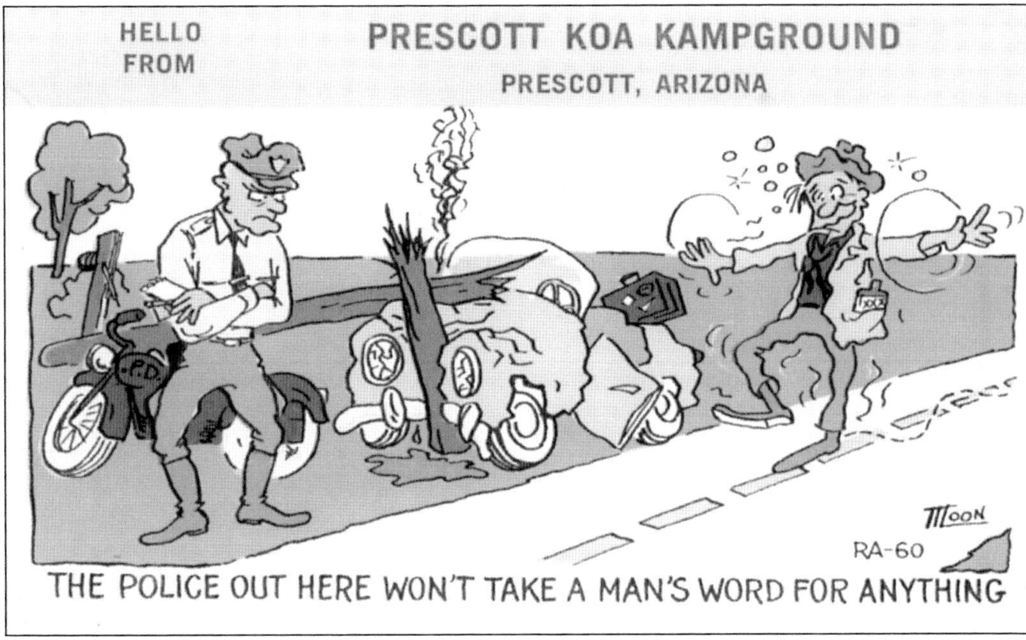

KOA KAMPGROUND, C. 1960S (ADVERTISING POSTCARD). This generic postcard was used by KOA Kampgrounds in the 1960s and 1970s to caution against drunk driving. The campground, located at Willow Lake, is now the Willow Lake RV Park. The park still has the familiar KOA-style A-frame office. (Courtesy KOA.)

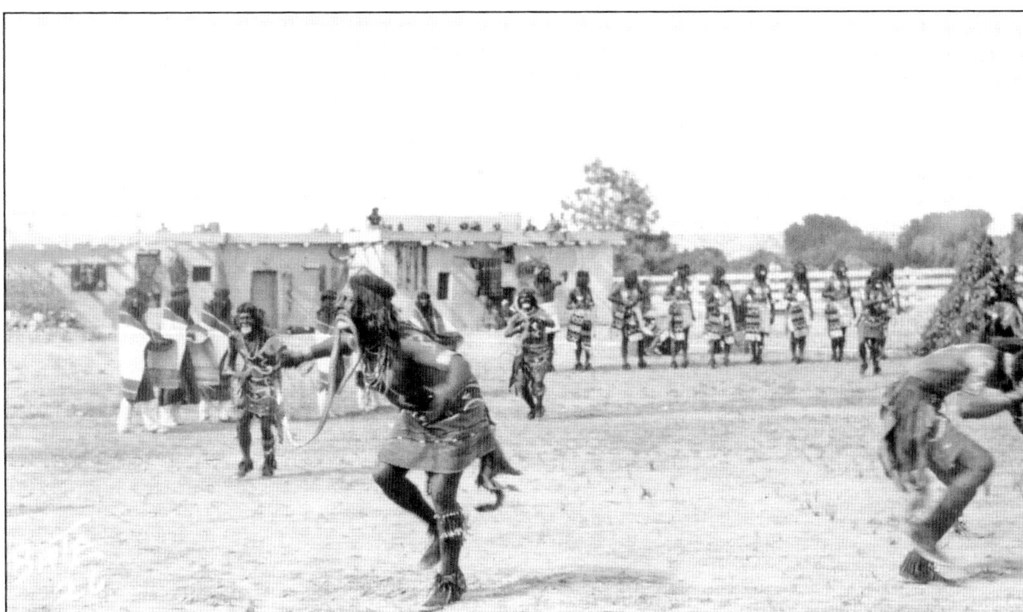

SMOKI DANCERS, C. 1930S (REAL PHOTO POSTCARD). By far the Smoki's most famous member was Barry Goldwater, a five-time US senator from Arizona and Republican presidential nominee in 1964. Goldwater danced the Antelope Dance competition in 1941 and the Snake Dance in 1947. (Published by Bate Studio, courtesy Smoki Museum.)

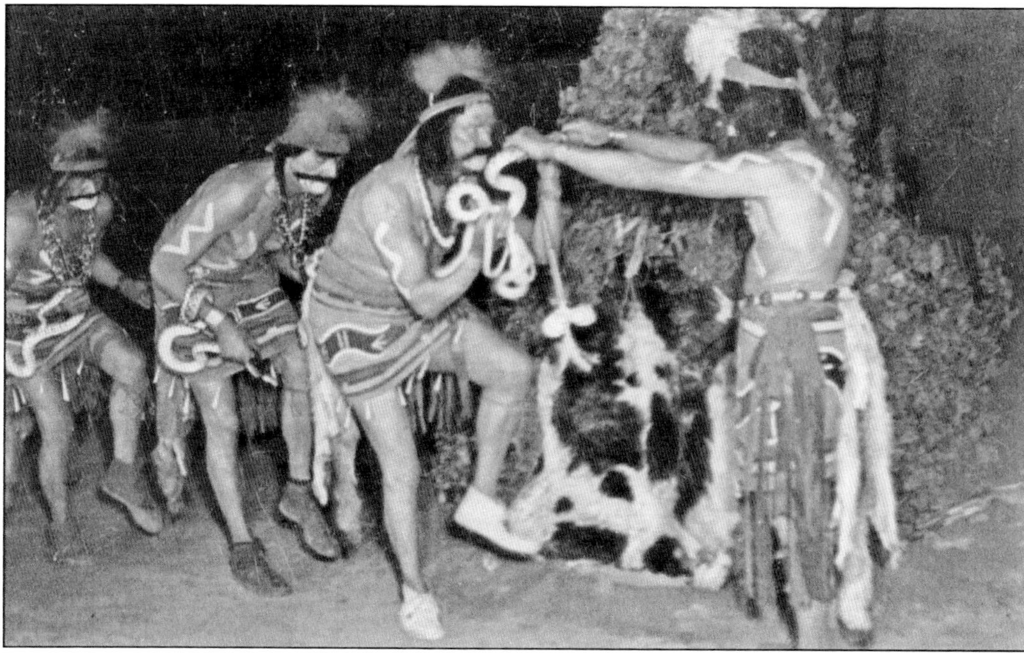

ABOVE: SMOKI DANCERS, C. 1960S (REAL PHOTO POSTCARD); BELOW: SMOKI DANCERS, C. 1942 (CURT TEICH HAND-COLORED POSTCARD). Started in 1921 as a way to raise funds for Prescott's Frontier Days, a group of local citizens organized a snake dance and charged $1 admission. Originally calling themselves the Moki, the club's name changed to Smoki shortly before their first performance. For their first performance, they ordered fake snakes, and finding they looked too unrealistic, they obtained live bull snakes. (Above, published by Bob Petley, photographed by Ray Manley; below, published by C.T. Art, distributed by Lollesgard Specialty Co.)

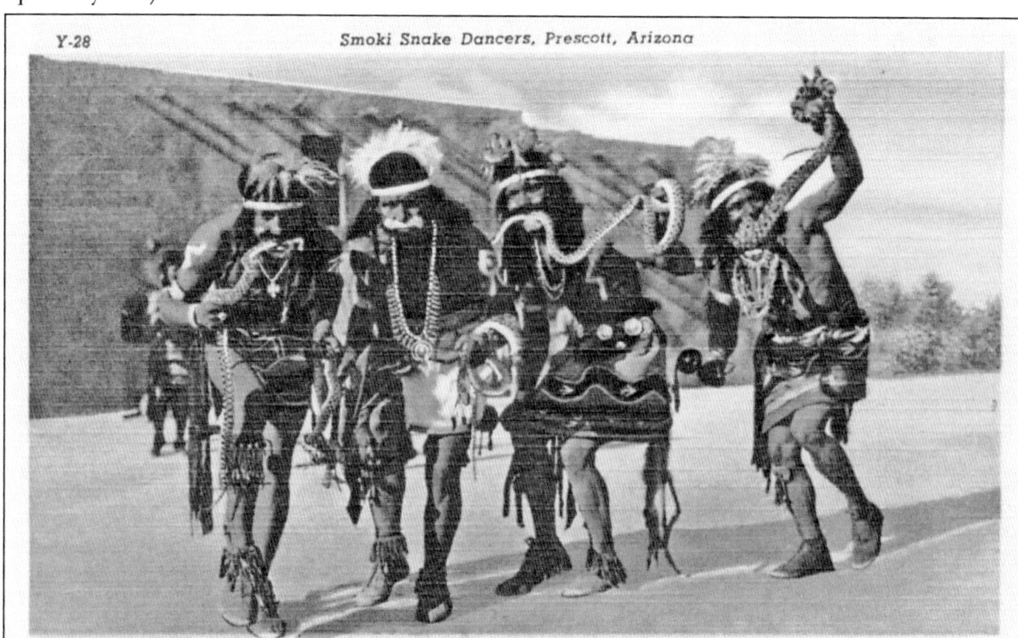

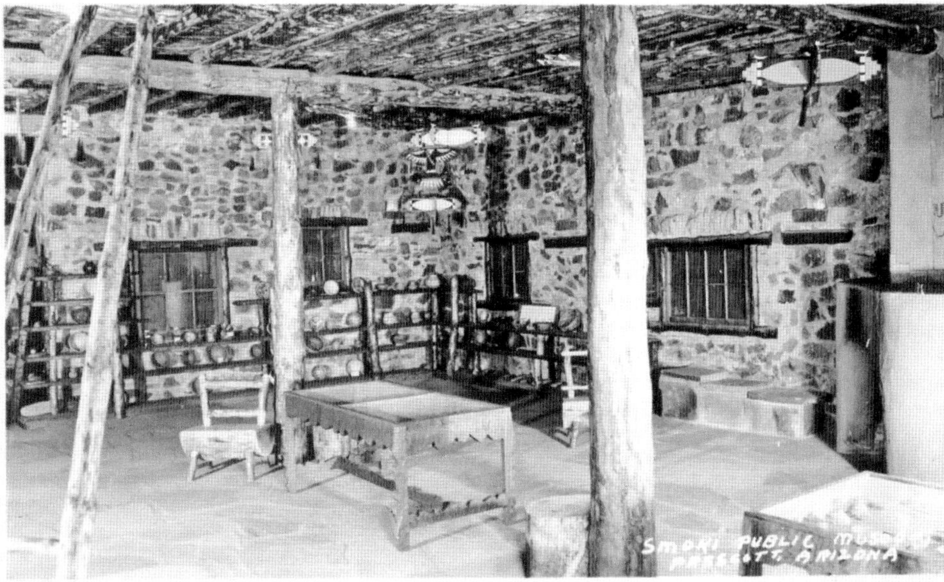

SMOKI PUBLIC MUSEUM, C. 1940S (REAL PHOTO POSTCARD). The original museum and clubhouse were built in 1932. Needing a larger space to house artifacts, the Smoki used funds in 1935 from the Emergency Relief Association of Arizona to construct a larger museum next to the clubhouse. The architect designed the museum to resemble a building one would see in an Indian pueblo, including a large double Zuni-styled fireplace. (Courtesy Andy Christenson.)

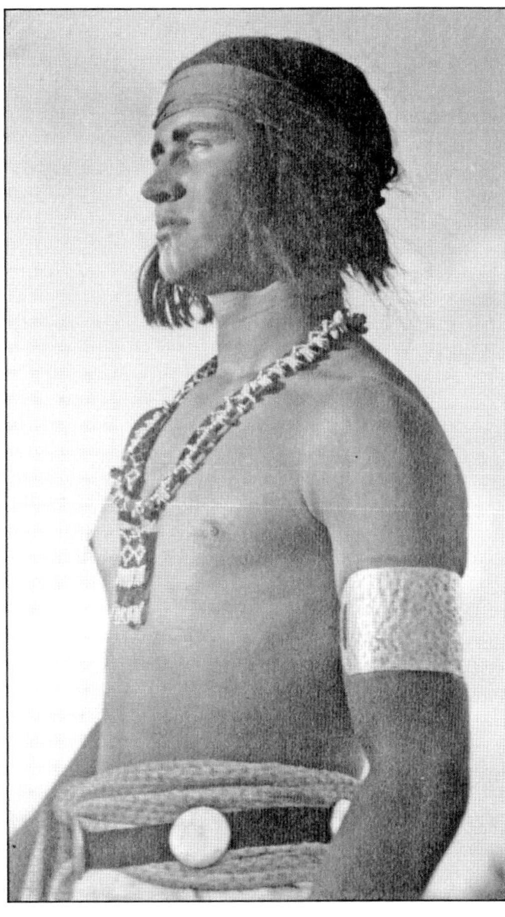

SMOKI DANCER, C. 1947 (REAL PHOTO POSTCARD). An unidentified dancer poses in a typical Smoki dance costume of the 1940s. By the 1980s, the Smoki had a difficult time recruiting new members, and with pressure from the Hopi and other Native American groups, the Smoki held their last dance in 1990. (Published by Leroy E. Eslow, courtesy Andy Christenson.)

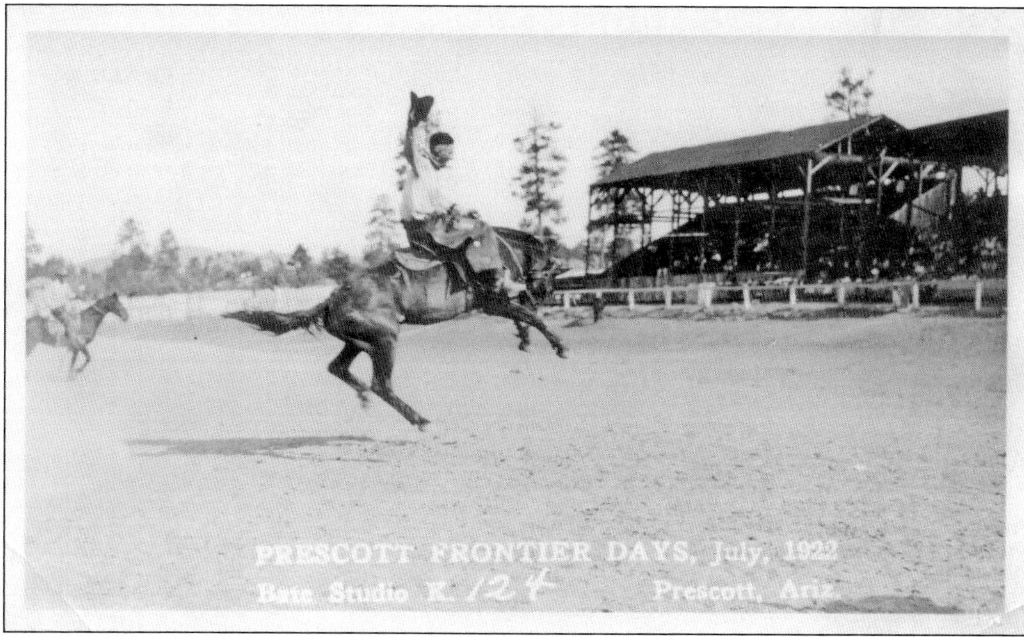

ABOVE: FRONTIER DAYS, C. 1922 (REAL PHOTO POSTCARD); BELOW: FRONTIER DAYS, HANDWRITTEN DATE JULY 4, 1919 (REAL PHOTO POSTCARD). Billed as the "World's Oldest Rodeo," Frontier Days in Prescott has been held annually over the Fourth of July weekend since its inception in 1888. Originally the rodeo was held at Forbing Park, a dirt lot off Iron Springs Road. It was not until 1913 that it moved to its current site at the old fairgrounds. That was also the same year the phrase "Frontier Days" came to be. (Above, published by Bate Studio; below, published by Bate Studio.)

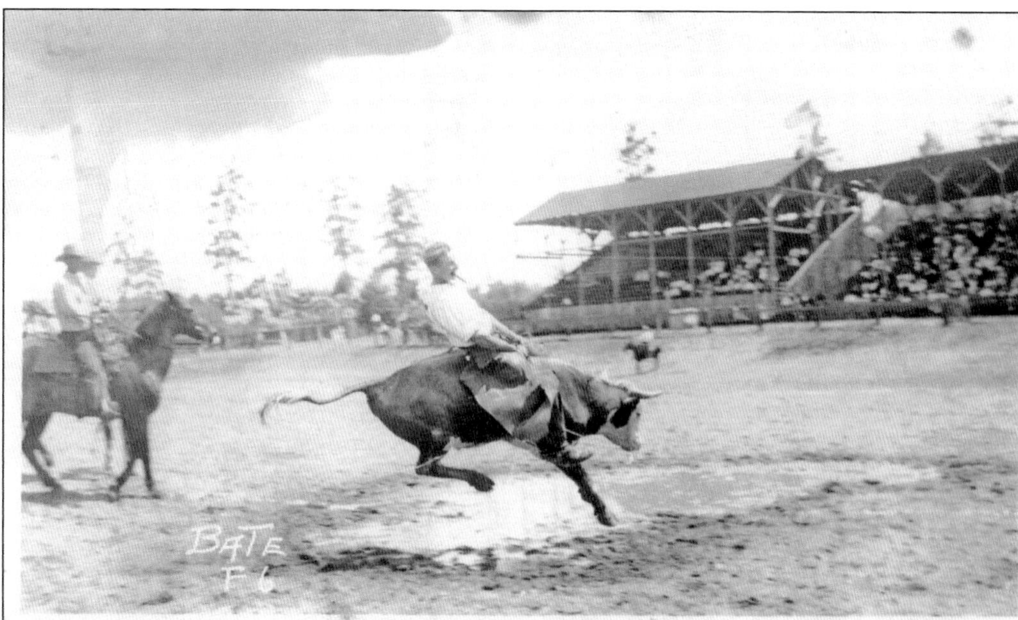

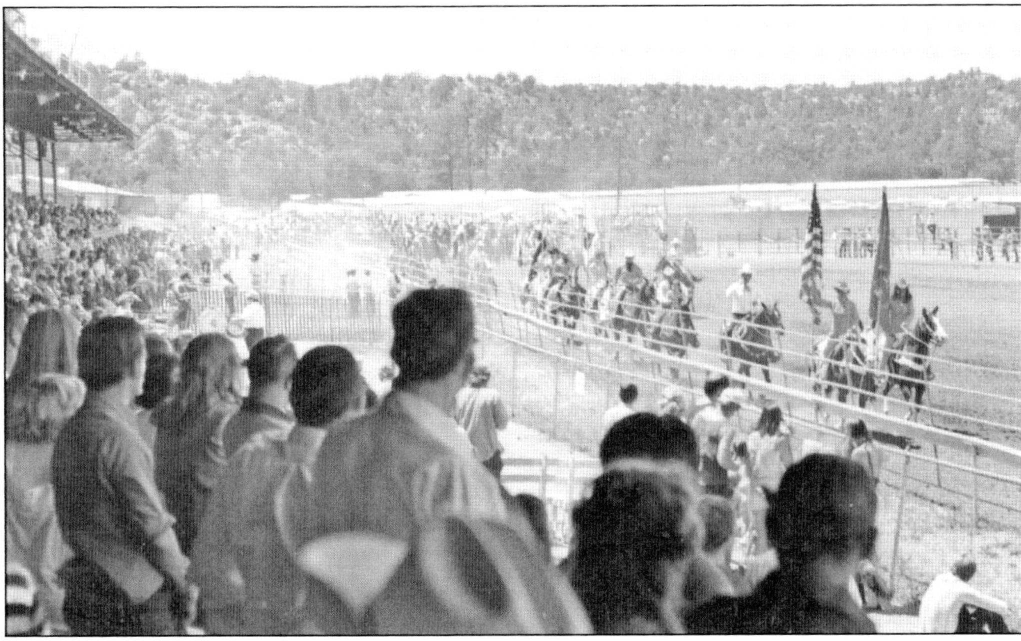

FRONTIER DAYS, C. 1960S (REAL PHOTO POSTCARD). Over the four-day holiday, with the rodeo and parade downtown, Prescott sees almost 30,000 people coming to town for the festivities. (Published by Kendall Photography, photograph by Charles P. Kendall.)

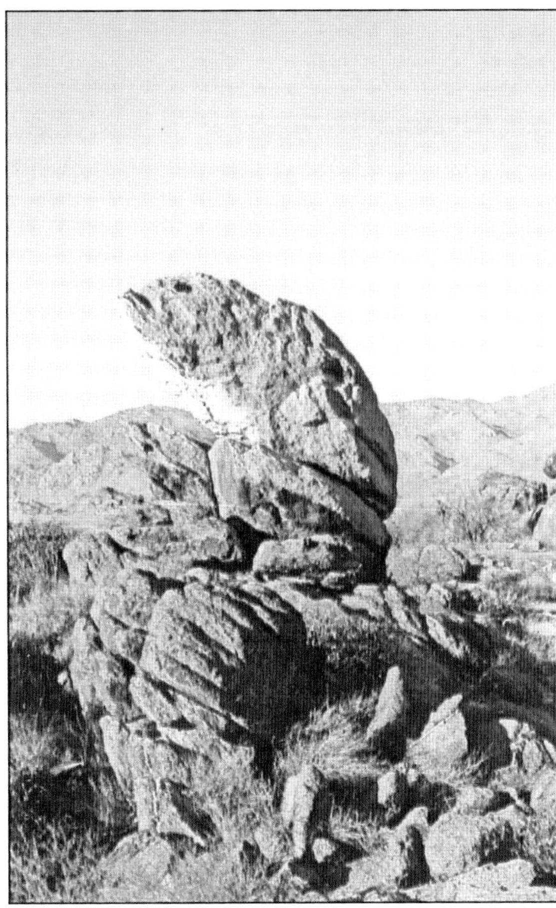

HIGHWAY 89, FROG NEAR CONGRESS, C. 1962 (REAL PHOTO POSTCARD). "Rocky the Frog" has existed longer than Highway 89. It was painted by Sara Perkins, who lived in the Martinez Wash, near the present-day Arrowhead Bar and Restaurant, with her husband, Eli. One day, Sara was walking with her sons when she spotted a rock formation resembling a huge frog. Soon the rock was painted with the familiar green and white paint that has been kept up over many years. (Published by Bradshaw Studios, photograph by Dick Carter.)

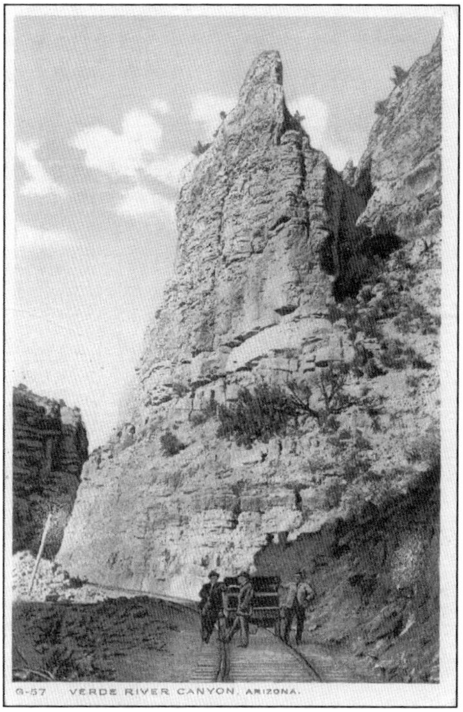

VERDE RIVER CANYON, POSTMARKED JULY 1913 (DIVIDED BACK HAND COLORED POSTCARD). An automobile on the United Verde and Pacific Railroad tracks in the Verde River Canyon. Ten miles of the tracks are now used by the Verde Canyon Railroad running between Clarkdale and Perkinsville. (Published by Fred Harvey, Courtesy Nancy Burgess.)

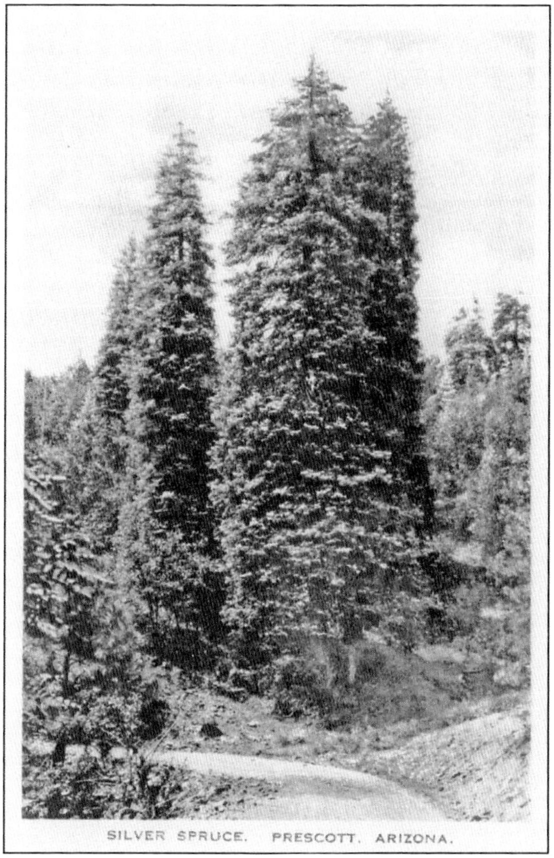

SILVER SPRUCE, C. 1915 (ALBERTYPE POSTCARD). Not as common as the ponderosa pine, the silver spruce is usually found in higher elevations from the Southwest to Canada. This large evergreen tree averages between 80 and 130 feet in height, but a few have been found as tall as 213 feet. (Published by Acker's Book Store, Prescott.)

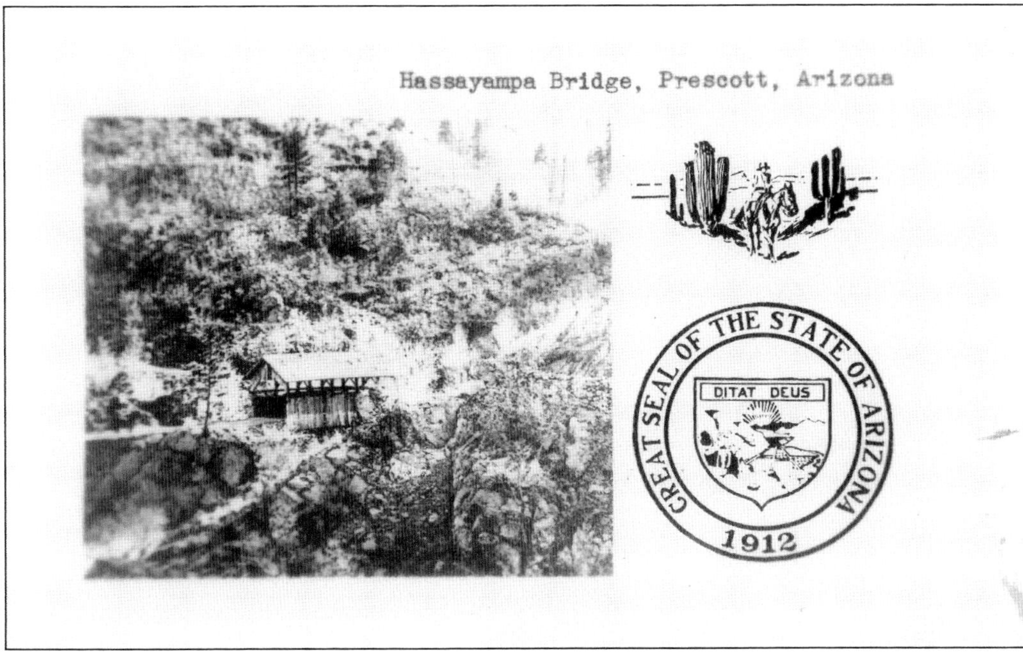

MAXTON, HASSAYAMPA BRIDGE, C. AFTER 1912. (REAL PHOTO POSTCARD). The covered bridge, built in 1890, was on the senator Highway where it crosses over the Hassaympa River near Maxton about three miles north of Venezia. (Courtesy Nancy Burgess.)

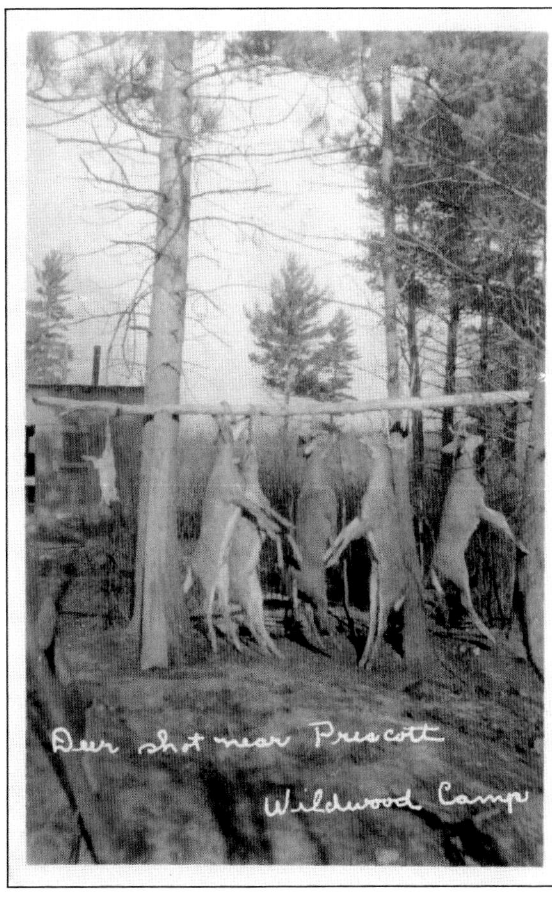

WILDWOOD CAMP, POSTMARKED JULY 20, 1936. (REAL PHOTO POSTCARD). Written on the card's back is the following: "We made 442 miles Sunday Arrived 7:30 PM. Everybody OK. But still crabby." There is no clear reference to a Wildwood Camp in Yavapai County. It could have possibly been a private hunting camp or perhaps near Camp Wood. There is, however, a Wildwood Estates off of Iron Springs Road.